Canadian Development Report 2008

Fragile States or
Failing Development?

The North-South Institute

The North-South Institute is a charitable, not-for-profit corporation established in 1976 to provide professional, policy-relevant research on North-South issues and relations between industrialized and developing countries. The results of this research are made available to policy-makers, interested groups, and the general public to help generate greater understanding and informed discussion of development questions. The Institute is independent, nonpartisan and cooperates with a wide range of Canadian, overseas, and international organizations working in related activities. The North-South Institute thanks the Canadian International Development Agency for providing a core grant. For more information about the Institute consult our website at www.nsi-ins.ca.

The editorial content of the Canadian Development Report represents the views and findings of the authors alone and not necessarily those of The North-South Institute's directors, sponsors, or supporters, or those consulted in its preparation.

Library and Archives Canada Cataloguing

Canadian development report.

1996/97-
Issued also in French under title: Rapport canadien sur le développement.
Includes bibliographical references.
ISSN 1206-2308
ISBN 978-1-897358-00-9 (2008 edition)

1. Developing countries-Social conditions-Periodicals.
2. Economic assistance, Canadian-Developing countries-Periodicals.
3. International economic relations-Periodicals.
4. Civil rights-Developing countries-Periodicals.
5. Developing countries-Foreign economic relations-Periodicals.

I. North-South Institute (Ottawa, Ont.)

HF1413.C36   337'.09172'4   C97-9300128-3

Managing Editor: Lois L. Ross
Layout and Cover Design: Green Communication Design inc.
Editorial Team: Ruth Bradley-St-Cyr, Peter Thornton, Marcelo Saavedra
Translation: Société Eskénazi Inc.
Cover and Title Page Photos: World Bank
© The North-South Institute/L'Institut Nord-Sud, 2007
Price: C$35.00

Available from: Renouf Publishing Co. Ltd.
                   5369 Canotek Road, Unit 1
                   Ottawa, Ontario K1J 9J3
                   Tel.: (613) 745-2665
                   Fax: (613) 745-7660

                   Email: order.dept@renoufbooks.com
                   Website: www.renoufbooks.com

FSC

The North-South Institute gratefully
acknowledges the generous financial
support of the following donors
in the publication of the
Canadian Development Report 2008

Benefactors
(Donations of more than $20,000)

 Canadian International
Development Agency

Agence canadienne de
développement international

Canadä

IDRC
International Development
Research Centre

CRDI
Centre de recherches pour le
développement international

Supporters

(Donations between $4,000 and $9,999)

Aga Khan Foundation Canada
Fondation Aga Khan Canada

Contributors
(Donations between $1,000 and $3,999)

Donors

We would also like to thank
Results – Résultats Canada

Canadian Development Report 2008

Fragile States or Failing Development?

Table of Contents

Foreword

by Roy Culpeper, President of The North-South Institute
and Stephen Baranyi, NSI Principal Researcher, Conflict Prevention

In 2002 the Bush Administration unveiled a U.S. National Security Strategy that identified fragile states as a major security threat. It held that the weakness of certain states left power vacuums that could be exploited by transnational terrorist and/or criminal networks. Al-Qaeda's use of the Afghan countryside, to train and command those who attacked U.S. targets in September 2001, was framed as symptomatic of a larger problem. The War on Terror, preemptive defense, regime change and the integration of defence and development — became pillars of the U.S. response.

For quite different reasons, donors have also been grappling with the problems of fragile and failing states. Aid is thought to be more effective in, and thus increasingly allocated to, countries demonstrating "good governance". Fragile states, in contrast, exhibit weak governance, but neglecting their needs by depriving them of aid could serve only to increase their fragility. The need to prevent such an outcome is motivated less by the prospect of transnational terrorism than by the spectre of growing human misery. Accordingly the World Bank developed a rationale for assisting Low-Income Countries Under Stress that produced recommendations for development interventions appropriate to the challenges faced by fragile states. Meanwhile, the Development Assistance Committee of the OECD launched a Learning and Advisory Process on "difficult partnerships". In 2005 the latter yielded draft Principles for International Engagement in Fragile States, to orient developmentally-sound approaches to international interventions in such contexts. These Principles are currently being pilot-tested in several states. Canada is leading the process in Haiti.

Against this backdrop, several Western states have developed policy frameworks and institutional mechanisms to reconcile these two very different rationales, namely the U.S.-led national security approach and the donor-led developmental approach. Canada's policy framework, codified in the last Liberal government's International Policy Statement in early 2005, is a blend of these perspectives. The mechanisms consolidated by the Harper government since then – namely whole-of-government approaches resting on the Stabilization and Reconstruction Taskforce (START) in DFAIT, the Rapid Deployment Brigade in Department of National Defence, and the growing Afghanistan and Haiti programs in CIDA – also reflect these international tendencies. It is important to remember that the West has not been alone in this regard. The preoccupation with state fragility and its tragic consequences has driven many African governments, and the African Union, to develop their own policy frameworks and mechanisms to respond to very real problems on the ground.

Despite these attempts intense debate continues as to whether it is possible to reconcile the "security" and "development" paradigms underlying these two alternative approaches to fragile states. Indeed, the very notion of "fragility" is contested, as well as the most appropriate and effective means of dealing with failed or failing states. It is all very well to endorse a whole-of-government approach, involving the simultaneous engagement of defence, diplomacy and development instruments (the "three Ds"). But is there a risk that such instruments are inconsistent rather than complementary? And, even if complementary, what should be the balance between these policies?

This edition of the *Canadian Development Report* highlights three axes of contestation:

1. **International normative foundations?** Writing from a Latin American perspective, Alejandro Bendaña maintains that many developing countries question fragile/failing/weak states concepts on the grounds that neither these concepts, nor the practices associated with them, are rooted in universally-accepted norms. Arguing that "fragility is in the eyes of the beholder," the prescription of military intervention often precedes a proper diagnosis of the causes of fragility. And often those causes can be global or external, citing the fact that chronic International Monetary Fund involvement in a number of states has served to heighten their fragility. Concerned about the prospects both for sovereignty and democracy, Bendaña cautions that high-minded principles such as the "responsibility to protect" populations vulnerable to egregious abuses may be humanitarian in theory, but are often imperial in practice.

2. **Security and sustainable development: integration or subordination?** Against the call by some Western leaders for deeper integration of the "3Ds", some critics warn that this trend subordinates development and diplomacy to the logic of national security. In his chapter Ernie Regehr shows how this is happening in Afghanistan. What he finds lacking, but imperative, if a sustainable peace is to be achieved in Afghanistan, is political consensus among its disparate regions, legitimate governance, socio-economic development, regional cooperation (particularly with Pakistan), and energetic peacebuilding efforts with the Taliban. Moreover, while resorting to force can play an important role, it risks making things worse when not restrained, leading to a high toll of civilian casualties.

3. **Gender equality and/or stabilization?** The promotion of women's rights has been used by certain Western governments to justify their interventions post hoc. In her chapter, Cheshmak Farhoumand-Simms shows how this is also problematic in Afghanistan. Yet she goes beyond a facile critique of the instrumentalization of womens' rights by arguing that a different approach to gender equality, more sensitive to cultural dynamics and linked to a broader strategy of development and dialogue, could more effectively promote changes in the relations between men and women as well as helping to reverse state fragility. Jennifer Salahub complements this analysis in her chapter on Haiti, showing how despite some advances, Canada could more consistently promote gender equality during the stabilization phase, to help lay solid foundations for building democracy and the reversal of state fragility in the long term.

There are many other issues raised by the current discourse on fragile states. Critics argue that it is too preoccupied with the state as the problem and solution; perpetuates fragility in countries that are not geopolitical priorities for the West; and that public relations trump learning in contexts like Afghanistan and Iraq.

These issues are important, but they are not examined systematically in this Canadian Development Report. They should be the object of deeper analysis and debate in the future.

Failed States and
the Limits to Force:
The Challenge of Afghanistan

Ernie Regehr

Failed States and the Limits to Force: The Challenge of Afghanistan

Ernie Regehr

The Last Resort?

The international community now turns rather frequently to the use of collective force in situations of advanced state failure, and it has even promised to protect populations in peril by the resort to force in extreme cases.[1] But it does so only inconsistently and with some reluctance. Force in the pursuit of the direct national interest comes easier, and since the end of the Cold War, the more prominent instances of the resort to major force by groups of states acting together — notably in Kosovo, Afghanistan, and Iraq — were initiated without the formal consent of the international community acting through the Security Council and were primarily a response to the perceived threats and interests of the force leaders, rather than the vulnerability of the people of the states that were attacked.

The 1999 NATO attack on Serbia was certainly a response to state failure and to the growing peril of the people of Kosovo, but the perception that NATO's reputation and future would be fatally affected if it ignored the descent into chaos in its own backyard was a major factor — and the prominent reliance on aerial bombardment owed much more to the convenience of the interveners than to the safety of either the Kosovars or Serbs. The attack on Afghanistan in 2001 was explicitly presented by the United States as an act of self-defence. Similarly, the attack on Iraq in 2003 was premised on the interests of the attackers, notwithstanding the string of broader international principles and interests that were marshalled in support of the action, and few can dispute that the results have been catastrophic for human security in Iraq.

Collective military action that was formally mandated by the international community through the Security Council in support of collectively defined objectives was taken with regard to Iraq and Kuwait in 1991 to reverse Iraqi aggression, Somalia in 1992 to facilitate humanitarian access to Somali victims of state collapse, and through several UN peace support operations, notably in Haiti and the Democratic Republic of Congo. But it is still the explicit refusals to act in support of masses of people in extraordinary peril that stand out — South Sudan, Rwanda, Darfur (Sudan), Somalia.

Reluctance regarding the collective mobilization of protection forces in situations of extreme human peril and complex emergencies has many sources, and whatever the particular grounds for that caution may be in each case, it clearly is reinforced by the compelling principle that force should be mobilized only as a last resort. The last resort principle is rooted in just war doctrine that counsels against any early turn to the war option in settling disputes between states not yet at war, but in situations of advanced inter-state violence, delays in remedial action by the international community can actually exacerbate violence and, ironically, betray excessive confidence in the utility of force. The very formulation tends to mythologize force as a reliable solution, to be held in reserve until all other options are exhausted. The implication is that when all else fails, the international community can still turn to military force to make things right.

Furthermore, delays in the resort to force, in the face of increasing state failure and escalating criminal and political violence, serve primarily to ensure that when force is finally used it will not be effective. When increasingly chaotic conditions finally trigger a response, there is a heightened risk of major clashes and more people caught in the crossfire, as well as a greater likelihood that nationalist sentiment against combat-intensive foreign military intervention will generate rather than quell insurgency.[2]

The reality is that the resort to collective force to reverse state failure and protect vulnerable people is least effective when all else has or is failing. Afghanistan is rich in lessons that force is in fact an international instrument of very limited utility, one that has a reasonable chance of making a positive contribution only if it is used with disciplined restraint and is accompanied by a range of vigorous diplomatic, political, economic, social, and domestic security measures that are not failing. If reserving the resort to force as a final option literally means that it is invoked only when other means have been tried and failed — in other words, when conditions have deteriorated to the point of widespread instability and violence — then the resort to force is unlikely to fare any better. The last resort principle may be premised on restraint, but the resort to force when all other options have failed actually and frequently defies restraint and leads to escalating violence.

The international community will not soon find it easy to resolve the complex and consequential questions of when and how the resort to force can be effective in its collective efforts to reverse state failure and to protect vulnerable people. However, research carried out through the NSI project, "What Kind of Peace is Possible?" (WKOP),[3] confirms that the more military interventions are drawn into war-fighting operations outside of a "negotiated, comprehensive approach to peacebuilding," the less likely they are to produce positive outcomes. The Afghanistan case makes it clear that the success of foreign military assistance depends heavily on both the kind of force that is used and the context in which it is employed.

A Threat to Homeland Defence or Human Security?

The assumption that the international community must respond to state failure is now a prominent feature of the post-Cold War and post-911 environment. But that doesn't mean it is the well-being of the local victims of state failure that drives such responses. There is an assumption that state failure is primarily a security challenge to states and communities far away from the failed states, and that sentiment is most clearly articulated in the introduction to the 2002 US National Security Strategy. It declares that "America is now threatened less by conquering states than... by failing ones."[4]

In its 2007 Failed States Index, *Foreign Policy* adopts a similar tone of alarm to explain why the world's weakest countries pose the greatest danger:

> "It is an accepted axiom of the modern age that distance no longer matters. Sectarian carnage can sway stock markets on the other side of the planet. Anarchic cities that host open-air arms bazaars imperil the security of the world's superpower. A hermit leader's erratic behavior not only makes life miserable for the impoverished millions he rules but also upends the world's nuclear nonproliferation regime. The threats of weak states, in other words, ripple far beyond their borders and endanger the development and security of nations that are their political and economic opposites." [5]

If the primary and, by such accounts, fervently held assumption about failing states is that they threaten the security of distant ones, even when those distant states are both powerful and stable, it is likely to follow that international responses to failed and failing states will be filtered through the security needs of the powerful rather than the welfare of the most vulnerable. One need look no further than the West's interest in Afghanistan in October 2001 to confirm that when the wealthy and powerful countries of the global North consider the phenomenon of failed states, the focus is the security requirements of the wealthy North rather than the security needs and well-being of the people of failing states. Concern about the extraordinary human rights situation in Afghanistan preceded September 11, but regard for the human security of Afghans was not what triggered the attacks that deposed the Taliban government of the day. The issue was the newly declared "war on terror" and the defence of the homelands of the attacking states.

When the United States, in the operation it called Enduring Freedom (OEF), first led the attack on Afghanistan, the formal mission was the defence of the United States and the legal framework was the right of self-defence under Article 51 of the UN Charter. America's NATO partners immediately reinforced the self-defence paradigm by invoking NATO's Article 5,[6] which declares that an attack on one is an attack on them all, that NATO states will come to the aid of any member under attack, and that such assistance is the exercise of self-defence. Canada as a NATO partner joined OEF and provided naval support for the initial attack on Afghanistan, as well as ground forces shortly thereafter.[7] While the US, Canada, and other OEF partners certainly identified additional objectives, such as the removal of a regime guilty of the gross and systematic violation of human rights and security support for the new Government in Afghanistan when it was established, the basic paradigm was self-defence.

The subsequent establishment of the International Security Assistance Force (ISAF), supported by Security Council resolutions,[8] was based on quite another paradigm, namely a request from the newly-constituted Government of Afghanistan for assistance in support of the security of Afghanistan, not North America. Canada shifted its primary role in Afghanistan to the ISAF operation in Kabul in 2003, and with that Canada's role shifted from the defence of North America to security assistance for Afghanistan. Indeed, by virtue of its focus on the greater Kabul area, the operation was very much within the minimal combat framework of traditional peacekeeping. The 2005 Canadian deployment to Kandahar Province was designed to launch ISAF there — and thus expand the range of the international community's security assistance in that much less stable and more dangerous Southern region. The initial operational involvement in Kandahar was through OEF, but when the switch to ISAF was accomplished in mid 2006, the formal basis of the operation switched from homeland defence to providing stabilization patrols in support of the overt peacebuilding efforts later defined in the ambitious Afghanistan Compact:[9] "…to overcome the legacy of conflict in Afghanistan by setting conditions for sustainable economic growth and development; strengthening state institutions and civil society; removing remaining terrorist threats; meeting the challenge of counter-narcotics; rebuilding capacity and infrastructure; reducing poverty; and meeting basic human needs."

At the time, however, Defence Minister Gordon O'Connor was making a particular point of continuing to invoke the homeland defence rationale. In the May 17, 2006 Parliamentary debate that preceded the vote on the Government's intention to extend Canada's involvement until February 2009, Mr. O'Connor highlighted the Government's "Canada first" defence strategy that "seeks to protect Canadians from threats that confront us at home, along our coastlines and from any place abroad. Right now this means being in Afghanistan".[10]

Prime Minister Stephen Harper adopted the same tone of hard-nosed defence of Canadian interests. "Our rationale for being in Afghanistan is clear. It is in the interests of this country." Warming to the Prime Minister's tone and his own "Canada first" approach, Mr. O'Connor became even bolder in the debate: "The bottom line is that the mission in Afghanistan supports one of the enduring goals of Canada's foreign and defence policy: to protect Canada's national interest. We must commit to seeing our mission through. Our national interest is straightforward: to ensure the security and prosperity of the Canadian people. This government has summed it up in two words: Canada first."

It was meant to be practical and tough, the bottom line defence of Canada in Afghanistan, but it is not the language that speaks to Canadians when they face the hard reality of the return home of the bodies of Canadian soldiers killed in Afghanistan. When the ultimate sacrifice is asked and courageously given, the language of self-interest fails us. At such a time Canadians turn to more fundamental values of justice and a common global humanity. When Prime Minister Harper was at the Vimy anniversary event in France it happened that he had to announce the deaths of more Canadian soldiers, and to his credit he could not find what needed to be said in the language of self-interest and Canada first. Instead he said, "When the cause is just, Canada will always be there to defend our values and our fellow human beings."[11]

The language that gives meaning to sacrifice is much more in tune with "the responsibility to protect" and "human security". And it is, in fact, these two paradigms that most clearly link to the formal objectives of foreign forces participating in ISAF. Whether the means currently pursued by OEF and ISAF forces are effective is another question, but in his intervention in the Parliamentary debate, Foreign Minister Peter MacKay focused almost exclusively on the protection paradigm and the Canadian values that drive it: "Protecting and ensuring a safe home, a chance at education, free from exploitation or worse — violence, abuse — building democracies, these are all such important bedrock pillars of our society. Why would we not want to share this with the people of Afghanistan? Canada is helping to create freedom from fear; a freedom that will allow ordinary Afghans to lead their daily lives without fear."

These are values that Canadians collectively at times honour and at other times betray, but they are part of our constructed national story and, as such, should help shape our action when it matters most. In places of state failure, like Afghanistan, it is obviously our responsibility, along with that of a responsible and responsive international community, to muster the resolve and especially the skills to effectively serve the values of justice and peacemaking that our national story invokes.

What is a Fragile State?

The resolve and skill needed for effectively responding to state failure begins with an understanding of the phenomenon itself. The OECD says "states are fragile when governments and state structures lack capacity — or in some cases, political will — to deliver public safety and security, good governance and poverty reduction to their citizens."[12] In other words, all states fail; the question is how much and how consistently. For the purposes of the *Foreign Policy*/Fund for Peace survey, "a failing state is one in which the government does not have effective control of its own territory, is not perceived as legitimate by a significant portion of its population, does not provide domestic security or basic public services to its citizens, and lacks a monopoly on the use of force."[13] Each of these criteria is a matter of degree,[14] making it useful to measure comparative levels of failure through a series of indicators in an effort to develop broad overall assessments of relative failure and of the risks of escalating failure. The degree of failure is proportional to a state's "ability and willingness… to provide basic public goods to most of its population. It is this capacity to provide public goods that forms the principal determinant of a state's position on the spectrum; the more diminished it is, the greater the state's propensity for failure".[15]

The Canadian International Development Agency (CIDA) developed a similar, though more comprehensive, definition as a follow-up to the International Policy Statement (IPS) produced in 2005 by the Government of Paul Martin. According to CIDA,[16] "…States are perceived as fragile when the government does not demonstrate the will and/or capacity to deliver on core state functions such as the enforcement of legitimate security and authority, the protection, promotion, and implementation of human rights and gender equality, the rule of law, and even the most basic provision of services (e.g. in health and education, in enabling the private sector, and in environmental protection). When these core state functions are unreliable and inaccessible, the legitimacy of the state erodes and is likely to result in a breakdown in the social 'pact' of trust and cooperation within civil society and between civil society and the state. States are fragile not only when they are *moving towards* failure, but also when they are *recovering from* failure."

Complete failure is reached, as in Somalia over the past 15 years, when there is no longer a government in place, or when governance is so fundamentally absent or incapable that the country or parts of it are in an ongoing state of crisis (for example, the Democratic Republic of Congo), or when a government lacks virtually all legitimacy domestically and internationally (as in Haiti at particular times).

CIDA also assembled a helpful and extensive list of "catalyzing factors," that is, "events, outcomes, and processes that can quickly shift a state's trajectory towards fragility because of their critical impact on will, capacity, political stability, and sustainable development." Examples include the lack of very basic and essential services for a large part of the population, widespread food insecurity, dramatic declines in livelihood opportunities for young men, rampant corruption, flagrant abuses of civil and political rights, the proliferation of small arms, and privatized security forces with off-budget revenue sources.[17]

The 2005 IPS made the reversal of state failure a centerpiece of its framework for defining a Canadian role in support of international peace and security, but the approach does not make the defence of Canada the exclusive or even primary concern. The failed state analysis in the IPS began with attention to the humanitarian consequences for populations directly affected, describing "the suffering that these situations create" as "an affront to Canadian values".[18] Of course, more immediate national interests are never absent from international engagements and elsewhere in this volume Alejandro Bendaña argues persuasively that the "threat" emanating from failing states is an "ideological construct" designed to justify responses that are closer to a new imperialism than humanitarianism.

An analysis prepared by the Policy Research Division of Foreign Affairs emphasized that the focus on failed states is rooted in both strategic and humanitarian imperatives. At the strategic level the paper echoes, but in more restrained terms, the analysis accompanying the *Foreign Policy*/Fund for Peace failed states index, referring to "the growing capacity of weak states to endanger Canadian strategic interests and threaten the welfare and security of Canadian citizens."[19] The same theme is reflected in the IPS attention to wider issues of regional stability and the implications for the security of Canadians: "More ominously, the weakness of failed states makes them obvious breeding grounds for terrorist networks and organized crime, which can directly threaten the security of Canadians."[20] But the human security of the immediate victims also figures prominently into the IPS emphasis on development as a means of preventing state breakdown. It noted that when prevention fails "members of the international community must also possess the capacity for rapid intervention that can stabilize the situation on the ground and restore security for the local population".[21]

Foreign Affairs officials confirm that the International Policy Statement is no longer, formally or informally, a guiding document for Canadian foreign policy, but it is still worth noting that it identified a number of Canadian initiatives that were specifically undertaken, and which continue, in response to failed state conditions:

- Contributions to international efforts "to stop ethnic cleansing and massive abuse of human rights" in Darfur;
- Promoting social, economic, and security reforms in Palestine;
- Supporting Afghanistan and the Kandahar Provincial Reconstruction Team;
- Helping to build an accountable police force in Haiti;
- Reconstruction and development in Iraq; and
- Action to help people deal with forced displacement (internally and across borders).

The establishment of the Stabilization and Reconstruction Task Force (START) and the Global Peace and Security Fund are also linked to the response to failed and failing states.[22]

What Works and What Doesn't?

State failure is easy enough to observe, but observation and description do not themselves yield prescription. The antidote to failed states is not revealed in its symptoms anymore than the antidote to any disease is revealed in its symptoms. Effective responses grow out of experimentation and long-term practice, gradually revealing, if we are attentive (as through the research of the NSI's WKOP project), what works and what doesn't.

The Canadian Council for International Cooperation identifies two important cautions regarding the contemporary state-building focus of international responses to "state-failure".[23] First, the focus on particular failing states does not sufficiently acknowledge that significant factors in state failure are not home-grown. The international system and other international actors contribute significantly to state failure, as Bendaña also points out in Chapter 4. Second, a "failed state" framework tends to assume a sovereignty vacuum into which the international community must come with its state-building initiatives. This can mean "highly directive state-building, in which 'democracy and ownership' are the goal but not the means, creating challenges for both the legitimacy and effectiveness of such interventions".[24] That is a persuasive summary of how not to do peacebuilding and it helpfully raises the question of whether top-down, security-dominated international interventions are intrinsic to the very concept of reversing state failure. It is, in effect, a return to the question of whether the rebuilding of failed states can be pursued with human security, rather than homeland defence, as the basic framework.

It is also the question of the fundamental utility of or limits to force: Can externally driven state-building exercises that involve significant military security operations successfully employ means that emphasize inclusive and participatory governance, respect for human rights, economic justice, and that put the people of the state under reconstruction in charge of the process?

State structures that are durable, even when they need to be defended from spoilers that seek to attack them, are essential to the development of human security. In other words, state security and human security are not in competition, and state-building that is effective pursues them both as inseparable. The point is to ensure that human security is in fact the objective and measure of state security and state competence, and thus to ensure that the state-building exercise is oriented toward building state institutions and processes that serve the needs, safety, and wellbeing of people and, as a consequence, enjoy high levels of public confidence. The Foreign Affairs discussion paper of failed states links six key peacebuilding lessons to state-building: the centrality of local ownership and direction; accommodation to local contexts, notably traditions and political dynamics; measures focused on developing local human and institutional capacity; effective coordination of the multiple stakeholders; sustainability, so that newly developed institutions and processes can be maintained even when donor support recedes; and recognition that state-building is a long-term process and requires commensurate commitment from the international community.[25]

Almost two decades of post-Cold War peacebuilding activity has been rooted in the indivisibility of human security — in the recognition that a globalized world is an interdependent world in which the consequences of the failures of some inevitably visit the many. The broad conclusion of that experience is no mystery: winning the peace in troubled societies is primarily a political, social, and economic enterprise that, in some circumstances, needs to be supported by military force. It is not the other way around; that is, primarily a military enterprise that needs to be supported by social and economic projects to win hearts and minds.

Can Force Help to Reverse State Failure?

The annual failed states index produced by the journal *Foreign Policy* and the Fund for Peace ranks state failure based on 12 indicators of a state's failure to meet basic human security needs.[26] Advanced levels of state failure correlate strongly with public violence and 14 of the 20 states with the highest state failure rankings in 2006[27] were in a state of war.[28] The link between declining state capacity and the loss of a state's monopoly on the use of force is part of what defines state failure. In other words, when state capacity declines and state authority is increasingly challenged, such challenges inevitably escalate to become armed challenges. In turn, threatened state authorities inevitably turn to military and police forces to retain their authority. In the post-Cold War era especially, it is state failure linked to armed conflict that tends to get the attention of the international community, which is itself then increasingly drawn to responses that include the deployment of international military stabilization forces. Hence, of the 20 states exhibiting the greatest degree of state failure in 2006, 12 were also hosts to UN-authorized interventions or peace operations. Of those, nine were authorized under Chapter VII of the UN Charter and thus included some declared element of military coercion.

It is a pattern that intensified in the post-9/11 era. The international resort to collective military coercion in response to individual state failure has a variety of sponsors — e.g., unilateral interveners, regional organizations, international coalitions of the willing, UN-authorized coalitions, UN-mandated and managed forces — with results and impacts that are far from certain.

What has the international community learned about the conditions and methods that are essential to, or conducive to, making the international resort to force an effective contribution to reversing state failure — that is, to advancing human safety, accountable governance, and sustainable development? Put another way, what are the limits to force in pursuit of human security?

Contrary to conventional wisdom, the effective employment of force in situations of failed or failing states is one of the least self-sufficient measures available. There is obvious recognition that there are situations in which reconstruction and development activities are extremely difficult because of the absence of security, but it is just as true that the establishment and maintenance of security is heavily dependent on a range of accompanying conditions:

- Political consensus around the new order that is being stabilized;
- Legitimacy of the emerging governance system and public institutions;
- Legitimacy of the methods, as well as the objectives, of foreign security assistance forces;
- Regional cooperation and buy-in to the new order; and
- Energetic peacebuilding.

a) Political consensus and the resort to force

For international military operations to be genuinely peace support actions, as opposed to combatants on one side of a war, they have to be supported by a political consensus that is either formalized through a negotiated peace agreement or is being promoted through an active and dynamic peace process that includes all the major stakeholders. International military forces operating in the absence of such a consensus will not manage to generate one by force of arms. In protection operations on behalf of vulnerable populations in the midst of ongoing conflict that has not found a political settlement, high-level diplomatic commitment to the pursuit of an inclusive political settlement is critical and should be seen to be pursued.

The primary role of international security forces in a peace support operation is to support the political order sanctioned by a new peace agreement that has buy-in from all the major stakeholders, or to support the process that pursues political settlement. In both instances, a key manifestation of support for the new political order is protection of vulnerable citizens — protection from isolated spoilers and the kind of unstable environment that saps public confidence in the institutions and processes, or from more generalized violence of an unresolved political conflict. International military operations against a determined insurgency will not force a political settlement, and it is now part of the conventional wisdom, regularly repeated by people like President George Bush, President Hamid Karzai of Afghanistan, and the Chief of Staff of the Canadian Armed Forces, General Rick Hillier, that determined insurgencies cannot be militarily defeated.

In Afghanistan, which has the benefit of a general peace accord through the Bonn agreement, it is increasingly clear that neither the agreement nor the subsequent elections managed to bring all of the major stakeholders into the national consensus. As Cheshmak Farhoumand-Sims points out in Chapter 2 in this volume, the Taliban and the Pashtun communities of the South and East were either not included or are marginalized in favour of the Northern Alliance partners of the international forces that launched the attacks in October 2001 — partners whose enthusiasm for democracy and an inclusive political order knows clear limits.[29] To a significant degree, therefore, current stabilization efforts in the South are premised on reinforcing a political order that many Southerners fundamentally distrust and reject. As long as they feel themselves outsiders to the political process it is reasonable to expect that they will seek to undermine it. And as Peggy Mason, a former Disarmament Ambassador for Canada and currently an instructor at the Pearson Peacekeeping Centre, points out, for foreign military stabilization forces to be successful, the key players have to want peace more than war — if that is the case, "individual spoilers can be effectively isolated and dealt with". But if significant stakeholders believe that peace will leave them indefinitely marginalized, they will prefer war to peace[30] — and Afghans wrote the book on the futility of trying to militarily defeat determined spoilers mounting armed insurgencies.

That means there is an urgent need to open the political process to renewed negotiations to bring dissident communities and regions into the political and governance process. Unfortunately, in the "war on terror" it is also the conventional wisdom that insurgencies that employ acts of terror against one's own interests are driven by fanaticism rather than grievance, and thus are not amenable to rational negotiation or compromise. Calls by some

Canadian NGOs and elements of the political opposition for talks by the Government of Afghanistan and its international backers with the resistors have been ridiculed by others, but such calls are actually rooted in realism. They recognize that rebuilding a country and restoring the effectiveness of the central government are not simply a matter of more effective fighting or even more effective reconstruction projects. State-building in Afghanistan, as elsewhere, depends on a commitment to political inclusiveness that reaches out to those now in opposition to the government. Winning the peace is fundamentally a political challenge, not a military one. Gordon Smith, a former deputy minister of foreign affairs, in a report for the Canadian Defence and Foreign Affairs Institute, also calls for incorporating the Taliban into the political process. He points out that this "will require far more than episodic, jirga-centred dialogue between the government and extremist anti-state elements, the tokenistic representation of former radical figures in official state agencies, or the negotiation of ad hoc, local, cease-fire agreements with militants. What is needed is a process of substantial conversion or reorientation of anti-state elements into an open and non-violent political dynamic."[31]

Opposition to the current Afghan Government is concentrated in the Southern and Eastern Pashtun regions — regions and communities that have historically resisted efforts by Kabul to exert authority over their tribal areas. An Afghanistan specialist at the US Naval Post-Graduate School in Monterey, Thomas H. Johnson, says, "While it would be incorrect to refer to the Taliban insurrection or resurrection as merely a Pashtun affair, it would not be far from the mark."[32] Taliban appeals to Pashtun communal solidarity are reinforced by reminders that foreign protectors will not be there forever. Combine those realities with the failure of both the international forces and the Kabul government to make effective strides in meeting the basic needs of people in the Pashtun areas, and the result is that "the villagers either remain neutral or provide assistance to the guerrillas".[33]

A pre-requisite to peace is that the majority of Afghans in all regions become persuaded that the central government has their interests at heart and deserves their support. But that is unlikely to happen without significant changes in the way the Pashtun regions relate to the central government, and that in turn cannot happen without a new round of intra-Afghan negotiations. The issue is not to negotiate with the Taliban as an ideological movement, but to talk to the representatives of the Pashtun regional interests, which by all accounts include at least some elements of the Taliban.

The calls for such negotiations have not been lacking. President Hamid Karzai has already asked a group of former Taliban to engage dissidents.[34] The Afghan Senate has called on the government in Kabul to open direct talks with native Taliban insurgents, and for NATO-led military operations against them to stop. The call distinguishes between Afghan members of the Taliban, and Pakistani and al-Qaeda fighters, which it says are the enemy of Afghanistan. For the action to become law it would also have to be passed by the lower house of the Afghan Parliament.[35] Last fall a group of village elders told a UN Security Council delegation that the international community should make peace with the Taliban and turn from fighting the Taliban to focus on reconstruction. They said stability would be advanced by increased financial aid and rebuilding the country's infrastructure.[36] A former Afghan (Taliban) minister, who now teaches at a university in New Zealand, writing in the *International Herald Tribune*, also argued last year that the international forces in Afghanistan have reached the limit of their contribution and that a new plan is called for, including renewed focus on development, greater focus on training Afghan army and police, a Muslim peacekeeping force, and, in particular, a new intra-Afghan dialogue: "A new intra-Afghan dialogue should include all prominent personalities from within and outside the country. No time limit should be set. The participants should have the opportunity to freely voice their grievances and express their views in detail. The process may take many months, but it is only through such a process that a new social contract can emerge."[37]

Negotiating with one's adversary is the rule, not the exception, in the successful termination of armed conflict. In the NDP's dissenting opinion to the report of the House of Commons Defence Committee on Afghanistan, MP Dawn Black suggests that the success of the diplomatic element of Canada's mission in Afghanistan "should be judged by its capacity to support, facilitate and catalyze efforts towards the peaceful resolution of the conflict in Afghanistan. Specifically, the diplomatic mission should be measured by progress in building international momentum for comprehensive peace negotiations at three levels: within Afghanistan; with international players; and in the regional context. Such international momentum might take the form of a UN Security Council resolution, the appointment of a UN special envoy, and/or the establishment of a safe place for negotiations to occur."[38]

Proposals to pursue negotiations toward a reformed political order that can earn the confidence of Southerners and Northerners alike tend to be reinterpreted by Kabul, as well as by Canadian officials, as proposals for amnesty to disaffected backers of the Taliban. The counter-insurgency effort does try at times to distinguish between first-tier Taliban — the committed ideologues — and the second-tier Taliban fighters — young men who do much of the movement's fighting but who are generally thought not to be driven by the movement's ideology. The second-tier fighters are part of a broad Pashtun community that is sufficiently disaffected with Kabul to be susceptible to the Taliban's offers of attractive pay envelopes. The main effort to get these young men to decline further service to the Taliban is therefore individual amnesty and an effort to win over their villages through accelerated reconstruction projects. In addition, Canadian military officials as well as UN representatives acknowledge that reconstruction with tangible and immediate returns to villages in the South — returns that display the benefits of the central government — is the only real source of evidence of a serious intention to meet local needs and earn loyalty to the new Afghanistan. And it is only a sense of this durable mutual commitment that will finally discourage young Southerners from becoming tier-two Taliban. But amnesty to individuals and even concrete benefits to communities are unlikely to address the fundamental wariness of the central government that seems to imbue the South. The government, with its international backers, will also have to take overt steps to convince Southerners that it is striving to be representative of and sympathetic to the needs and interests of the people of the South.

If current reconstruction efforts are to have the desired political impact — that is, growing support for the government — Kabul will have to demonstrate that it is not in the hands of the traditional adversaries of the people of the South (i.e. that it is not dominated by the Northern Alliance at the expense of the Pashtun). Only then, say other analysts, will Southerners be persuaded that short-term benefits will be converted into a long-term commitment to the well-being of the South. If the South continues to view the regime as untrustworthy and not inclusive, loyalty will not be bought with projects delivered by Canadian soldiers. Farhoumand-Sims describes (in Chapter 2) a large contingent of poor farmers in the South that is driven to link to the Taliban as a consequence of their economic reality. As a result such farmers are labelled as part of the insurgency and treated accordingly, with grave consequences for the "hearts and minds" efforts of the government and its backers.

If, as Prime Minister Harper has suggested, Canada's mission in Afghanistan is linked to this country being a serious player on the global stage,[39] his Government will have to build on the extraordinary effort and sacrifice that this country has already made in Afghanistan to be at the forefront of proposing renewed peace efforts to engage politically with those political-military entities that are now in conflict with the government and that represent genuine grievances and aspirations of Afghans.

b) Legitimacy of the government and public institutions

Another critical condition for the success of foreign stabilization forces is that the national institutions and government that the foreign forces support operate in such a way as to continuously earn the loyalty and support of the population. The legitimacy of ISAF, in other words, is directly dependent upon the ongoing legitimacy of the Government of Afghanistan. At the present time that is not good news for ISAF.

In his March 2006 report on Afghanistan, UN Secretary-General Kofi Annan said he is "increasingly concerned that the insecurity that is poisoning the lives of Afghans in several provinces of the country and that denies them the ability to enjoy the benefits of the peace process, is whittling away at the support for the institutions that have emerged under the Bonn process."[40] Since then, insecurity has escalated, including in hitherto stable parts of the country, bringing the legitimacy of the government into growing disrepute. In his March 2007 report, the Secretary-General revisited the same theme: "Popular alienation remains a key factor behind the revitalized insurgency, and stems from inappropriate Government appointments, tribal nepotism and monopolization of power, and the marginalization of those outside the dominant social and political groups. The central Government's frequent tolerance of weak governance has diminished public confidence in its responsiveness and its readiness to hold officials accountable for their transgressions."[41] And as the legitimacy of the still fledgling Government falters, the legitimacy of the foreign troops that are there to support it and help extend its influence is obviously also brought into question.

Afghanistan appears to illustrate the problem of ineffective or misplaced state-building undermining peacebuilding and exacerbating insecurity. "Where external donors (and one could add external military forces) provide resources to corrupt, predatory central governments in the name of strengthening their institutions (think of Zaire during the Cold War), then state-building only advances abusive authority and fuels resentment and armed resistance."[42] Effective or strong state institutions are essential to human security, but if they are unaccountable they can also obviously be sources of abuse that produce acute human insecurity.

The Secretary-General's most recent report describes reform of the Ministry of the Interior, responsible for the Afghan police, as "a precondition for achieving a sustainable peace in Afghanistan" in part "through the creation of a more capable and motivated [police] force."[43]

Training and mentoring the Afghan army and police are key to building confidence in public institutions, and General Hillier has indicated that in the remainder of the current Canadian mission (to February 2009) that will be the focus. Development of the Afghan army is making better progress than is police training, as the Secretary-General's report indicates.[44]

Building local security institutions, like the police and judiciary, that are experienced by the people as fair and operating in the interests of all, is essential to legitimacy, as is the demobilization and disarming of combatants to give the civilian population the assurance of a serious effort to control crime and sectarian violence and to give former combatants the hope of a new future. At the same time, the security sector requires special care inasmuch as "… efforts to establish national coercive capacity — whether in the form of armies, police, or other forces — can end up empowering some segments of the population at the expense of others in a way that militates against political moderation and reconciliation".[45]

The declining legitimacy of both Kabul and ISAF is also reflected in a report by the UK-based Senlis Council, an extensive 2007 survey of Afghans in Kandahar and Helmand provinces, which showed the majority to be skeptical of the help coming from international forces and willing to admit their support of the Taliban. Particularly telling is the widespread belief in the Southern provinces that the international community will not be able to defeat the Taliban.[46] But, with the government and its military leaders in apparently growing disrepute, the least desirable and least effective response is to intensify the military effort to expand the reach and influence of a thoroughly unpopular government. It is attention to the shortcomings listed by the Secretary-General, not more military backing, that will improve the Government's political standing.

c) Restraint and the civilian death toll

Just as ISAF derives its legitimacy or lack of it in substantial measure from the government it is supporting, the Government of Afghanistan also derives, or loses, legitimacy in part from the international forces on which it relies. That also means that the intervening forces must operate in such a way as to continuously earn the loyalty and support of the population. At the present time that is not such good news for the Government.

When a *Times of London* reporter asked an Afghan Southerner what his compatriots in the Pashtun heartlands thought of the international troops operating there, the response was: "People hate NATO more than the Russians."[47] The source of the anger was the continuous flow of reports of American and ISAF killings of civilians. It should not be forgotten that the insurgent forces are responsible for the vast majority of civilian killings in Afghanistan — according to Human Rights Watch, in 2006 there were 492 civilians killed in bombings and another 177 by other attacks and executions.[48] Nevertheless, Afghan authorities report that in the first 6 months of 2007 American and ISAF forces killed more than 130 civilians,[49] and other reports claim that in the first half of 2007 more civilians were killed by ISAF and OEF forces than by insurgents.[50] The growing death toll and its impact on popular support for foreign forces are producing growing concern within ISAF. The German defence minister has called for a major re-think of military tactics: "We need to make sure that in future, operations don't take place in this way. We don't want the population against us."[51] Afghan President Hamid Karzai has also called for foreign troops to take more effective action to prevent civilian deaths, and Afghan Member of Parliament Khalid Farouqi reflected the rising anger in Afghanistan when he said: "Nobody can accept the killing of women and children. It is not acceptable in either Islam or international law." Apologies, he said, are no longer adequate.[52]

The principle at issue is restraint. In skilled domestic police action there is a presumption of care and restraint that privileges the safety of innocent bystanders over the safety of police personnel and even over the objective of capturing suspects. The report of the International Commission on Intervention and State Sovereignty emphasized the obvious importance of conducting military protection operations in ways that will not "result in widespread hatred against the intervening nations… This means accepting limitations and demonstrating through the use of restraint that the operation is not a war to defeat a state but an operation to protect populations in that state from being harassed, persecuted, or killed."[53]

But the reports of civilian casualties at the hands of international forces in Afghanistan have not abated:

- At least 14 civilians died in bombings of suspected Taliban compounds as part of the Canadian-led offensive against insurgents in the district of Panjwai.[54]

- Canadian troops mistakenly gunned down an Afghan National Police officer and a homeless beggar after their convoy was ambushed in Kandahar City.[55]

- Nine members of a family, including five women and three children, were killed in an American air strike in central Afghanistan.[56]

- American troops opened fire on a highway filled with civilian cars and bystanders, leaving 16 civilians dead and 24 wounded after a suicide car bombing in Eastern Afghanistan. One American was also wounded.[57]

- At least 40 civilians were killed in an air strike in Afghanistan by foreign forces, according to witnesses. US officials said only rebels were hit.[58]

- In mid-June NATO reported that 50 to 60 insurgents had been killed in a few days of fighting in Uruzgan province, but the head of the provincial council in Uruzgan, Mulvi Hamdullah, said the toll among civilians was far higher with at least 50 to 60 dead, with the fighting continuing.[59]

July reports from Afghan elders, that 108 civilians were killed in bombing raids in Western Afghanistan, and from villagers, that 25 civilians were killed in air strikes in the Northeast, highlight the growing problem that such reports cannot be confirmed because they come from areas under insurgent control — the problem being that, even if unconfirmed, they have a devastating political impact. The ISAF and OEF record on air strikes is such that the reports are credible and believable by local populations.[60] NATO officials say they have reviewed their operations but major changes are not planned. Instead, the strategy has been to shift responsibility to the Taliban by accusing them of using Afghan civilians as human shields. NATO defence ministers meeting in Brussels in June 2007 issued a statement saying, "We strongly condemn the insurgents' practice of deliberately endangering the civilian population, as well as the disregard for human life shown by suicide bombings and the use of improvised explosive devices."[61]

Whether or not the Taliban actually use human shields (and respect for human rights and international humanitarian law is not their hallmark), a Canadian military official in one off-the-record briefing admitted that the Taliban are skilled in luring ISAF into attacks that inflict tactical defeats on the Taliban but, by creating civilian deaths and extreme community distress, also alienate local communities from the foreign attackers and inexorably advance Taliban strategic objectives. The Taliban accept tactical defeats in the interests of strategic gains, while ISAF and the Americans pursue tactical victories at the expense of strategic objectives.

Demonstrable respect for the people of Afghanistan must illuminate every action by foreign personnel and operations — civilian and military. The high level of killings of civilians, however, indicates that American and ISAF forces have defined objectives which trump the safety and well-being of the people they are supposed to be there supporting. A separate but related issue is obviously the treatment of detainees.

d) The regional dimension

Zones of conflict are not hermetic enclaves. Moral, political, and materiel intrusions from neighbours cannot be blocked by military prowess, which means that those neighbours must be influenced and accommodated, especially in conflicts that span decades and in regions of entrenched patterns of interaction. Analysts therefore never fail to raise the Pakistan problem, which of course is the rest haven and ideological and human re-supply centre that is available in Pakistan to first-tier or hard-line Taliban combatants and leaders.

Pakistan has managed the unlikely feat of positioning itself as an ardent ally in Washington's "war on terror" while actively frustrating Washington's objectives in neighbouring Afghanistan. The well known Pakistani journalist Ahmed Rashid says that today Pakistan "is the centre of global Islamic terrorism, with Osama bin Laden and Taliban leader Mohammed Omar probably living here," with President Pervez Musharraf and his army remaining focused only on "keeping Musharraf in power".[62] Writing in *Foreign Affairs*, Barnet Rubin is a little more understanding of Pakistan's interests, pointing out that "the haven and support the Taliban receive in Pakistan are partly a response to claims Afghanistan has made against Pakistan and are also due to Islamabad's concern about both Indian influence, through the pro-India Northern Alliance, in Afghanistan and Afghan backing for Pashtun and Baluch nationalists" in Pakistan.[63]

Foreign Minister Peter MacKay used his January visit to Pakistan to join the intensified public and quiet diplomacy now underway to persuade Pakistan to try harder to stop the free move-ment of insurgents and their supplies between the two countries. A Canadian Senate Defence Committee report[64] also calls for "a defensible buffer zone" on the Afghan side of the border with Pakistan. But an intensified NATO military presence will not succeed without some parallel political work. The cooperation of Pakistan is clearly necessary, and that, in turn, requires demonstrating to Islamabad that a stable Afghanistan is in Pakistan's best interests. In other words, Pakistan's full cooperation in denying the Taliban sanctuary will depend on Kabul recognizing Pakistan's legitimate security concerns, accepting the Durand line as the boundary between the two countries, and on adopting a posture of explicit Afghan neutrality in the Pakistan-India conflict.[65] The Secretary-General rightly concludes that regional cooperation must be a "strategic priority" for Afghanistan.[66]

e) Peacebuilding: The essential context

If foreign security forces are to make an effective contribution to reversing state failure they must, above all, be accompanied by a pervasive sense that the everyday lives of people are improving. That requirement inevitably comes up against the enduring conundrum that faces peacebuilding efforts in situations of advanced instability — namely, that peacebuilding cannot proceed without a reasonable measure of security, while security forces are not trusted or supported if they are not linked to early and measurable change in the welfare and well-being of people.

A primary lesson learned through efforts to end and prevent armed conflict, and thus to set the stage for building conditions for a sustainable peace, is that stabilization/peacekeeping and peacebuilding need to be pursued simultaneously. "The comparative vulnerability of negotiated settlements to renewed conflict can be offset if a settlement is comprehensive and if its implementation involves a multidimensional peace operation. Importantly, this positive correlation between international efforts and enduring peace only characterizes peace operations that include a range of peacebuilding components and not those — such as traditional peacekeeping or more limited diplomatic efforts — that do not."[67]

It is a fact of practical politics and communal solidarity that if public institutions are not trusted and if the pursuit of livelihood is not supported by national programs, people will revert to the pursuit of sub-state interests and groups in the effort to work out their basic (human) security arrangements on their own. That is a particularly disturbing prospect in Afghanistan's North, where the insurgency is largely absent but where "the potential for wider intra-ethnic and intra-regional conflict remains", especially if the development and reconciliation objectives of the Afghanistan Compact are not pursued more effectively. As the International Crisis Group reports, there is a need to engage peaceful areas actively to prevent conflict from spreading beyond the South and the East where the insurgency is concentrated.[68]

Hence, there are regularly calls for greater balance in the international community's engagement. Currently, the extraordinarily expensive military campaigns dwarf the chronically underfunded peacebuilding/reconstruction efforts. That in turn means that the military intervention takes place in a context that makes progress next to impossible. The resort to force is not an option to be pursued when all others fail. For the use of force to be effective in reducing violence and establishing stability it must be pursued in contexts in which peacebuilding is vigorously pursued and is making a demonstrable difference.

The Threefold Dilemma of the Resort to Force in Afghanistan

It is only six years since the Bonn Agreement and the establishment of a transitional government in Afghanistan. But that came only after 30 years of war, so the obvious fact that Afghanistan is a place of ongoing instability is not itself conclusive evidence of the futility of the current peacebuilding/state-building enterprise. The real surprise would be if recovery from decades of war, human rights violations, and endemically weak governance were accomplished without a hitch in a matter of a few years.

Nevertheless, foreign military forces in Afghanistan continue to face a complicated threefold reality: First it is broadly recognized that there will be no military solution to the continuing crisis and conflict in Afghanistan; second, it is also broadly understood that foreign military assistance continues to be essential to the pursuit of a sustainable solution; and third, the lack of restraint in military operations and the use of force outside of a credible context of political consensus-building and peacebuilding produce consequences that both undermine peace efforts and generate more demand for military assistance.

The question is not whether a military-driven strategy can work, or whether alternatives (such as strategies that focus on reconciliation, political inclusion, reconstruction) should be pursued. Conflict resolution, peacebuilding, and reconstruction are not an optional alternative strategy; they must, in fact, be regarded as the only strategy. There is only one (complex) game in town — only one solution — and that involves attention to the resolution of the civil conflict that is still ongoing, and by some accounts predates the 2001 invasion, addressing the economic and other roots of conflict and widespread public grievance, building economic viability, training police and other security forces to meet security needs of people and communities, and all the other things that effective peacebuilding requires. In fact, these are the clearly articulated aims of the Afghanistan Compact's Action Plan for Peace, Justice, and Reconciliation.[69] The challenge is to employ the international military forces in support of that Plan; they obviously cannot be successfully deployed as an alternative to such a plan.

That brings us back to the basic question of the limits to force: To what extent can state-building efforts be successful if they are linked with significant military operations?

As has been argued in the foregoing, the resort to force in support of state recovery and human security depends substantially on context and methodology: political consensus, legitimate governance, the restrained and lawful application of force, regional cooperation, and energetic peacebuilding. In fragile state situations each of these will by definition be works in progress, but the absence of discernable action on any one of them jeopardizes the entire state-building effort and, in particular, threatens to convert the military effort into a counterproductive engagement that will, in a descending spiral, undermine state-building efforts and embolden the spoilers. The evidence in Afghanistan suggests that each of these five conditions is in serious deficit, and if no new remedial action is taken, the people of Afghanistan will be condemned to endure still more conflict and acute human insecurity.

Some critics of the Afghanistan operation charge that a major reason the Taliban insurgency has not been quashed is the failure of the international community to muster the level of force needed,[70] but such a claim ignores the evidence that the effective resort to force in reversing state failure and protecting vulnerable people depends on political reconciliation and peace-building efforts that are working:

- Force in the absence of a credible political consensus regarding the new order becomes hostile action on one side of a war in which not only fanatics and extremists oppose foreign military action but also broad swaths of the affected public.

- Force in support of governmental authorities and public institutions that do not have the confidence of the majority of the population is experienced by people as a hostile effort to give power to leaders that are not trusted and to strengthen institutions that are regarded by many as antithetical to the interests of their community.

- Force that abandons restraint and does not respect the safety of civilians caught in the crossfire undermines support for foreign security forces and in turn undermines support for the leadership and institutions that those forces are their to support.
- Force in a conflict zone that does not have the cooperation of neighbours courts the danger of ongoing malaise and even spreading armed conflict.
- Ongoing resort to force in the absence of measurable improvement in the daily lives of people becomes yet another adversity, the scourge of increased violence on a social and economic landscape that is already overwhelmed by trial and hardship.

In Afghanistan the international community, including Canada, has made an extraordinary and sacrificial commitment to the resort to force in pursuit of a stable and democratic Afghanistan. But the international community has not yet shown the same commitment to creating a context in which that resort to force can be fully effective. The window for remedial action is undoubtedly closing — but certain imperatives present themselves.

When leaders dutifully repeat that the struggle for a peaceful and accountable social/political order in Afghanistan will not be won militarily it is a welcome recognition of the limits to force — but it is a meaningless recognition if it is not accompanied by aggressive non-military action. There is an urgent need for a renewed pursuit of political consensus, which means talking to the Southern Pashtun and the Taliban in the interests of more inclusive and trusted political order. There is an urgent requirement for new infusions of funding and energy in support of good governance and the training of security forces that respect the rights of Afghans and that develop policing measures that will win the respect of Afghans. The ISAF forces need a fundamental rethink of their military tactics, especially the extensive resort to air strikes, that lead to an inordinate and demoralizing loss of civilian life. The governments of Afghanistan and Pakistan also need to develop persuasive mutual assurances that they are not a threat to each others' interests, and the international community needs to help Pakistan make renewed efforts to eliminate the haven that Taliban forces have been enjoying there. Finally, there is a need to rebalance the use of military and non-military instruments through a major increase in funding and delivery mechanisms to mount accelerated peacebuilding efforts, both in the areas of Afghanistan that are still relatively stable and in the chronically unstable South.

The outcome of such efforts, even if they are undertaken early and energetically, remains uncertain. On the other hand, if such efforts are not pursued, the outcome will not be in doubt. The failure in Afghanistan will deepen, public support for peacebuilding in troubled societies elsewhere will erode, and enthusiasm for efforts to protect people in extraordinary peril will be further damaged.

ERNIE REGEHR is co-founder of Project Ploughshares and Adjunct Associate Professor in Peace and Conflict Studies at Conrad Grebel University College, University of Waterloo. He has served as NGO representative and expert advisor on numerous Government of Canada delegations to multilateral disarmament forums and has published various works on peace and security. His current engagements include the Board of the Africa Peace Forum of Nairobi, Kenya. He is an Officer of the Order of Canada.

Endnotes

1 United Nations General Assembly. *2005 World Summit Outcome*, Resolution, A/Res/60/1, October 24, 2005, paras 138-139.

2 Bendsahel, Nora, "Preventing Insurgencies After Major Combat Operations," *Defence Studies*, Vol. 6, No. 3 (September 2006), pp. 278–291. http://www.rand.org/pubs/reprints/RP1242/.

3 Baranyi, Stephen, Principal Researcher for The North-South Institute Project entitled "What Kind of Peace is Possible?" conclusions and reports available online at: http://www.nsi-ins.ca/english/research/progress/28.asp Also forthcoming from UBC Press in spring 2008 — *The Paradoxes of Peacebuilding Post 9/11* (working title)

4 United States of America. *The National Security Strategy of the United States of America.* Washington: The White House, September 2002, p. 1. http://www.whitehouse.gov/nsc/nssall.html

5 *Foreign Policy* and The Fund for Peace. "The Failed States Index, *Foreign Policy* May/June 2006, p. 1. http://www.foreignpolicy.com/story/cms.php?story_id=3420.

6 "The Parties agree that an armed attack against one or more of them in Europe or North America shall be considered an attack against them all and consequently they agree that, if such an armed attack occurs, each of them, in exercise of the right of individual or collective self-defence recognized by Article 51 of the Charter of the United Nations, will assist the Party or Parties so attacked by taking forthwith, individually and in concert with the other Parties, such action as it deems necessary, including the use of armed force, to restore and maintain the security of the North Atlantic area."

7 A full account of Canadian Force contributions to OEF and ISAF operations in Afghanistan is provided in the, "Canadian Forces in Afghanistan: Report of the House of Commons Standing Committee on National Defence" (39th Parliament, 1st Session, June 2007), Chair, Rick Casson, MP.

8 UN Security Council Resolution 1386 (Dec. 20/01) and Resolution 1510 (Oct 13/03).

9 The Afghanistan Compact, approved at The London Conference on Afghanistan, January 31 — February 1, 2006. http://www.fco.gov.uk/Files/kfile20060130%20Afghanistan%20Compact%20Final%20Final,0.doc.

10 References to the May 17 debate on Afghanistan are taken from Hansard of that day. http://www.parl.gc.ca/39/1/parlbus/chambus/house/debates/025_2006-05-17/HAN025-E.htm.

11 Prime Minister Stephen Harper speaks at an Easter dinner with veterans in Verlinghem, France, April 8, 2007. http://www.pm.gc.ca/eng/media.asp?id=1618.

12 OECD. Principles for Good International Engagement in Fragile States, Development Cooperation Directorate of the Organisation for Economic Co-operation and Development, April 7, 2005. DCD(2005)8/REV2, http://www.oecd.org/dataoecd/59/55/34700989.pdf.

13 *Foreign Policy* and The Fund for Peace, "The Failed States Index, *Foreign Policy* May/June 2006 (http://www.foreignpolicy.com/story/cms.php?story_id=3420), p. 1.

14 Baranyi, Stephen and Kristiana Powell. "Fragile States, Gender Equality and Aid Effectiveness: A Review of Donor Perspectives, CIDA, August 11, 2005. http://www.nsi-ins.ca/english/pdf/Gender_FS_Paper_Donor_Perspectives.pdf.

15 Canada. "Confronting the Threat of Failed and Fragile States," drafted by Mark Sedra and Nathan Naidoo of the Policy Research Division for the Deputy Ministers' Committee on Global Affairs, Foreign Affairs Canada, 2005 (mimeo), p. 2.

16 CIDA. "On the Road to Recovery: Breaking the Cycle of Poverty and Fragility, Guidelines for Effective Development Cooperation in Fragile States (Canadian International Development Agency, November 2005 — mimeo), p. 6.

17 CIDA, pp. 28–29.

18 Canada. Canada's International Policy Statement (IPS). *Defence: A Role of Pride and Influence in the World.* Department of National Defence (Ottawa, 2005), p. 5

19 Canada. "Confronting the Threat of Failed and Fragile States," p. 1.

20 Canada. Canada's International Policy Statement (IPS). Overview: A Role of Pride and Influence in the World. Department of Foreign Affairs and International Trade (Ottawa, 2005), p. 13.

21 Canada. IPS. Overview, p. 13.

22 Canada. IPS. Overview, pp. 13–14.

23 "Failed States: Canadian Action in Conflict-Affected States," Discussion Papers by CCIC (December 2006 – mimeo).

24 Ibid, p. 3.

25 Canada. "Confronting the Threat of Failed and Fragile States."

26 Demographic pressures, human displacement, group paranoia, human flight, uneven economic development, severe economic decline, criminalization of the state, deterioration of public services, human rights violations, unaccountable security apparatuses, factionalized elites, and external interveners (elaborated on The Fund for Peace site — http://www.fundforpeace.org/web/index.php?option=com_content&task=view&id=104&Itemid=324).

27 The 2007 report: Sudan, Iraq, Somalia, Zimbabwe, Chad, Cote d'Ivoire, DRC, Afghanistan, Guinea, Central African Republic, Haiti, Pakistan, North Korea, Burma, Uganda, Bangladesh, Nigeria, Ethiopia, Burundi, Timor-Leste. (http://www.foreignpolicy.com/story/cms.php?story_id=3865&print=1)

28 Project Ploughshares, *Armed Conflicts Report 2006* (http://www.ploughshares.ca/libraries/ACRText/ACR-TitlePageRev.htm).

29 Baranyi, Stephen and Kristiana Powell. WKOP, Chapter 11, Conclusions.

30 Masson, Peggy. "Canadian strategy making matters worse," *Mondial*, June 2006 (World Federalists of Canada).

31 Smith, Gordon. "Canada in Afghanistan: Is it working?" Canadian Defence and Foreign Affairs Institute, March 2007. http://www.cdfai.org/PDF/Canada%20in%20Afghanistan%20Is%20it%20Working.pdf.

32 Johnson, Thomas. H. "On the Edge of the Bid Muddy: The Taliban Resurgence in Afghanistan," China and Eurasia Forum Quarterly, Vol. 5, No. 2 (2007), p. 122. http://www.silkroadstudies.org/new/docs/CEF/Quarterly/May_2007/Johnson.pdf

33 Johnson, Thomas. H. and M. Chris Mason. "Understanding the Taliban and Insurgency in Afghanistan," Orbis, Vol. 51, No. 1 (Winter 2007), p. 87.

34 Friel, Terry. "Only peace talks can save Afghanistan — former rebel," Reuters, April 12, 2007 http://www.afghanistannewscenter.com/news/2007/april/apr122007.html#4

35 Afghan Senate urges Taliban talks, BBC News, May 9, 2007. http://news.bbc.co.uk/2/hi/south_asia/6637473.stm

36 "Make peace with the Taliban, village elders tell UN," CBC News, November 14, 2006. http://www.cbc.ca/world/story/2006/11/14/delegation-afghanistan.html

37 Lafraie, Najibullah. "The Way Out of Afghanistan Is to Get Out," International Herald Tribune, September 6, 2006. http://www.spiegel.de/international/0,1518,435388,00.html

38 Black, Dawn. Dissenting opinion of the New Democratic Party to the Standing Committee on National Defence, Canadian Forces in Afghanistan: Report of the Standing Committee on National Defence, June 2007, 39th Parliament, 1st Session. http://cmte.parl.gc.ca/Content/HOC/committee/391/nddn/reports/rp3034719/391_NDDN_Rpt01_Pdf/391_NDDN_Rpt01_Pdf-e.pdf

39 Speech to the Economic Club of New York, September 20, 2006. http://www.pm.gc.ca/eng/media.asp?category=2&id=1327

40 Report to the Security Council, "The Situation in Afghanistan and its implications for international peace and security," A/60/712 — S/2006/145, March 7, 2006. http://daccessdds.un.org/doc/UNDOC/GEN/N06/260/77/PDF/N0626077.pdf?OpenElement

41 Annan, Kofi. Secretary General's report to the General Assembly, "The situation in Afghanistan and its implications for international peace and security," March 15, 2007 (Sixty-first session, Agenda item 16) and the Security Council (A/61/799–S/2007/152).

42 Call, Charles. T. and Elizabeth M. Cousens. "Ending Wars and Building Peace," Coping with Crisis Working paper Series (International Peace Academy, 2007), p. 9.

43 Annan.

44 "Hillier says training Afghan Army now first priority," Globe and Mail, June 17, 2007. http://www.theglobeandmail.com/servlet/story/RTGAM.20070617.whillier0617/BNStory/National/

45 Call and Cousens, p. 9.

46 Senlis Afghanistan, "On a Knife Edge: Rapid Assessment Field Survey Southern and Easter Afghanistan, March 2007. http://www.senliscouncil.net/modules/publications

47 Albone, Tim, "Civilian deaths are making NATO the enemy," The Times, March 5, 2007. http://www.timesonline.co.uk/tol/news/world/asia/article1473092.ece

48 "Taliban accused of war crimes for killing civilians," Associated Press, International Herald Tribune (Asia Pacific), April 16, 2007. http://www.iht.com/articles/2007/04/16/asia/afghan.php

49 Bearak, Barry and Taimoor Shah. "7 Children Killed in Airstrike in Afghanistan," The New York Times, June 19, 2007. http://www.nytimes.com/2007/06/19/world/asia/19afghan.html?ex=1182830400&en=c7cda1ad17b2a811&ei=5099&partner=TOPIXNEWS

50 "Afghan investigation finds 62 Taliban, 45 civilians killed in southern battle," International Herald Tribune, June 30, 2007. http://www.iht.com/bin/print.php?id=6428190

51 "German Criticizes US Over Afghan Civilian Deaths," Deutsche Welle, May 14, 2007. http://www.dw-world.de/dw/article/0,2144,2514088,00.html

52 Bearak and Shah, "7 Children Killed..."

53 The Responsibility to Protect. Report of the International Commission on Intervention and State Sovereignty, December 2001 (Ottawa: International Development Research Centre), p. 63.

54 Smith, Graeme. "Civilian deaths reported in Operation Medusa," Globe and Mail, September 8, 2006.

55 Canadian troops kill Afghan civilian, officer," CTV.ca, February 19, 2007. http://www.cbc.ca/world/story/2007/02/19/afghan-canadian.html

56 Gall, Carlotta and Abdul Waheed Wafa. "US Strike Kills 9 Family Members Near Kabul, Afghans say," New York Times, March 6, 2007.

57 Gall, Carlotta. "16 Civilians Die as US Troops Fire on Afghan Road, New York Times, March 5, 2007.

58 Achakzai, Saeed Ali. "US-led Raid Kills 40 Civilians in Afghanistan, Witnesses," Reuters, May 10, 2007. http://www.alertnet.org/thenews/newsdesk/ISL305008.htm

59 Witte, Griff and Javed Hamdard. "Dozens Die in NATO's Offensive in Afghanistan," Washington Post, June 19, 2007. http://www.washingtonpost.com/wp-dyn/content/article/2007/06/18/AR2007061800305.html?hpid=sec-world

60 Strziuso, Jason. "Afghan elders claim rising fatalities in NATO campaign," The Chronicle Herald, Halifax, July 8, 2007.

61 John, Mark and Andrew Gray. "NATO says review reducing Afghan civilian casualties," Globe and Mail, June 15, 2007. http://www.theglobeandmail.com/servlet/story/RTGAM.20070615.wnatoafghan0615/BNStory/Afghanistan/home

62 Rashid, Ahmed. "US duped into support for Musharraf," Kitchener-Waterloo Record, June 21, 2007.

63 Karzai's government is linked to India, according to Pakistan, through strong personal and political ties and Pakistan is concerned that a strategic alliance with India will not only undermine Pakistan's traditional influence in Afghanistan but will give India a foothold from which to further threaten Pakistan. ["Musharraf's Taliban Problem," Backgrounder, Council on Foreign Relations, September 11, 2006. http://www.cfr.org/publication/11401/musharrafs_taliban_problem.html]

64 "Canadian Troops in Afghanistan: Taking a Hard Look at a Hard Mission," An interim Report of the Standing Committee on National Security and Defence, February 2007. http://www.parl.gc.ca/39/1/parlbus/commbus/senate/com-e/defe-e/rep-e/repFeb07-e.pdf

65 Rubin, Barnet. "Saving Afghanistan," Foreign Affairs, January/February 2007. http://www.foreignaffairs.org

66 Annan.

67 Call and Cousens refer to Michael W. Doyle and Nicholas Sambanis, Making War and Building Peace: United Nations Peace Operations, Princeton: Princeton University Press, 2006.

68 ICG, Afghanistan's Endangered Compact, International Crisis Group Policy Briefing, Asia Briefing No. 59, January 29, 2007.

69 Peace, Reconciliation and Justice in Afghanistan Action Plan of the Government of the Islamic Republic of Afghanistan, 6–7 June, 2005. http://www.aihrc.org.af/tj_actionplan_19_dec_05.htm#_ftn2#_ftn2

70 "We need more boots on the ground," Canadian Press, Edmonton Sun, July 5, 2007. http://www.edmontonsun.com/News/Canada/2007/07/05/4315974.html

Canada's Contribution to Gender Equity in Afghanistan

Cheshmak Farhoumand-Sims

Canada's Contribution to Gender Equity in Afghanistan

Cheshmak Farhoumand-Sims

Almost three decades of war have devastated Afghanistan's economy and destroyed the social, political, economic, and physical infrastructures, leaving the country with one of highest rates of poverty, underdevelopment, illiteracy, and infant and maternal mortality in the world. The departure of the Taliban brought new opportunities and a renewed hope and optimism to Afghanistan. Within weeks, the international aid community had descended on Kabul, with hundreds of millions of dollars in aid, and the dream of transforming Afghanistan after decades of violence and underdevelopment. The years since have been marked by unprecedented achievements, as well as difficult challenges. Canada has been one of Afghanistan's partners in this endeavour, committing hundreds of millions of dollars in aid as well as providing troops to NATO forces engaged in security efforts.

Special attention is being focused on Afghan women and efforts to promote their equality. While the whole of the Afghan population has suffered greatly during the last three decades of conflict, women were particularly effected by it, especially under the Mujahedeen and Taliban rules. While women activists, human rights organizations, and the United Nations tried to draw attention to the plight of Afghan women throughout the 1990s, international response was largely muted. Then came the tragic events of September 11, 2001, propelling Afghanistan back into international consciousness, and the plight of Afghan women became a rallying cry of the United States and its allies in the "war on terror". The last six years have seen some progress on the gender equality front, but progress has been slow and laboured and the level of progress anticipated is yet to be achieved.

The premise of the paper is that women's equal access to rights and opportunities is a prerequisite to sustainable peace and development in Afghanistan, making gender equality programming an essential component of international engagement in Afghanistan. The paper will consider Canada's efforts to promote gender equality in Afghanistan; discuss the ways in which gender dynamics in Afghanistan have been, and continue to be influenced by culture, tradition, and religion, historical realities, and militarism; and suggest that Afghan women are not victims but empowered with the agency and determination necessary to lead the fight for equality, with support from their international partners. The paper will argue that effective gender equality programming must account for the Afghan context, ensure that policies are formulated and implemented in a religiously and culturally sensitive manner, and facilitate the full participation of Afghan women towards sustainable peacebuilding and reconstruction efforts. I believe that strengthening the Afghan women's movement and connecting it to like-minded regional and international feminist networks will serve to promote Afghan-led and directed transformation of patriarchal attitudes and institutions that sustain gender inequality.

The Instrumentalization of Women's Rights in Afghanistan

Within days of the 9/11 tragedy, news shifted to the Taliban's "gender apartheid". Pictures of burqa-clad women and accounts of human rights violations against Afghanistan's women dominated Western media.[1] The instrumentalization of Afghan women's rights became part of a deliberate strategy to gain support for the "war on terror", justifying the impending military campaign named "Operation Enduring Freedom", and elicited fierce debate within the feminist community. Many feminists supported the government's approach, while others expressed skepticism at this "sudden interest in the Taliban's treatment of women in Afghanistan" and offered their own analysis on this co-optation of women's rights for military purposes.[2] This latter group criticized the linking of violence with efforts to protect and promote women's rights and argued that military response would not decrease but exacerbate the suffering of Afghan women and their families. Women in Afghanistan were pleading that their children not be exposed to further violence and suffering, while the US first lady was helping to gain support for the violence by stating that Afghan women were rejoicing at the retreat of the Taliban who had made the "lives of children and women in Afghanistan miserable".[3] The general feeling among those of us working on Afghan women's issues was well articulated by Katha Pollitt of *The Nation* who said:

> "This war is not about freeing women from government-mandated burqas, or teaching girls to read, or improving Afghan women's ghastly maternal mortality rate of 17 in 1,000 births — the second highest in the world. Those things may happen as a by-product of realpolitik, or they may not. But if women's rights and well-being were aims of US Afghan policy, the Carter, Reagan, and Bush administrations would never have financed the mujahedeen, whose neanderthal treatment of women, including throwing acid at unveiled women, was well documented from the start; the Clinton Administration would not have initially accepted the Taliban even after they closed the girls' schools in Herat; and the current Bush Administration would have inundated the millions of Afghan women and girls in Pakistan's refugee camps with teachers, nurses, doctors and food."[4]

The fall of the Taliban in November 2001, and the Bonn Agreement that was drafted one month later, signalled the beginning of international efforts to bring peace, security, reconstruction and development to Afghanistan.[5] For women's rights activists, the highlight of the Agreement was the promotion of gender equality principles, and the establishment of the first Ministry of Women's Affairs (MOWA) in Afghanistan.[6] Achievements such as the guaranteeing of equality rights in the new Afghan Constitution, the participation of women in Presidential and Parliamentary elections, the election of women to Parliament, and the efforts to increase women's rights and opportunities are hailed by Western leaders as the successes of their interventions. Still Afghan women are only guardedly optimistic. They celebrate the explicit inclusion of gender equality but "remain cautious due to other constitutional provisions that proclaim Afghanistan an 'Islamic Republic' and declare that the beliefs and provisions of the sacred religion of Islam have precedence over any law in Afghanistan".[7] This apparent conflict will pose an obstacle to the advancement of women if extremist interpretations of Shari'a are used to determine women's rights and responsibilities in Afghanistan. Furthermore, many women were barred from participating in the elections by their male "guardian", or intimidated into casting ballots for a particular individual, and women candidates and parliamentarians were and continue to be subjected to verbal assaults, insults, intimidation, and threats by their male counterparts. Clearly, deeply-rooted patriarchal attitudes and institutions still operate, and much more time, commitment by national and international actors, and financial and human resources will be needed for positive change to take root. In the meantime, as much as the US and other Western countries wish to justify their past and current policies in Afghanistan by linking them to advancements by women, it is inappropriate, and indeed unethical, to continue co-opting women's rights issues in Afghanistan to advance or justify our own policies, until such time that the victories we claim are indisputable.

Gender Equality and State Fragility: Considering Afghanistan's History and Context

While peacebuilding, reconstruction, and development are challenging endeavours in any conflict and post-conflict environment, they are particularly difficult in contexts of "fragile"[8] and "failed" states. According to Baranyi and Powell:

"...fragility refers to certain states' inability and/or unwillingness to provide essential public goods like protection from external threat, rule of law, and basic social services to most of their citizens..."[9]

In Afghanistan, there are many factors contributing to state fragility, all of which have implications for the advancement of women. I will focus on two. First is the central government's lack of institutional capacity, internal corruption, and limited reach outside of Kabul. The international community has responded to this with financial support and extensive training programs. But "the reconstruction of Afghanistan desperately needs the expertise of technocrats, professionals, and intellectuals, most of whom have fled the country"[10] or been killed since the start of the violence. It will take many years to reverse the impact of this. Second is the continued power and influence of warlords who continue to dominate the political scene and greatly undermine Afghanistan's ability to move forward socially, politically, and economically. Many of these power brokers are complicit in the decades of violence — some of them have been implicated in war crimes — and yet they are fully integrated into the political system where they have brought their culture of criminality and impunity.[11] This issue has contributed to frustration and cynicism among the general public, the majority of whom are committed to peace, and supportive of the government, but wish to see these warlords marginalized and brought to justice.[12]

Western actors argue that marginalizing warlords from the political process would present a threat to peace, security, reconstruction, and development. This may be true, but casting them as the "heroes" of Afghanistan's war against foreign occupation, and their effortless entry into Afghanistan's new power structures, is contributing to state fragility, exposing the dilemmas and contradictions inherent in rebuilding fragile states, and raising normative questions about the international community's roles and responsibilities in conflict and post-conflict contexts, and the ways in which support of former power holders can and does undermine achieving sustainable peace and development. Warlordism also has implications for Afghan women. Most warlords are known for their misogynistic attitudes and despised for a disturbing history of human rights violations against the Afghan population, including women.[13] It is unclear how Afghanistan can have successful gender equality (GE) within this context.

Gender inequality is both a feature of state fragility, and a prerequisite to rebuilding state capacity.[14] Considering gender in efforts to transform fragile states is important because men and women experience and are impacted differently in situations of conflict, violence, and underdevelopment, and the consequences for them in these contexts vary tremendously due to their dissimilar social roles, responsibilities, and access to rights and opportunities. While the international community has emphasized the situation of women under the Taliban, Huma Ahmed-Gosh argues that the treatment of women cannot be neatly categorized into pre-Taliban and post-Taliban frameworks of analysis, but requires an understanding that "There is a history over the centuries of women's subjugation" in that country.[15] Historically, efforts to advance women's rights and opportunities met with severe opposition and resistance among the powerful clergy and tribal leaders, even leading to violence.[16] Today, women's rights are viewed as part of a Western agenda, used by all sides as a propaganda tool linked to cultural and religious values. "Every possible roadblock to the realization of women's rights and to the participation of women in decision-making processes has been installed: the perpetuation of warlordism, the lack of security, and the lack of effective gender policy coordination." [17]

Ahmed-Gosh asserts that, "Afghanistan may be the only country in the world where during the last century kings and politicians have been made and undone by struggles relating to women's status."[18] In the 1960s and 1970s, there was some improvement in women's access to education and employment opportunities but these were short-lived and, due to the pervasive urban/rural divide, largely benefited upper-class women in urban centres and not impacting women's lives in rural areas. This resistance to gender equality efforts is rooted in deeply patriarchal attitudes stemming from strong cultural norms and narrow interpretations of Islam. Years of conflict, fraught with religious undertones, have further deepened these cultural and religious attitudes toward women and their roles in society, despite Islam and Afghanistan's history of having strong women heroines and social actors. This context demands that GE programming be culturally and religiously sensitive while at the same time not allowing these considerations to be used as justification for discrimination.[19]

Canada in Afghanistan: An Agenda for Peace and Development[20]

Canada has been at the forefront of efforts to promote peace and development in Afghanistan. It has been one of Afghanistan's most consistent donors, and has made gender equality a central component of its programming there.[21] Since 2002, Afghanistan has been CIDA's largest recipient of donor funds.[22] These funds are being spent on four program areas: sustainable rural livelihoods and community based development projects; democratic development and effective governance; supporting the role of women and girls, including access to education; and meeting the basic human needs of vulnerable Afghans.[23] Since February 2006, Canada's involvement in Afghanistan has been based on the goals and outcome objectives outlined in the Afghanistan Compact.[24] The Compact represents the goals and objectives that define a framework for co-operation for 2006–2011 and aims to "establish an effective mechanism for coordinating Afghan and international efforts" in order to improve impact.[25] The Compact notes that the country's "transition from peace and security is not yet assured" requiring continued "strong international engagement" and focuses on four areas: security; governance, rule of law, and human rights; economic and social development; and counter-narcotics.[26] Canada is approaching its efforts in Afghanistan as a "whole of government" approach, which is an extension of the 3D approach (diplomacy, development, defence) by engaging all relevant government departments and units — such as the RCMP, Elections Canada, Statistics Canada and others as appropriate — that can address the "unique challenges facing Afghanistan" and supporting stabilization and reconstruction there.[27]

Canada's largest disbursement of funds are to the Afghanistan Reconstruction Trust Fund (ARTF),[28] the National Solidarity Program (NSP),[29] the Microfinance Investment Support Facility for Afghanistan (MISFA)[30] and the United Nations Mine Action Centre in Afghanistan, which has received a total of $13.8 million.[31] Of these, the NSP has received the most attention for its aim of engaging local communities in their own social and economic development.[32] The program provides cash grants from the Afghan Government directly to locally-elected community development councils (CDCs) who then lead their communities through the process of identifying, planning, managing, and monitoring their own development projects. To receive funding the CDCs must allocate 10 per cent of their budget to women's activities, something that they rarely achieve, yet their failure to do so is tolerated.[33]

Clearly "many recipient organizations adopt 'gender friendly' projects to acquire donor funding, but do not fulfill this mandate, raising questions about how seriously these groups are committed to and capable of achieving gender equality for Afghan women."[34] Funders of NSP argue that more female staff are needed to guide and facilitate the development process through women's CDCs but say that insecurity is inhibiting efforts to hire women and send them out into communities. The Afghanistan Research and Education Unit (AREU) agrees that increasing female staff is a critical component of success but suggests this must be coupled with increasing gender awareness, soliciting support for women's participation and legitimacy by engaging power holders (such as religious and tribal leaders), creating communication links between men's and women's CDCs, and improving accountability structures, which do not adequately hold recipient organizations to account.[35] This accountability must be uniformly imposed on all partners, including the Government of Afghanistan (GOA). Presently CIDA does not extend the same level of scrutiny to the Afghan government as it does to other partners; "it does not conduct formal evaluations of funds allocated to the Afghan government,"[36] nor are funds withheld for non-compliance. CIDA must address this issue immediately, especially at a time when the vast majority of CIDA's spending in Afghanistan is channelled through the Government of Afghanistan, an apparatus that is wracked by lack of capacity, corruption, and a lack of visible commitment to GE.

Several reasons motivated the decision to fund projects through the GOA rather than grassroots organizations. The decision was largely rooted in the "nation building" project in Afghanistan and the fact that, historically, governments in Kabul have had little reach or perceived relevance outside of the capital region. It was believed that this perception had to be modified for the sake of future peace and development so that a relationship between the GOA and the Afghan populace could be made. Hence, providing funds to the government to implement projects throughout the country was thought to strengthen capacity and reinforce popular support and allegiance. A second issue leading to the transfer of funds through the GOA was a growing resentment in Afghanistan against the NGO community, both local and foreign. The infusion of donor money into Afghanistan led to a rapidly expanding presence of foreign NGOs and the formation of Afghan ones, creating what Antonio Donini refers to as the "Kabul Bubble".[37] Small local NGOs, with "little or no capacity for implementing development projects and results-based management", were simply created to "capture a portion of the vast donor funds available for gender programming",[38] while international NGOs and their staff depleted donor funds with exorbitant salaries, rent, security needs, support staff, and so on.

The explosion of NGOs also meant duplication, lack of coordination, and the unfortunate waste of precious donor funds and human resources. To Afghans it appeared that the conflict was enriching foreigners and the Afghan "elite" while very little of the donor funds seemed to be entering the local economy and benefiting poor local populations. The infusion of funds was also creating and exacerbating class differences and contributing to social fissures. Those who spoke English, were literate, and had the skills needed by the international agencies had access to jobs and good salaries while those working in the local economy continued to struggle on less than $20 a month. Kabul residents and returning refugees could not find housing while undamaged houses were being rented to aid organizations for $10,000 to $15,000 a month. The growing resentment of Western NGOs created pressure on the Afghan government to reign in the proliferation of NGOs and regulate their activity so channelling all funds through the GOA was seen as a possible solution to this growing dilemma. But this approach has not proven wholly successful or beneficial either. The GOA itself is weakened by corruption, lack of capacity, and lack of absorption capability. But more importantly, the emphasis on government capacity building has taken attention away from the equally important tasks of building a strong civil society, developing capacity within the grassroots and local NGO communities — which is central to community peacebuilding, development, and poverty reduction — and counteracting the growing insurgency — which is having deadly impact on Afghans and the foreigners trying to assist them.

This growing insurgency is a threat to peace and development in Afghanistan and of particular importance to Canada and Canadians given our military involvement with NATO in the South of the country. Canada has been militarily engaged in Afghanistan since December 2001 when a naval task force was deployed to the Persian Gulf. This was followed in February 2002 by the deployment of a battle group from the Princess Patricia's Canadian Light Infantry to support the US Operation Enduring Freedom (OEF) in Kandahar Province. But our greatest involvement has been with the NATO-led International Security Assistance Forces (ISAF). Initially, ISAF was mandated to provide security in the Kabul area allowing for stabilization and reconstruction to begin, but this mandate changed in 2006 when NATO assumed command of all military operations, and the Canadian military joined counterinsurgency military operations against growing Taliban resurgence in the South, as well as participating in the work of Canada's Provincial Reconstruction Team (PRT). The PRTs are part of the "whole of government" approach to Afghanistan, and bring together personnel from Foreign Affairs, CIDA, and the RCMP, with the aim of providing security while working with local leaders and populations to expand on development and reconstruction efforts.

This military engagement has resulted in the death of 66 soldiers and one diplomat so far,[39] and is greatly impacting all aspects of Canadian policy in Afghanistan. My interviews with CIDA officials revealed the challenges of working on such a high profile portfolio. One official noted that the organization is under a lot of pressure because Afghanistan is a particular and distinct case. It is not only a recipient country for development assistance, but also a theatre of war fighting by Canadian Forces, resulting in unprecedented scrutiny, not only from government but also the Canadian public. This has led to "a strong foreign policy imperative on the part of the Prime Minister and the Canadian government" which "sets up a nexus of foreign policy interests globally — i.e. global security — and lends Afghanistan a very high profile that is much, much higher than any other country we've ever been involved in". While this high profile and scrutiny has its benefits such as added resources, attention of senior officials, et cetera, it also "limits our ability at times to implement and design programs with aid effectiveness profiles. On the one hand, we need to be in line with goals in the country and coordinate our efforts with other aid agencies, but on the other hand, when there is such a high profile and time pressures, you can't always do that effectively. The pressure is on to show what you're doing, demonstrate that you're active on the aid front and to show there is partnership with other departments. Afghanistan's profile makes it so that domestic pressures impact time lines and take focus away from development milestones."[40]

An Analysis of Canada's Engagement in Afghanistan

While there has been some progress in Afghanistan, a number of recently written studies and papers[41] suggest that the slow rate of reconstruction along with the worsening security situation is threatening short- and long-term progress. These reports express concerns about the consequences of limited visible impact. The reports point to, among other things: the inadequate level of aid; government incapacity and absorption capacity; state building efforts in a country that has never seen a central government with reach outside of its capital; high levels of corruption, criminality, and insecurity; the impact of military operations on peace-building and reconstruction efforts; and the slow rate of reconstruction and development, which has resulted in relatively low impact, particularly outside of Kabul. They point out that the near future will be decisive.

Canada's efforts (both development and military) have not been without criticism and controversy. The military engagement in the South — although vital to preventing another civil war — is seen as an expensive enterprise, which is in some ways deepening violence rather than ameliorating it. NATO and US military efforts are causing an unacceptable number of civilian deaths, and making it difficult for development aid to reach the needy population. The military is labelling all insurgent fighters as terrorists without distinguishing between ideologically motivated fighters and poor farmers and villagers who are picking up arms and fighting alongside the Taliban in exchange for the salary needed to feed their families.[42] So in addition to the large number of civilians being killed in major operations, there is a significant contingent of poor farmers who are being labelled as insurgents and arrested or killed, with grave consequences in the quest to "win hearts and minds". Another concern about the military engagement is its impact on development efforts. Aid organizations argue that the militarization of aid, and the blurring of lines between military operations and aid provision, is making it extremely difficult and dangerous for them to access the Southern region, thus contributing to the cycle of poverty impacting the insurgency and the violence impeding development.[43] Certainly, security is imperative. It provides an enabling environment for development, reconstruction, economic growth, and community building, but as more and more observers are suggesting, the roots of the insurgency are extremely complex and a military solution without diplomatic pressure on neighbouring states and an accelerated development agenda will prove costly and fruitless and only serve to strengthen the insurgency. One report notes that, "If major conflict continues at the present rate, there is a very real risk that the local population will become increasingly frustrated by the lack of security (engendering various negative responses), and that some allies will head home."[44]

On the development front, there are major concerns that the slow rate of reconstruction and development despite six years of international engagement and billions of dollars spent on these efforts, is leading to donor fatigue as well as disappointment and frustration among the Afghan population. Many argue that underdevelopment and abject poverty are significant factors contributing to the rising insurgency, and that "development failure" is impeding progress on the military front in this vicious circle where "each is paradoxically, both cause and symptom of the other."[45]

As one report articulates:

> *"In Afghanistan, security and development are integrally linked; it is futile to proceed with one without the other. It has been argued that Canada's current civilian development policies are not achieving the necessary success, because they are compromised through close association with the military presence. At the same time, the limited nature of reconstruction and economic opportunities in the South likewise impacts negatively on the Canadian military presence, putting Canadian soldiers at further risk and jeopardizing success."[46]*

It is well known that Afghanistan has received a significantly lower proportion of aid per capita than most other post-conflict nations. Moreover, the disproportionate amount of funds being invested in the military campaign as compared to development spending is not lost on local populations. Afghan researchers, think tanks, activists and Afghanis themselves highlight the link between poverty and the rising insurgency and warn that unless something is done quickly to remedy the situation, the insurgency will continue to grow. History has shown us that foreign armies do not fare well in Afghanistan and that insurgencies cannot be fought and won with military might.

Given Canada's military commitment in the South, "one would expect to see a comparable level of humanitarian assistance, and where possible, development assistance in the province"[47] yet reconstruction and development efforts in the South remain largely insufficient and the Canadian non-military presence is very limited. Analysts suggest that this lack of Canadian presence and impact in Kandahar is having negative consequences on the military efforts and hurting the Kandaharis. Food aid is not meeting the needs of the starving population,[48] the health sector continues to be grossly underfunded and inadequate to meet the needs of an increasing number of casualties of violence between coalition fighters and the Taliban, and there is yet to be an increase in the number of schools to meet the needs of the local population.[49]

CIDA officials respond to these criticisms by explaining that Canada is indeed investing in Kandahar province, and collaborating with the Afghan government to increase development spending in the province, but does not want to focus its efforts solely on Kandahar simply because of the military aspect of our engagement. One CIDA officer explained that:

"In Kandahar, you have a careful balancing act. You want to pay specific attention to the place because of the military aspect of Canada's engagement but you don't want to sacrifice your national approach. Yes, the fires are in the Southeast, but there is potential for instability in the North so you have to create programs that aim at a stabilizing front. This is important in Afghanistan because unless you can strengthen the central government and make it visible in the North and West as well as the South, you are actually weakening things. That is why CIDA is focusing on having strong national programs going through the central government in Kabul. If there is a sense of exclusion, if lots of resources are devoted to the South, that could actually destabilize other parts of the country." [50]

To have a more balanced approach then, the organization has allocated $20 million (of its planned $100 million disbursement), to development programs in Kandahar, and is also financially contributing to the Afghan government's recent announcement of $21 million in development spending in Kandahar for "building irrigation and drinking water systems, as well as roads, clinics, and schools".[51] They explain that while the interest and motivation for increasing impact in the South is there, the dangerous and worsening security situation continues to impede its efforts.

Oates and others say the lack of spending in Kandahar has not been the only concern related to Canada's program in Afghanistan. They point to several issues that have exacerbated CIDA's difficulties in planning and implementing projects and programs in Afghanistan. Although some improvements are underway, discussing and analyzing these issues provides valuable "lessons learned" for future Canadian engagement in Afghanistan and elsewhere. The first concern has been weaknesses within the Afghanistan Desk itself.[52] "At a time when Canada was investing hundreds of millions of dollars in Afghanistan, the unit had only a handful of officers, most of whom were based in Canada, and few of whom had country expertise making it very difficult for them to undertake strategic planning and base projects on local needs and lived experience."[53] And, instead of using country-based research and needs assessments, programming was largely ad hoc:

"CIDA would get unsolicited proposals and decided if they would fund it or not rather than having an overarching plan and then seeking out proposals that matched their objectives. Although things have improved, this is still happening to some extent. It might come together at the end, but the absence of an initial needs assessment, failing to look for partners and projects, and a lack of communication and coordination has resulted in years of loss and wasteful spending." [54]

Furthermore, the organization's culture, which involves regular shifting of responsibilities from one unit to another, has made it difficult to sustain expertise, while the extremely tedious funding application process is severely impacting the ability of legitimate organizations to secure funding and support GE and other CIDA-funded projects.[55] While some of these issues are institutional and difficult to address in the immediate future, others can be more easily addressed.

In recent months, Canada's rising casualty rate in Afghanistan and public pressure to better explain and demonstrate the impact Canada is having in Afghanistan has resulted in government response. Presently, there is a significant recruiting campaign under way aimed at considerably expanding the Afghanistan Task Force both in terms of number of personnel as well as country experience and expertise. Another positive step has been the hiring of point people with specific expertise on relevant issues, such as education and gender. There are also efforts to increase the number of staff on the ground in Afghanistan, and particularly in Kandahar. Currently, there is only one CIDA employee in Kandahar as part of the PRT and security concerns have impeded an increase in numbers. There is a general consensus that this lack of ability to get out into the community to determine needs is a serious impediment to Canada's success in Afghanistan in general, and Kandahar in particular. As several of my interviews revealed, "CIDA is under heavy guard in their Kabul office, and cannot leave the PRT in Kandahar without force protection. This is leading to policies that are out of touch with on the ground realities and can only be rectified if and when officers can access communities to determine needs."[56] Partnering with local organizations[57] may help to address this disconnect between CIDA and the South. An additional option would be for CIDA to increase its consultation and collaboration with individuals and organizations within Canada that have expertise, experience and a knowledge base to offer.[58] Many of these individuals and organizations have reached out to CIDA and offered their assistance but have never been called upon.[59]

Closer collaboration would be extremely beneficial in breaking down the existing barriers that exist between academics, practitioners, and policy makers and my interviews with all three groups indicated a willingness and openness to such a partnership, as well as a deep commitment among all groups to increase Canada's positive impact in Afghanistan. In June 2007, a team of CIDA officers, including a development consultant, travelled to Afghanistan to assess current projects, scope out new programs, and map, as much as possible, the work of other donors in supporting the work on women and girls in Afghanistan. They are committed to translating their experience into improved GE programming in Afghanistan.

GE Programming in Afghanistan: Challenges and Opportunities

Gender equality is one of Canada's key policy objectives in Afghanistan and a cross-cutting theme that is "systematically and explicitly integrated across all CIDA programming, including Afghanistan".[60] But in addition to being a cross-cutting theme, gender equality is also an explicit sector of focus in Afghanistan with gender-specific programming at its core. The GOA has also expressed a commitment to gender equality, positioning it as one of the five cross-cutting themes in its Interim-Afghanistan National Development Strategy (I-ANDS) in 2001, which it re-endorsed at the London conference in 2006. The I-ANDS outlines a three-pronged goal for promoting gender equality in Afghanistan, which includes "eliminating all forms of discrimination against women; developing their human capital; and ensuring their full participation and leadership in all aspects of life in Afghanistan".[61] Further, it established formal equality between men and women before the law in its Constitution in January 2003 — followed by ratification of the UN Convention on the Elimination of All Forms of Discrimination Against Women (CEDAW) in March 2003 — and endorsed the Millennium Development Goals (MDGs). While these instruments have yet to be translated into visible, widespread, and sustainable change in the lives of Afghan women, they provide forces within Afghanistan — such as women's organizations — and outside of the country, such as the UN, donor countries and international NGOs an opportunity to bring pressure to bear on the Afghan government to transform rights on paper to tangible rights. The role that Canada can play through diplomacy and development assistance in this regard cannot be overemphasized.

Discussions of GE programming in Afghanistan must include reference to the Ministry of Women's Affairs and its role in supporting these efforts. In its 2003 report, *Afghanistan: Women and Reconstruction*, the International Crisis Group (ICG) notes that since its inception, the Ministry of Women's Affairs (MOWA) has been seen by the international community as a victory for Afghan women and a focal point for the development of policies and programs that would impact women in both the urban and rural areas. It was thought to be "the logical vehicle for developing strategies to embed gender in the planning activities of the line ministries".[62] This initial euphoria detracted attention from "the critical factors that had made past reforms on women's human rights unsustainable and the task of identifying strategies for mainstreaming gender issues in the development process as a whole" resulting in "donor assistance being channelled into projects likely to prove at most symbolic"[63] and in time MOWA proved incapable of achieving anything close to its original mandate.[64] This is largely due to institutional weakness, lack of absorption power and professional capacity, "and a hierarchical structure that impedes collaboration between its departments".[65] What I observed while working in Afghanistan and visiting MOWA, was what many gender specialists refer to as a Ministry that operates more like a "large NGO", and a "a black hole for money"[66] that was created in order to "ghettoize" gender[67] and keep women's issues quiet but argue that something is being done about women's rights.[68]

The ICG report also points to failures by the international community in its efforts to promote GE. It notes that there has been a failure to "incorporate gender effectively into the national budget or the policy calculation of the line ministries"; it states that "donor assistance, both to government and civil society, has been directly toward quick-impact, high visibility projects" with "relatively little research into their sustainability and accessibility to women, particularly in rural areas." It highlights the fact that grassroots women's NGOs are not being sufficiently supported and "the small grants they receive restrict their capacity for growth and limit their activities to vocational training, literacy programs, and other activities that have marginal impact on women's economic empowerment." Finally, it emphasizes that insecurity continues to hinder women's rights activists in their efforts to "educate and mobilize women around issues related to political participation."[69] These weaknesses within MOWA are symptomatic of the fundamental issues underlying the lack of progress on women's issues in Afghanistan. While there has been marked progress in six brief years, we need to appreciate that gender equality efforts will continue to face resistance, and cannot unfold quickly or on Western terms. These weaknesses have also made it more difficult for international aid organizations to engage in sustainable GE programming.

For its part, CIDA has "positioned gender equality, and specifically the 'role of women and girls' in society, as one of the three pillars of its interim programming strategy", with the primary areas of focus being: education, sustainable livelihoods, and women's economic empowerment; and legal protection and women's rights.[70] In its efforts, CIDA focuses on "integrating gender equality into all projects, programs, and grants; and supporting specific gender equality programming to enhance the role of women and girls in society" but also "acknowledges the importance of working with men in Afghanistan to affect change in the role of women and girls in society."[71]

Currently there are 50 projects being supported by CIDA in Afghanistan. Of these, fourteen are in Kandahar province, with the remaining projects spread throughout the country. Among these projects, six are "women-specific" and supported by the bilateral program. They include:

1. The deployment of a Gender Advisor to the Afghan Ministry of Interior to assist in the development of policies and programs that will help advance the representation of women in the Afghan National Police;

2. Partnering with the Mennonite Economic Development Associates (MEDA) to help 1500 women develop horticulture operations in home-based gardens, growing fruits and vegetables to supplement family diets and generate income;

3. Working with WUSC-CARE to assist 2000 vulnerable women acquire employable skills and help them integrate into the labour market;

4. Working with UNDP and through the MOWA to build GOA's capacity for stronger policy formulation and gender mainstreaming practices to overcome deep-rooted gender inequalities;

5. Working with Rights and Democracy to support Afghan civil society to conduct research and design advocacy/awareness strategies in favour of Afghan family law reform, as well as engage local community leaders;

6. Working with Building Resources Across Communities-Afghanistan (BRAC-AF) and the Ministry of Education to establish up to 4000 community-based schools, as well as after-school learning programs, and to provide training for 9000 schoolteachers, at least 4000 of them women. About 120,000 schoolchildren in 11 provinces (including Kandahar province) will benefit from this project, 85 per cent of them girls. The project also aims to promote gender equality in education by improving access to quality of basic education and life skills development focused on girls.[72]

7. Women's Rights in Afghanistan Fund (WRAF)[73] which has facilitated 30 projects promoting women's rights around the country by providing funds directly to local women's organizations. Projects have included education; human rights and legal awareness training; a radio program; training on human rights and gender equality for religious leaders; health services; and provision of legal aid.

Responding to calls to increase development spending to better match our military spending, and to reiterate Canada's commitments to gender equality, on April 12, 2007, the Minister for International Cooperation, Josée Verner announced new spending in Afghanistan. This latest package will include an additional $9 million to support initiatives that will help strengthen the rights of women in Afghanistan. Of the money, $5 million will be used to create "stronger programs dedicated to enhancing the role and voice of Afghan women, including establishing a Gender Studies Institute at Kabul University; $4 million will support locally proposed initiatives that will create economic and educational opportunities for women and girls, with a focus on projects that emphasize women's economic independence, skill development, training and advocacy on eliminating violence against women, and education and literacy programs for women and girls."[74] This is in addition to existing programs, which include $14.5 million for a girls' education project and training of new teachers; $5 million to integrate women into markets; $1.75 million to support maternal health and women's literacy in Kandahar province;

and $16 million for a microfinance investment support facility that will provide small loans and financial services to poor Afghans, particularly women.[75] Everyone interested in seeing Afghanistan succeed acknowledges that these types of programs are important for advancing women's rights and opportunities and building a foundation for sustainable norm diffusion despite concerns about efficacy and impact.

Two of the recent projects announced that hold the most promise of sustained gender impact are the Gender Fund and the Gender Studies Institute (GSI) at Kabul University. The Gender Fund grew out of the need to support high calibre and genuine women's NGOs that have been identified through networks and consultations in Afghanistan. Strong support from the field, and advocacy by gender specialists, led to the announcement of this fund which, once established, will provide CIDA with a stronger mechanism to support grassroots, community-based gender initiatives, including small women's NGOs in rural areas.[76] The funds, with a high capacity coordinator, could prove to be extremely effective in strengthening CIDA's ability to improve its GE programming and extend greater support for initiatives by local women's NGOs throughout Afghanistan. Afghanistan activists have been seeking this type of programming for years and it is hoped that the project will be expedited through CIDA pipelines as soon as possible to allow for more immediate action and maximized impact.

The second project — the GSI — is being established in partnership with MOWA, the UNDP, UNESCO, and UNIFEM within the framework of the University of Kabul. Once fully operational, the GSI will "operate, not only as an academic institute — offering graduate level courses and specialized training and certificate courses — but also a policy research organ that can nurture national gender expertise and identify gaps in data, research, and knowledge to feed into policy development. The idea is that the GSI will inform development initiatives, institutional priorities, and policies for the promotion of gender equality in the country." The objective of the Institute is to minimize the capacity gaps in gender technical capacity and nurture gender expertise throughout Afghan institutions. The GSI will be led by a team of national and international experts, and establish and maintain technical co-operation with like-minded academic and research institutions, nationally, regionally, and globally, and may include an internship component. In order to meet its objectives, "An oversight committee of key stakeholders will ensure quality of the institute's outputs, a steering committee will provide general guidance for the implementation of the planned activities, and a project team, led by a Project Manager, will carry out day-to-day functions."[77]

Several people with extensive experience in Afghanistan have expressed reservations about the efficacy of the GSI, unless it is armed with sufficient funds and personnel to undertake research and programming that would effect change throughout the country and be accessible to rural as well as urban women.[78] Presently, rural women have extremely limited access to Kabul University: many do not have the required level of literacy and education, and those who do are either unable to leave their communities due to cultural restrictions on women's movement without a male chaperone, or have to compete within a system where admission is based on nepotism and bribery, not merit, making Kabul University a largely elite-based institution.[79] CIDA must take these limitations into consideration and address them with creativity and based on consultation with rural women. Enabling the GSI to provide short-term certificate courses in rural communities as well as at its home base in

Kabul; reserving a certain number of seats for rural women and providing them with scholarships; and holding consultations in rural communities to discuss what steps can be taken to facilitate young women leaving their communities for higher education, might be some starting points for ensuring universal access to and benefit from the GSI. CIDA can also respond to questions about the GSI's value added. Some argue that the money could be better spent increasing women's access to existing programs, or starting programs that better correspond to Afghanistan's needs, such as a faculty of social work, or college-based programs that enable women to gain valuable skills that can take them from creating products, budgeting, marketing, and sales.[80] One gender specialist suggested that "economic development activity is a key GE issue in Afghanistan but should be coupled with additional support mechanisms (legal, advocacy, medical, psychosocial) as well as skills (literacy, savings)". Consultation with these and other Afghan experts as well as local women and their organizations would be extremely useful in ensuring that the GSI can make a long term impact.

It would be instructive to conclude this portion of the paper by discussing some of the challenges of implementing GE programming in Afghanistan, as presented by CIDA officers and consultants, and offer some reflections. According to CIDA, one of the most pervasive impediments to effective programming is the dangerous security situation in Afghanistan and the difficulty in finding experienced staff, particularly women, who are willing or able to operate within this context.[81] Insecurity and cultural restraints on women's freedom of movement make it difficult, if not impossible, for female staff to visit project sites outside of Kabul, which severely limits CIDA's ability to engage local populations in project design and impedes the monitoring of gender integration into programs.[82] A second challenge facing CIDA is a lack of information about existing GE programs in Afghanistan. In this vain, the consultant I spoke to highlighted the importance of mapping all existing GE related projects and programs in Afghanistan. She suggested that such a "map" would be invaluable not only to CIDA but for all NGOs and aid organizations operating in Afghanistan, providing important information about existing projects, identifying gaps in programming, and reducing duplication and lack of coordination.[83] Finally, CIDA points to lack of capacity throughout the country as a fundamental challenge of working in Afghanistan. "There are a small number of high capacity women's NGOs who receive the bulk of the support of many donors, but they are overstretched in terms of staffing and management. Most of these women's NGOs are Kabul-based with little contact with the peri-urban areas or concerns for the challenges facing rural women, so there is little substantive gender equality programming outside of Kabul. And the NGOs and CBOs that do exist in the rural areas, and there are very few, have low capacity."[84] It is particularly difficult to find qualified gender specialists whose expertise is essential for successful implementation, follow up, and evaluation of projects.[85]

What I observed in Afghanistan in 2003 leads me to believe that the concept of "capacity" needs to be problematized and re-evaluated. It is true that the Afghan women's movement is still in its infancy, but our interactions revealed "a rich, diverse, and extensive network of Afghan women's resistance, organizing, public participation, and political activism".[86] But many of these women,[87] and their organizations felt marginalized from the international aid community, and the ways in which women's organizing was being institutionalized in order to create "functional and efficient" NGOs that are structured to operate like their international counterparts. This approach has encouraged an urban-based humanitarian aid framework which has alienated rural women's organizations who are conceived of as lacking capacity.[88] This has led to tensions and the imposition of policies and practices that have disempowered the illiterate, rural-based Afghan feminist networks in the "periphery" and put them in competition with more formal, urban-based, educated and professional Afghan women's organizations, because they are perceived as inexperienced, culturally and religiously conservative, and unable to manage their financial resources. These perceptions have contributed to inequalities within a very loose network of Afghan women's organizing across the country, exacerbating cleavages that can potentially lead to the further fragmentation of the women's movement in the country. This failure to fully understand and incorporate the perspectives of a broader base of Afghan women is already leading to a further disavowal of women's rights in a great majority of the rural population, and further exacerbating animosities among women, whose contributions are critical given the reality that Afghanistan's economy is largely rural and family-based. The protracted exclusion of these women not only dislocates their agency as co-constructors of a women's rights agenda, but will have a detrimental impact on Afghanistan's overall capacity to instigate long-term changes in attitudes and perceptions. Implementing more flexible approaches that depart from practices that, so far, have focused on hierarchical, institutionalized, and internationally directed and designed programs for Afghanistan will result in far greater impact.[89]

Addressing these challenges and changing women's lived experience in Afghanistan will require a long-term and multi-faceted approach that is aimed at a bottom-up transformation of attitudes, beliefs, and opinions about the status of women in society, and a top-down dimension that protects women's rights and prosecutes offenders with the full force of the law, all within a culturally- and religiously-minded framework that is grassroots based and supported by domestic, regional, and international forces. Creating these links with external actors — such as women's movements and women's human rights organizations in other Muslim states — would be indispensable to offering Afghan women workable strategies for operating within a conservative Islamic context. Organizations such as Women Living Under Muslim Laws (WLUML),[90] Shirkat Gah, and The Women Action Forum in Pakistan, Women's Solidarity Association of Iran and Raahi (Path to Empowerment) in Iran, and Networking for Women's Rights Organizations (NWRO) in Egypt have long-term experience advocating for women's rights within a conservative context where narrow interpretations of Islam prevail. Their experiences would provide valuable insights into effective strategies that have worked in similar contexts, as well as providing Afghan women with inspiration, encouragement, and solidarity.[91]

Conclusion

The last six years of international engagement in Afghanistan have been marked by crisis and victory. The road ahead offers both challenges and opportunities, but we stand at a critical juncture where the accomplishments of the next year will determine Afghanistan's future. The rising insurgency, poppy production, divisive politics,[92] poverty, and the weak economy are all issues that need immediate attention. But foremost among the challenges facing Afghanistan is gender inequality rooted in culture, religious interpretation, and the culture of war that has permeated Afghan society for almost 30 years. Success depends on the ability of local and international actors to demonstrate the indispensable link between gender equality and sustainable peace, security and development, and gain the support of a broad spectrum of Afghan society. If this proven principle takes root, there will be unprecedented progress on all fronts. To support this process, GE programming must include sustained investment in universal education, the propagation of well-informed religious instruction to combat narrow interpretations of Islam by uneducated and illiterate clerics; poverty reduction and job creation, among other things. This will require committed perseverance, strategic action, and the support and collaboration of men, particularly tribal and religious leaders, to undermine the prevailing patriarchal attitudes, structures, and institutions that impede women's equality. And it will take time. So there must be patience, and sustained and long-term commitment, as we work to establish the building blocks for women's equality. We must also allow the work to be done by Afghans themselves, but offer support, technical assistance, and resources.

We must be particularly mindful that GE programming does not marginalize the male population, which can and has had negative consequences in Afghanistan and elsewhere. Advancing women's rights necessitates the engagement and commitment of men, and support for their personal development as well. Clearly, educating girls at the expense of educating boys in a patriarchal culture will only serve to deepen resentment and result in negative consequences. Men must not be presented as part of the problem, but as indispensable to the solution of gender inequality in Afghanistan. Their engagement must be approached in both a bottom-up and top-down manner. At the grassroots, radio and television programs, as well as the arts such as drama, can be extremely effective tools for education in a country where literacy is low but entertainment and culture are extremely important.[93] Finally, and perhaps most importantly, the success of GE in Afghanistan lies in supporting the nascent Afghan women's movement and grassroots women's organizing, through partnership, capacity building, and collaboration with women's organizations and movements throughout the Muslim world. Helping to create these links will create an existing momentum of empowered women who are advocating for equal rights and opportunities. In many instances these women are successfully influencing policy, law, and social norms with "a good deal of sustained effort, careful strategic work, and negotiating with key powerbrokers and stakeholders for positive change".[94]

It's been four years since I travelled to Afghanistan. The country and its people left a deep impression on me. I had the privilege of meeting many inspiring women and men whose eyes were filled with both pain and hope. They wanted a better future for their children and grandchildren and listening to their stories of courage, fortitude, and perseverance, I strongly felt that if Afghanistan was given a true opportunity — one that was not marred by power politics and competing national and international interests — there would be hope for more peaceful days. It is what the Afghans I met craved and worked for. And it is what I committed to working for along with them. I hope this paper will contribute to that end.

CHESHMAK FARHOUMAND-SIMS is Assistant Professor in the MA program in conflict studies at St. Paul University. Her research focuses on the gendered impact of violence on women and the critical role of women in peacebuilding in Afghanistan. Cheshmak worked in Afghanistan in 2003 providing human rights and peace advocacy training to Afghan women, working for grass roots organizations, NGOs, and government ministries.

Endnotes

[1] Ironically, there was no discussion of the similar gender apartheid suffered by women under the US-backed Mujahedeen leadership, nor the many ways in which the Taliban, despite their oppressive rule, were able to disarm these warlords and protect communities from their indiscriminate acts of violence, such as the rape of women and the murder of men.

[2] Hunt, Krista, "The Strategic Co-optation of Women's Rights," *International Feminist Journal of Politics*, 4:1, p. 116. See also Whitworth, Sandra, "September 11th and the Aftermath — A Comment," in Studies in Political Economy, 67 (Spring 2002), pp. 33-38.

[3] Please see http://www.whitehouse.gov/news/releases/2001/11/print/20011117.html

[4] Please see http://www.thenation.com/doc/20011217/pollitt

[5] For the Bonn Agreement, please see http://www.afghangovernment.com/AfghanAgreementBonn.htm

[6] The weaknesses of this Ministry will be discussed later in the paper.

[7] Oates, L. & Isabelle Solon-Helal, *At the Cross-Roads of Conflict and Democracy: Women and Afghanistan's Constitutional Loya Jirga, Rights and Democracy*, May 2004.
note : A loya jirga is the traditional way that Afghans engage in consultation until a decision by consensus is reached. The words come from the Pashto meaning grand assembly, and although it was originally a Pashtun tradition, other ethnic groups routinely engage in loya jirgas. Afghan coming together of people in Afghanistan involving consultation and decision making. Participants are usually those in positions of power including tribal and religious leaders, politicians, military and government officials. They are traditionally male-dominated gatherings although, since 2001, there have been efforts to ensure a more active participation by women as well.

[8] While concepts such as fragility and failure are useful in providing a context, it must be acknowledged that they are terms that have been developed in the West to describe states who may not apply these concepts to themselves if given the opportunity.

[9] Baranyi, S. & Powell, K. (2005). "Fragile States, Gender Equality and Aid Effectiveness: A Review of Donor Perspectives", p. 1.

[10] Alvi, H. "Reconstruction in Post Taliban Afghanistan," Report from the Reconstruction Workshop held in Cairo, Egypt, in October 2002.

[11] In February 2007, warlords in Parliament presented and passed a resolution providing themselves complete amnesty from prosecution for war crimes. Please see Jared Ferrie's "Amnesty for Afghan War Criminals," http://thetyee.ca/News/2007/03/12/Amnesty/

[12] However, the ongoing insecurity, lack of services, etc. is starting to impact the government's popularity. For statistical information, please see "Afghans Speak Out?" and www.worldpublicopinion.org/pipa/articles/brasiapacificra/290.php?nid=&id=&pnt=290&lb=bras

[13] See Gagnon, *I is for Infidel*, Rashid, *Taliban*, as well as reports by Human Rights Watch and Amnesty International such as: *Women in Afghanistan: A Human Rights Catastrophe* http://www.amnesty.org/ailib/intcam/afgan/afgtoc.htm , *Women in Afghanistan: Pawns in Men's Struggle for Power* http://web.amnesty.org/library/Index/engASA110111999 , *Afghanistan: Humanity Denied, Systematic Violations of Women's Rights in Afghanistan*, http://www.hrw.org/reports/2001/afghan3/

[14] Baranyi, S. & Powell, K. (2005). "Fragile States, Gender Equality and Aid Effectiveness: A Review of Donor Perspectives", p. 1.

[15] Ahmed-Gosh, H. "A History of Women in Afghanistan: Lessons Learned for the Future, or Yesterdays and Tomorrow: Women in Afghanistan." In *Journal of International Women's Studies*, 4 :3 (May 2003), p. 1.

[16] Farhoumand-Sims, Cheshmak. Unpublished PhD dissertation, York University – Supervisor: Dr. David Dewitt. *Overcoming Religious and Cultural Barriers to Women's Full Participation in Post-Conflict Peacebuilding and Reconstruction Efforts. The Relationship between Women's Human Rights and Peacebuilding in Afghanistan.*

[17] *Seizing the Opportunity: Afghan Women and the Constitution-Making Process*, Rights and Democracy Mission Report, May–June 2003. Montreal: Rights and Democracy, September 2003.

[18] Ahmed-Gosh 2003, p. 1.

[19] When I was working in Afghanistan, many Afghan women would say that culture and religion are instrumentalized by men to prevent women's advancement, and that although women themselves want their religion and culture respected, they do not want external actors to be so careful and sensitive as to perpetuate patriarchal structures. I learned from them that the solution lies in using moderation, wisdom, and consultation with and inclusion of Afghan men and women in the planning and implementation of programs. They argued that if they were incorporated into international efforts more inclusively, and equally, they could serve to bridge this gap and help facilitate the process of change.

[20] For suggestions on best practices, please refer to *Women Living Under Muslim Laws* www.wluml.org. For a more detailed discussion of the gender equality programming and development efforts in Afghanistan, please see Farhoumand-Sims *Development in Muslim Societies: Constraints and Opportunities for Afghan women*. www.asiapacificresearch.ca/caprn/afghan_project/c_sims.pdf.

[21] It is not uncommon in patriarchal societies for powerbrokers to relegate women's rights issues as something to be addressed "later" when other, more pressing priorities have been dealt with. However it has been shown that when GE commitments are deferred until "later," gender inequality is exacerbated and progress on all fronts is compromised.

[22] According to Foreign Affairs, Canada has, so far, allocated $616.5 million to Afghanistan for 2001–2009, with $100 million committed per year between 2002 and 2011, and $139 million already spent in the 2006–2007 fiscal year.

[23] For a complete list of projects please see http://www.acdi-cida.gc.ca/CIDAWEB/acdicida.nsf/En/JUD-12514940-QGL#2.

[24] For a detailed explanation of the Afghanistan Compact, please see http://www.fco.gov.uk/servlet/Front?pagename=OpenMarket/Xcelerate/ShowPage&c=Page&cid=1132599286730.

[25] *The Afghanistan Compact: Building on Success*. Available on the internet at: www.unama-afg.org/news/_londonConf/_docs/06jan30-AfghanistanCompact-Final.pdf.

[26] Ibid., p. 3

[27] CIDA website, http://www.acdi-cida.gc.ca/CIDAWEB/acdicida.nsf/En/JUD-129153625-S6T.

[28] For description of this project, please see, http://www.acdi-cida.gc.ca/CIDAWEB/acdicida.nsf/En/JUD-1267497-H2R

[29] For a description of this project, please see http://www.acdi-cida.gc.ca/CIDAWEB/acdicida.nsf/En/JUD-1267121-GBL

[30] For a description of this project, please see http://www.acdi-cida.gc.ca/CIDAWEB/acdicida.nsf/En/JUD-1251644-SQ4

31 For 2006–2007 breakdown of disbursements, please see Afghanistan: Development Resources and Results 2006–2007 in Appendix 1.

32 The NSP seeks to "reduce poverty by empowering communities to take initiative, improving local governance, and increasing social, human, and economic capital" while increasing the exposure of the central government and therefore "its legitimacy and capacity." For NSP see, http://www.acdi-cida.gc.ca/CIDAWEB/acdicida.nsf/En/JUD-1267121-GBL.

33 Interviewee wishes to remain anonymous, but see also "Fine Tuning the NSP: Discussions of Problems and Solutions with Facilitating Partners" http://www.cmi.no/pdf/?file=/afghanistan/doc/AREU%20Nov%2005%20Fine-tuning%20the%20NSP.pdf.

34 Gender specialist working in Afghanistan. Email correspondence with gender specialist working in Afghanistan on April 23, 2007

35 The AREU report "Fine Tuning the NSP: Discussions of Problems and Solutions with Facilitating Partners" can be found at http://www.cmi.no/pdf/?file=/afghanistan/doc/AREU%20Nov%2005%20Fine-tuning%20the%20NSP.pdf.

36 Interviewee wished to remain anonymous. Telephone interview with Afghanistan activist on May 15, 2007

37 Donini, Antonio, Norah Niland, and Karin Wermester. (2004). *Nation Building Unraveled? Aid, Peace and Justice in Afghanistan.* Kumarian Press, quoted in Maliha Chishti and Cheshmak Farhoumand-Sims, "Transnational Feminism and the Women's Rights Agenda in Afghanistan," in Z. Jalalzai and D. Jefferess, *Globalizing Afghanistan: Terrorism, War, and the Rhetoric of Nation-Building*, Duke University Press (forthcoming in 2008).

38 Development consultant conveying information provided to her by staffers and researchers. Email correspondence with Development consultant conveying information provided to her by staffers and researchers on May 9, 2007

39 As of the time of writing, July 2007.

40 CIDA official. Telephone interview with CIDA official who wishes to remain anonymous on June 14, 2007

41 Please see USAID, "Breaking Point," February 2007; Swiss Peace Semi-Annual Risk Assessment (November 2006); ACBAR Briefing Paper (November 2006); Womankind, "Taking Stock Update" (October 2006); S. Zia-Zarifi, "Losing the Peace"; Smith et al., "Canada in Afghanistan: Is it Working?"

42 See Farhoumand-Sims, C. "Canada in Afghanistan: Is the Three Block War Working?" In *Three Block Wars and Humanitarianism*, proceedings from a consultation sponsored jointly by the Pearson Peacekeeping Centre and Humber College, September 2006, forthcoming Fall 2007. See also, Sarah Chayes and Norine McDonald's presentations to the Senate Committee on Foreign Relations from May 2007.

43 For a discussion of issues pertaining to the militarization of aid, please see March issue of *Human Security Bulletin*, http://www.humansecuritybulletin.info/.

44 Smith, Gordon (2007). "Canada in Afghanistan: Is it Working?" Published by the Canadian Defence and Foreign Relations Institute. Can be found at http://www.cdfai.org/PDF/Canada%20in%20Afghanistan%20Is%20it%20Working.pdf.

45 Ferrie, J. "A Development Surge: Rebuilding Kandahar before it is too late," http://thetyee.ca/News/2007/05/17/AidAfghan/.

46 Smith, Gordon. "Canada in Afghanistan: Is it Working?"

47 Ibid.

48 There is debate on this issue. Organizations such as The Senlis Council http://www.senliscouncil.net/documents/macdonald_testimony insisting that there are camps of starving Kandaharis in close proximity to the Canadian base, while the WFP challenges this contention in press releases such as on May 30, 2007, http://www.wfp.org/english/?ModuleID=137&Key=2502

49 Lauryn Oates, an independent expert with extensive experience in Afghanistan argues that increased investment and visibility in Kandahar should have been done much earlier and must not be delayed now. She notes that the British government, whose troops are serving in Helmand province, invested $55 million in development funding there in order to improve livelihoods in the province. Their investment has had a positive impact on both the local population and the British military efforts in the province.

50 CIDA official who wishes to remain anonymous. Telephone interview with CIDA official who wishes to remain anonymous on June 14, 2007

51 Smith, Gordon (2007). "Canada in Afghanistan: Is it Working?" Published by the Canadian Defence and Foreign Relations Institute. Can be found at http://www.cdfai.org/PDF/Canada%20in%20Afghanistan%20Is%20it%20Working.pdf

52 Please note that since April 1, 2007, the Afghanistan Desk has been renamed the Afghanistan Task Force.

53 Interview with Lauryn Oates, Vancouver-based independent human rights researcher and activist. Telephone interview with Lauryn Oates on June 13, 2007

54 Ibid.

55 In her presentation to the Senate Committee on Foreign Affairs, Sarah Chayes, the director of Arghand, a community-based, small business in Kandahar that uses local products to make beauty products states that, "I think CIDA procedures need to be streamlined. Like every public development agency, it is way too bureaucratic. I'm in the process of applying for some money from CIDA, I looked at the application form, and I have a MA and I can't read the thing." Transcript from Sarah Chayes' presentation to the Senate Committee on Foreign Affairs.

56 Anonymous interview with gender specialist and Afghan researcher. Email correspondence with gender specialist working in Afghanistan on April 23, 2007

57 Arghand in Kandahar and Turquoise Mountain.

58 Interview with Lauryn Oates. Telephone interview with Lauryn Oates on June 13, 2007

59 CARE Canada, Women for Afghan Women, The Afghan Women's Advocacy Committee of Canada, and other organizations and individuals have valuable knowledge about Afghanistan and long-term experience there and could serve as effective in-house experts for CIDA.

60 CIDA website, http://www.acdi-cida.gc.ca/CIDAWEB/acdicida.nsf/En/JUD-12514940-QGL#2.

61 "Afghanistan National Development Strategy," document provided to me at CIDA.

62 ICG, *Afghanistan and Reconstruction*, March 14, 2003. Please see http://www.reliefweb.int/library/documents/2003/icg-afg-14mar.pdf.

63 International Crisis Group, (2003). *Afghanistan: Women and Reconstruction*. http://www.reliefweb.int/rw/rwb.nsf/AllDocsByUNID/cba795f1da7d2a5285256cec007c88b6.

64 ICG, *Afghanistan and Reconstruction*, March 14, 2003. Please see http://www.reliefweb.int/library/documents/2003/icg-afg-14mar.pdf.

65 Ibid. Please note CIDA does not directly fund programs through MOWA because of these internal weaknesses but they have provided funds to other organizations with projects and programs at MOWA.

66 The Afghan gender specialist I spoke to suggested, for example, that instead of funding yet another MOWA study on "vulnerable women," which has little impact on government policy or development, the money would be better spent as seed capital for the women to start their own businesses.

67 It is unfortunate that some powerbrokers have relegated women and issues relating to their wellbeing and advancement to the MOWA, without appreciating the importance of mainstreaming gender across Ministries and government departments. A gender specialist I spoke to said this mainstreaming effort needs to be led by Afghans and pushed by donors that are responsible for that sector.

68 Consultation with a gender specialist working in Afghanistan who asked to remain anonymous. Email correspondence with gender specialist working in Afghanistan on April 23, 2007

69 International Crisis Group, (2003). *Afghanistan: Women and Reconstruction*. http://www.reliefweb.int/rw/rwb.nsf/AllDocsByUNID/cba795f1da7d2a5285256cec007c88b6.

70 "CIDA's Support to Women and Girls in Afghanistan," document provided to me on email by CIDA officer on May 7, 2007

71 Ibid., p. 1.

72 Please see CIDA website http://www.acdi-cida.gc.ca/CIDAWEB/acdicida.nsf/En/JUD-12514940-QGL.

73 Please see www.wraf.ca.

74 CIDA press release, April 12, 2007. http://www.acdi-cida.gc.ca/CIDAWEB/acdicida.nsf/En/ANI-41116275-RYY.

75 Meeting at CIDA with Afghanistan officers, May 7, 2007.

76 Currently these are being supported through a variety of funds including the Canada Fund for Afghanistan, the former WRAF project, the current Rights and Democracy project, Canadian Partnership Branch, Multilateral and even UN projects supporting small NGO initiatives.

77 All the information in this section are derived from interviews and email communication with CIDA officers as well the UNDP's proposal to CIDA for its program "Institutional Capacity Building for Promotion of Gender Equality: Strengthening Public Sector Response," which was provided to me on email. Dates for interviews are as follows: June 7, 2007, June 11, 2007 and July 3, 2007.

78 I was privy to an email consultation among several Afghan researchers, activists, gender specialists, and other individuals presently based in Afghanistan who were discussing the announcement of the GSI. The information contained in this section reflects some of the discussion that took place and all participants in the consultation wished to remain anonymous. The dates of correspondence were: April 23, 2007, May 11, 2007, June 11, 2007.

79 Email communication with gender specialist working in Kabul. Email correspondence with gender specialist working in Afghanistan on April 23, 2007

80 Gender specialist commenting on the GSI in email communication. May 3, 2007

81 One of two female staff working with the Kandahar PRT has already quit due to threats to her and her family's safety, and there are reports of a local mosque offering money to those who will harm foreigners and their local partners.

82 It is worth noting that this lack of capacity within Afghanistan exists both at the government level and within the NGO community, making it difficult to find partners to work with, especially in the rural areas.

83 For instance, CIDA was called upon to support a program. It agreed, found funds, and, upon arrival, found out that most of the work had already been allocated to other donors, leaving a very minor role for CIDA.

84 Development consultant working with CIDA on Afghanistan portfolio, summarizing comments by staffers and Afghan Canadians who work or have worked in Afghanistan. May 9, 2007, and May 11, 2007.

85 According to one of my interviewees who is a consultant working for CIDA on gender issues right now, gender specialists are few in number, in high demand, and usually drawn to the larger organizations that can offer much higher salaries. She noted that this shortage of gender specialists is facing the larger NGO community and not restricted to CIDA and Afghanistan. By email communication on June 1, 2007.

86 See Elaheh Rostami Povey's "Women in Afghanistan: Passive Victims of the Borga or Active Social Participants," in Haleh Afshar and Deborah Eade (eds.) *Development, Women, and War: Feminist Perspectives*. Oxford: Oxfam Publishing, 2003, pp. 172–187.

87 I would not include RAWA, The Revolutionary Association of the Women of Afghanistan in my description of the Afghan women's movement. Most Afghan women I have spoken to talk about RAWA with disregard. They feel RAWA has been picked up by Western feminist networks because of its aggressive and radical approach to advocacy, but say very few Afghans agree with RAWA's agenda and their approach, or feel that it represents them as Afghan women.

88 Chishti and Farhoumand-Sims, "Transnational Feminism and the Women's Rights Agenda in Afghanistan." In our paper, we define transnational feminist apparatus as the spectrum of actors, instruments, policies, and programs that bring gender issues into the forefront of politics and society in Afghanistan that have either been formulated, and/or supported by those located in the West, often within a Western liberal feminist discourse. The transnational feminist apparatus consists of the gender policies and programs alongside individual consultants, advisors, international women's rights NGOs, international agencies (UNIFEM) and international instruments such as The Convention on the Elimination of All Forms of Discrimination Against Women, Security Council Resolution 1325, Beijing Platform for Action, that have arrived more or less in Afghanistan after the fall of the Taliban government.

89 This paragraph summarized from Chishti and Farhoumand-Sims, "Transnational Feminism and the Women's Rights Agenda in Afghanistan."

90 Women Living Under Muslim Laws is an international solidarity network that provides information, support, and a collective space for women whose lives are shaped, conditioned, or governed by laws and customs said to derive from Islam. Please see www.wluml.org.

91 When I worked with Rights and Democracy providing a training workshop to women in preparation for the constitutional loya jirga, we had partners from Shirkat Gah and WLUML participating and offering training based on their advocacy experiences and success stories. The Afghan women participants said hearing these stories about women's activism in Iran and Pakistan was some of the most helpful information they had received and gave them courage to try new things and think creatively but forcefully.

92 Recently, a group of parliamentarians, led by powerful warlords, have created a new political party aimed at bringing down the Karzai government. For more information, please see http://www.rferl.org/featuresarticle/2007/05/ 64CCC722-13EB-4F66-8C60-EB7785EB64BB.html.

93 Poetry, storytelling, classical forms of music, and other forms of arts such as drama have a long and rich history in Afghanistan and can be better utilized.

94 *Memorandum on International Development* http://www.publications.parliament.uk/pa/cm200203/cmselect/ cmintdev/84/84ap06.htm.

Canada, Haiti, and Gender Equality in a "Fragile State"

Jennifer Erin Salahub

Canada, Haiti, and Gender Equality in a "Fragile State"

Jennifer Erin Salahub[1]

Introduction

The history of Haiti since its revolutionary beginnings has been a troubled one at best. Dictatorship, foreign military occupation, domestic military coups d'etat, fickle international engagement, and pervasive humanitarian crises exacerbated by environmental degradation and furious tropical storms have contributed to making Haiti the poorest country in the Western Hemisphere, as well as one of the least equitable. Women in particular have shouldered much of the burden of Haiti's poverty, but have seen little benefit from the few advances that have been made.

International cooperation has been integral to Haiti's development, such as it is; Canada has been among the most consistent and generous donors, with development cooperation in Haiti beginning in the late 1960s. Canada's engagement with Haiti has been continuous since that time, with the exception of a brief hiatus during military rule in Haiti in the early 1990s. Following its disputed role in the controversial ouster of President Jean-Bertrand Aristide,[2] Canada re-engaged with Haiti with renewed vigour in 2004 and greatly supported the development of Haiti's Interim Cooperation Framework (ICF), a development strategy to address the challenges Haiti faces post-Aristide. Canada was closely involved in the process of developing both the ICF and the United Nations Stabilization Mission in Haiti (MINUSTAH), and has been a key development partner in Haiti since that time. Indeed, Haiti is Canada's priority country for development partnership in the Americas and receives the second-most Canadian development assistance, behind Afghanistan.

Interestingly, Canada's adoption of the term "fragile state" coincided with the flurry of activity surrounding Aristide's departure, including Canada's renewed commitment to Haiti. Indeed, Haiti is identified by most stakeholders, including Canada, as a fragile state. The specific term "fragile state" has a short, yet troubled history: no universal definition has so far been agreed to and the term is contentious at best.[3] But, for Canada's purposes, a fragile state is loosely defined as a state that is unable or unwilling to provide basic services to the majority of its population, and is thus relatively at greater risk of failure.[4] Use of the term became commonplace around 2004, when Canada joined many other Western countries in following the United States, which identified "fragile states" as a threat to US security in the 2002 *National Security Strategy*.

Many issues, such as good governance or the promotion of human rights, surround the central themes of the fragile state discourse. One issue that is not yet receiving substantial attention is the question of promoting gender equality (GE) in fragile states as part of building a sustainable and equitable society. Linking the promotion of gender equality with engagement in fragile states may not seem obvious to many given, for example, the general perspective that the minimalist needs of fragile states to create secure environments and deliver basic services should be addressed before any other. Gender equality concerns may often be postponed as stakeholders focus on stabilizing a country before moving on to more robust development issues. Yet, such a perspective ignores the fact that men and women — and the relations among them — can contribute to state fragility in both positive and negative ways. Women's and men's different experiences of state fragility mean that an understanding of "gender roles and relations [is] crucial to understanding opportunities and obstacles to state building".[5]

The challenge to donors then is how to integrate the promotion of gender equality into their work in and with fragile states from the beginning, including while addressing initial security concerns and other immediate priorities. A failure to do so could ultimately undermine the work of donors in these fragile states. Canada — the Canadian International Development Agency (CIDA) in particular — is well-known for its work in promoting gender equality through its development work, writ large. Indeed, CIDA works to integrate gender equality as a "cross-cutting theme" into all programs and projects, with many successes and innovative approaches.[6] Moreover, Canada has been a vocal supporter of United Nations Security Council Resolution 1325 on Women, Peace, and Security, which sets out specific guidelines for member states with regard to women's rights in times of conflict and post-conflict.[7] Given Canada's commitment to gender equality — seen most comprehensively in CIDA policy — one wonders how well Canada has been able to integrate GE into its programs in such a challenging environment as Haiti.

This chapter explores the extent to which Canada has been successful in integrating GE as a cross-cutting priority by scanning Canadian policies and programming in Haiti since 2004. It identifies certain successes in and challenges to fully integrating gender equality as a truly cross-cutting theme. This chapter posits that the links between GE and state fragility need to be actively and profoundly made through policy and programming, especially in those areas that are priorities for fragile states, such as security and justice. The chapter then takes a closer look at a small sample of key interventions, focusing on the areas of women's political participation, socio-economic development, and public security. It concludes with some preliminary thinking on how Canadian programming in gender equality is influencing state fragility in Haiti, and about its potential to have greater influence in the future.

Linking Gender Equality to "Fragile States"

As Baranyi and Powell identify in their insightful analysis of donor policy on GE and fragile states, the links between gender equality and state fragility are not being made clear by either academia or policy-makers.[8] However, as they intuit, "one would think that gender would be a strong thread running through donor thinking in [the domain of state fragility/capacity]."[9] Eighteen months on, little evidence exists that the donor community is making these links in their programming. Indeed, the World Bank's most recent *Global Monitoring Report* is subtitled "Confronting the Challenges of Gender Equality and Fragile States" yet throughout the publication, these two themes are generally treated as distinct and unlinked.[10] Given that the links between these two discourses form an important starting point for the argument that follows, let us briefly explore those links.

The logic of the link between GE and fragile states is simultaneously simple and intuitive on the one hand, and somewhat convoluted and complex on the other. Its basis rests on the assumption that what we perceive to be the "strongest" states (i.e. the least fragile states) are those with robust, institutionalized democracies that are well-advanced along the path of human development.[11] Key characteristics of such states include: a fair and equitable division of power and resources; space to exercise both personal agency and voice, and recognition thereof; and integration of the principles of social justice (including equality), not to mention low levels of poverty and social violence. Equality of all people is a basic tenet of democracy and is fundamentally linked to the idea of gender equality. Recognizing and acknowledging the value of gender equality is essential to a robust conceptualization of equality more broadly and vice versa. Following this logic, if the process of engaging with fragile states is to assist them in moving along the path toward becoming states with such characteristics, steps should be taken to nurture the growth of these attributes throughout donor engagement with them.

However, many fragile states face severe instability and/or violence which, many argue, must be addressed first and foremost. The process of simple stabilization (as opposed to proactive development) is, I argue, the process of building the foundation upon which we hope to foster a strong, institutionalized democracy. If we fail to address key issues such as the equitable negotiation of power relations — of which the division of power between genders is a key component — in the initial stages of building this foundation, we risk building a structure that will be unable to support the requirements of democracy over the long term. Put more directly, if during the process of stabilization we solidify and institutionalize gender *in*equalities, thereby skewing the division of power, when we later try to rectify them during the process of consolidating a democracy, we risk destabilizing the democracy. Pulling the brick of inequality out of the fundamental power infrastructure of the state in an effort to create a more stable democracy could weaken the entire structure for a time.[12] During this weakened state, those who hold the reins of power would have an incentive to maintain their control with potentially brutal results as we have seen in many cases, such as Robert Mugabe's Zimbabwe or Charles Taylor's Liberia.

Adding an analysis beyond the purely realist, power-based, or geostrategic, and moving towards the principles of sustainable development, to see the importance of gender equality we need to focus on women's rights to agency, voice, and social justice. Importantly, many international commitments have recognized the essential role, place, and responsibility of women in achieving both sustainable peace and sustainable development. United Nations Security Council Resolution 1325 on Women, Peace, and Security identifies active participation of women as essential for truly sustainable peace.[13] Moreover, the Mission Statement of the Beijing Platform for Action states that:

> "… *Equality between women and men is a matter of human rights and a condition for social justice and is also a necessary and fundamental prerequisite for equality, development, and peace. A transformed partnership based on equality between women and men is a condition for people-centred sustainable development…*"[14]

Indeed, both of these documents, along with a host of others, identify the crucial role that women have to play in consolidating peace and building sustainable societies.

To follow this line of thinking through to the realm of socio-economic development and the important roles women have to play in that sphere, we need only recall the importance of sustainable human development in creating a strong, capable state. Indeed, as has been shown many times, a development focus on women can have far-reaching social effects. This is particularly true in the education of women and girls who are then better able to make sound decisions regarding the physical and social health of their families as well as themselves.[15] Moreover, as the World Bank has begun to promote, gender equality makes for smart economics: reducing barriers for women to enter the workforce increases productive capacity and generally leads to improved growth and the associated financial benefits.[16]

Above I have explored the links between gender equality and state fragility. It remains to be stated, however, that continuing to follow this line of thinking one comes to the following question: can the promotion of gender equality help to reverse state fragility? Intuitively, this seems to be the case: if solidifying inequalities at the stabilization phase of engagement with a fragile state can lead to likely destabilization at a later point, then consolidating equalities during reconstruction should allow for the creation of a virtuous circle. Moreover, there are early signals that this could be the case: for example, Rwanda's post-genocide constitution includes quotas for female members of Parliament, a system that is showing positive results and likening Rwanda to the European social democracies in terms of female political participation. Returning to the analogy of the foundation of a building, one could argue that equality between women and men is a key support in the foundation of sustainable democracy. I will now turn to explore how Canada has been translating these principles into action in a key fragile state, Haiti.

Gender Equality as a Cross-cutting Theme: How Are We Doing?

As mentioned briefly above, Canada has a long history of engagement with Haiti. Focussing on the period since 2004, we see that this history has been somewhat coloured by the fragile states paradigm. While Canada has remained involved as an important Haitian development partner, it has also been implicated in the controversial departure of former-president Jean-Bertrand Aristide. The circumstances surrounding Aristide's departure from Haiti remain clouded. Some — including Aristide himself [17] — claim that he was forcibly removed from the presidency in a US-led coup, in which Canada participated.[18] Others, including Canada, claim he left voluntarily in the face of mounting civil unrest.[19] Recently, parliamentarians recognized that Canada's role in Aristide's departure remains controversial.[20] Currently, it appears that Aristide's influence and support in Haiti are waning as he remains in exile in South Africa.[21]

On the more positive side, yet still working within the fragile states paradigm, Canada has focused in recent years on encouraging Haiti's stabilization. To that end, Canada has been an important member of the Friends of Haiti group, has been supportive of MINUSTAH (in both financial and human resource terms), was a key supporter of the development of the ICF and has provided both technical and financial support to elections in Haiti, helping that country to complete the first full electoral cycle in quite some time. More specifically, Elections Canada played a strong role in support of free and fair elections in Haiti, through both bilateral and multilateral means.[22] Financially, Canada has provided approximately C$100 million per year since 2004[23] and, in 2006, announced C$520 million in new funds over the five year period 2006–2011.

A key decision in Canadian engagement with Haiti in recent years has been taking on the task, in 2005, of piloting the Organisation for Economic Cooperation and Development — Development Assistance Committee's (OECD DAC) Principles for Good International Engagement in Fragile States in Haiti. As part of this agreement, Canada committed to coordinating the work of its departments in its engagement with that country in a "whole-of-government approach".[24] From the perspective of integrating GE into a whole-of-government approach, Canada seems well-placed: CIDA has a long history of effectively and efficiently promoting GE in its development programming, experience and tools that other government departments could draw upon. However, while some departments such as CIDA can claim some success in integrating gender equality into a range of programming in Haiti, overall Canada has yet to draw fully on the resources available to it to realize a whole-of-government commitment to integrating GE as a cross-cutting theme in this fragile state.

One example of the insufficiency of Canada's integration of GE as a cross-cutting theme in a whole-of-government approach is found in the House of Commons Standing Committee on Foreign Affairs and International Development's (SCFAID) report, *Canada's International Policy Put to the Test in Haiti*. House Standing Committees are comprised of both government and opposition members of Parliament; their reports should not be viewed as statements of government policy, but rather accounts of how that policy has been translated into practice. Published in December 2006, this report holistically reviews recent Canadian involvement in Haiti and makes recommendations for future policies and programs. The report undertakes "a study of Canada's role in complex international interventions that involve multiple foreign policy instruments focussing on Canada's efforts in Haiti…".[25] Its process involved assessing Canada's engagement and making recommendations for future practice, across the panoply of foreign policy 'instruments'. In this way, it can be seen as a reasonably reliable report of Canada's current priority interests in and for Haiti and can be used as a tool to evaluate the relevance and appropriateness of those priorities. SCFAID's assessment is explicitly framed by the concept of state fragility in Haiti and much of the report focuses on the obvious challenges faced by fragile states: increasing security, reforming the justice system, reducing poverty, and ensuring long-term commitments from donors, but it neglects to link these themes to issues of and surrounding gender equality and women's rights.

The process for compiling the SCFAID report saw testimony from a broad range of groups, including representatives from CIDA, the Department of Foreign Affairs and International Trade (DFAIT), the Royal Canadian Mounted Police (RCMP), Elections Canada, university academics, and civil society groups. Yet despite (or perhaps because of [26]) the wealth of experience and the broad range of perspectives of SCFAID members and witnesses, not once is gender equality specifically mentioned. The only time issues of equality between women and men are addressed is when "women's empowerment" makes a cameo appearance nineteen pages into the report, and is subsequently included in one recommendation along with a grab-bag of other focal points:

> *Recommendation 5 … Overall development strategy should also pay particular attention to: rural and local development, including agricultural production and food security; basic education for children; the empowerment of women; the formation of strong civil society and labour organizations; and the creation of a climate conducive to private-sector investment.*[27]

Clearly each of these other focal points is crucial to equitable and sustainable development in fragile states. The point is not to diminish their value; it is rather to draw attention to the fact that grouping these somewhat dissimilar issues together — or in not making explicitly clear the links among them and among other issues faced by fragile states — implies that these themes are of less importance than others.

As part of the procedure associated with a Standing Committee report, the Government prepared a response that addressed the concerns and recommendations raised by the Committee. Although the Government response is modestly more cognizant of integrating GE as one of two cross-cutting themes, it does so in an extremely limited way, mentioning gender only four times, including once in its repetition of the SCFAID recommendation and once in singling gender equality out as a cross-cutting theme. While the Government response is structured in such a way that it addresses each recommendation in turn, and thus could fall victim to the absence of robust treatment of GE in the SCFAID report, the response could have been an opportune venue for the Government to set a strong leading example by proactively integrating GE across the board in its discussion of future plans for engagement with Haiti.

Moreover, if GE is being legitimately integrated in Canadian programming in Haiti as a truly *cross-cutting* theme, one would expect to see mention of gender equality, women and/or girls, much more frequently than it appears in either document, and in a variety of contexts — such as security, justice, political participation, and poverty reduction — and with an explicit focus on the unique challenges faced by Haitian women and by those who work towards a more equitable Haitian society, both inside and outside of government. In fully recognizing the links between GE and other, more immediate challenges, we become more aware of the role that gender equality has to play in creating a sustainable, legitimate, democratic government and we are better able to work towards that goal.

Political Participation

While Canada has more work to do to fully integrate its knowledge and experience in promoting GE into an approach that includes departments beyond CIDA and reaching up to the seats of political power, the successes Canada has realized in the realm of political participation must be recognized. Indeed, Canada — especially through CIDA — has invested significant resources in promoting GE in Haiti since the beginning of the ICF. The keystone of CIDA's work in this area has been the Fonds Kore Fanm (FKF), a funding envelope specifically aimed at promoting gender equality in a number of areas, including reducing violence against women and promoting women's political participation.

As the only donor program in Haiti specifically aimed at promoting women's empowerment and women's rights, the Fonds Kore Fanm has made a significant impact on the promotion of GE in Haiti and CIDA must be recognized for its innovation and the risks Canada has taken in establishing this fund. Through the FKF a number of civil society organizations as well as the Ministère à la Condition Feminine et aux Droits des Femmes (MCFDF) have made significant progress in public awareness-raising, institutional capacity-building, access to medical services and political participation. What remains unclear is whether or not the programs sponsored by CIDA, including those described below, are reaching all levels of society. In promoting gender equality in Haiti and elsewhere, it is important to reach out to the *cadres populaires*, or general public — especially those in poor, rural settings — in order to ensure that their voices are heard equally with those of women of means. Replacing elite men with elite women is unlikely to result in positive social change or hold true to the principle of equality.

Nevertheless, one excellent example of the relative success of the Fonds Koré Fanm is a program for awareness-raising among political parties and for promoting women's political participation in the spaces of decision-making and power. Coordinated by Fanm Yo La (Women Are Here), a Haitian civil society organization dedicated to increasing the political participation of women, the project linked awareness-raising, training, and advocacy. It began by working with political parties to raise their awareness of women's issues, as well as to promote increased participation by women members at higher levels of decision-making. Women were also engaged and encouraged to run for political office; support was given to female candidates during their campaigns. A program to further support successful candidates has been implemented as well. The final leg of the project — advocacy — has worked towards encouraging change in Haitian laws to recognize and resolve the gender inequity in many Haitian statutes. For example, until two years ago, rape was considered nothing more than a "crime against one's honour" (*crime d'honneur*). As a result of concerted efforts by several feminist civil society organizations and the MCFDF, rape has been reclassified as a criminal offence, with a maximum penalty of life in prison.[28]

Other successes associated with this project relate to increased participation rates among women in recent Haitian elections. Through the combined efforts of Fanm Yo La and the MCFDF, women throughout Haiti were encouraged to vote, resulting in higher voter registration and turnout among women compared with the previous election. Moreover, 4000 women presented themselves as candidates across the country from the federal to the municipal level (29,500 positions were open). At the federal level, eight women were elected to the 129-member Parliament (National Assembly and Senate). At the local level, approximately 400 women were elected to municipal governments. This represents a significant increase from the previous elections in 2000. For appointed positions, Fanm Yo La proposed a list of about 150 women for positions in all sectors. Although their goal of having 30 per cent of appointed posts filled by women was not met, they did see several women appointed as directors general, a significant step in the right direction.[29] Given the strong history of inequality — not just related to women, but also more broadly — in Haitian society, while these steps are small, they remain significant and encouraging of further change to come. What is clear is that these changes could not have occurred without the financial and institutional support of Canada through the Fonds Koré Fanm.

However, in focussing much of its GE-promotion effort on the FKF, Canada may be missing opportunities to integrate GE into other areas, especially those outside of CIDA's responsibility. As many have noted, targeted spending, such as the FKF, must accompany broader cross-cutting work to promote GE; alone, neither is sufficient to achieve the goals these programs work towards. In CIDA-specific programming and projects, it seems that about 50 per cent of projects in the 2004–2006 period had impacts on gender equality and/or involved women or girls enough to merit mention in CIDA's ICF Result Summary for that period (see Table 1, following page).[30] Significantly, the pillar "Improve Access to Basic Services (including Humanitarian Assistance and Emergency Bilateral Aid)" showed the weakest recognition among participatory projects of an impact on GE, a topic that will be discussed in the following section. (The pillar "Targeted Budgetary Support" showed the weakest support overall.) This result could easily be due to a bias in the reporting, and women's rights and equality are in fact being addressed through these programs, but are just not making it into the results summary.

Nevertheless, given the importance of the principle of equality in the provision of such basic services and subsistence needs, such a reporting oversight remains telling. As explained in the document itself, the result summary "was compiled using a summary approach [and thus does] not represent the details of all results achieved by all Canadian cooperation stakeholders in Haiti during the period concerned. Rather, [it represents] a cross section that *highlights the most significant results*."[31] Clearly, as is suggested by the SCFAID report, some results are more significant than others. The inclusion of gender equality results in the results summary only about half the time suggests that either these results are not being tracked effectively, that they are non-existent or not yet visible, or that they are not significant enough to merit attention. Each of these options is out of step with either CIDA's GE policy, or with general Government of Canada accountability and results-reporting practices. If Canada truly seeks to promote equality between women and men, should it not start with ensuring that provision of the most basic of human needs is done in a fashion that is both aware of and respectful towards women and women's rights?

Table 1: CIDA project results in Haiti and the mention of women, girls, or gender-specific issues

Pillar	Total projects	Project Results mentioning women		Project Results NOT mentioning women	
		Quantity	% of total	Quantity	% of total
Strengthen Political Governance & Promote National Dialogue	29	15	52%	14	48%
Strengthen Economic Governance & Institutional Development	14	9	64%	5	36%
Promote Economic Recovery	8	4	50%	4	50%
Improve Access to Basic Services	33	15	46%	18	54%
Cross-cutting Themes	4	4	100%	0	0%
Targeted Budget Support	3	0	0%	3	100%
All Pillars	*91*	*47*	*52%*	*44*	*48%*

Source: CIDA, "Canada-Haiti Cooperation: Interim Cooperation Framework Result Summary (April 2004–March 2006) Final Report." Unpublished report, July 2006.

The same holds true for the pillar "Strengthen Political Governance and Promote National Dialogue (Including Security)" where only 52 per cent of the results presented mention the specific involvement of, or a focus on, women. This is of particular concern given the nature of the pillar and its focus on security as gender-based violence is consistently identified as a pressing concern in Haiti, as well as many other fragile states. In these sectors, which touch most profoundly on vulnerable populations, efforts to take a gender-sensitive approach to programming (and to reporting) should be redoubled. As mentioned above, one of the key challenges to integrating the promotion of GE is to actively make the links between issues surrounding women and women's rights and issues at the forefront of the fragile states discourse: security, justice, and good governance through strong state institutions. Canada is cognizant of these links, as noted on the DFAIT website:

> "Canada is committed to the view that gender equality is not only a human rights issue, but is also an essential component of sustainable development, social justice, peace, and security. These goals will only be achieved if women are able to participate as equal partners, decision-makers, and beneficiaries of the sustainable development of their societies."[32]

Clearly the recognition is there; the challenge may be in taking the policy and rhetoric and applying it, often 'on the fly', to challenging situations with difficult partnerships.

Finally, CIDA has recently developed an interim strategy to guide its operations in Haiti over the coming months through the extension of the ICF and while Haiti's Poverty Reduction Strategy Paper is being developed. The strategy document does seem to suggest that CIDA at least is focused on maintaining and increasing the integration of GE as a cross-cutting theme. *CIDA's Policy on Gender Equality* states that the first of eight guiding principles is: "Gender equality must be considered as an integral part of all CIDA policies, programs, and projects."[33] This concept is the essence of the "cross-cutting theme" and the manner in which the policy is operationalized. At the very least, inclusion of a gender analysis in project proposals and descriptions sets expectations for results and contributes to awareness-raising of the unique challenges faced by women and by men.

Reading the project descriptions included in CIDA's interim strategy, one is struck at how few of them mention how they will address gender equality (see Table 2, following page). Especially given CIDA's renewed focus on providing for basic services in Haiti,[34] all of which impact women and their families, it is disheartening to see that a gender analysis and steps to promote GE make such a poor showing. While, as with the ICF Results Summary described above, this could be a simple reporting error or bias, it is telling inasmuch as it reduces expected results in the area of gender equality promotion and misses an opportunity to raise awareness about these important issues, issues that CIDA clearly claims to support.

Table 2: CIDA Operational Projects in Haiti (Interim Strategy) and the mention of women, girls, or gender-specific issues

Theme	Total programs/ projects	Descriptions mentioning women		Descriptions NOT mentioning women	
		Quantity	% of total	Quantity	% of total
Bilateral Projects					
Reinforce the State	13	2*	15%	11	85%
Access to Basic Services	10	1	10%	9	90%
Social Peace	6	2	33%	4	67%
Others	6	0	0%	6	100%
Canadian Partnership Programs					
Projects with the Haitian diaspora	9	1	11%	8	89%
Promotion of the Protection of Human Rights	11	3	27%	8	73%
Satisfaction of Basic Human Needs and Access to Services	23	7	30%	16	70%
Development of Small Business and Cooperatives	4	2	50%	2	50%
College and University Teaching	2	1	50%	1	50%
Industrial Cooperation	1	0	0%	1	100%
Multilateral Programs (all)	3	0	0%	3	100%
All Themes	*88*	*18*	*21%*	*70*	*79%*
All Themes — approximate dollar amounts (millions of C$)	*420.67*	*48.83**	*11.6%*	*371.84*	*88.4%*

Source: CIDA, "Operational Projects, Canadian Cooperation Program in Haiti." Unpublished document, March 2007.

*One of these programs is the C$4 million Fonds Kore Famn II.

Socio-economic Development

As mentioned above, of the projects reported in the ICF result summary the pillar with the lowest percentage of projects with a gender equality focus was Improve Access to Basic Services. Although the information presented in Table 2 (above) does not follow the same pillar system, this trend is reflected in the interim strategy, in the themes that relate to socio-economic development. In fact, the trend is getting worse: of the projects covered by the interim strategy that relate to provision of basic services, and economic and social development, only approximately 24 per cent mention a specific focus on women.

These results seem counterintuitive and, I would suggest, reflect a reporting bias rather than neglect on the part of CIDA. For example, many of the programs related to health and education, with which Canada is having some success, fail to disaggregate data on the basis of gender in the ICF result summary. Surely these projects are accessing women and girls, especially those involving primary education and health. One cannot imagine that with CIDA's wealth of experience in these areas that women and girls were being excluded from these programs; however, many of the project descriptions do not mention girls or women. Moreover, CIDA is demonstrating a strong focus on education, both primary schooling and technical training. Over the next five years, CIDA will contribute C$100 million a year to basic education. Education will soon become the focus of the majority of Canadian development assistance in Haiti. Key to CIDA's strategy is a push to make education in Haiti public, free, and accessible to *all* young Haitians.[35] This perspective is reinforced by the work of certain Canadian partnership NGOs working in the education sector, which are witnessing gender-parity, if not a slight bias in favour of girls, in their primary education programs.[36] Investing in education could be the most cost-effective way of contributing to the reversal of state fragility by instilling the principles of a gender equal society in children through primary school curricula and working to change traditional societal biases. In this way, as these children grow and become political actors, they should carry these attitudes with them.

In terms of other socio-economic spheres, many of the projects related to infrastructure improvement do not mention the gender impact of the work, whether those impacts are positive or negative. As these projects create employment and impact the physical environment in which women work and live, it is important to be aware of and engage with the issues these projects create for women and girls, as well as for men in their communities. The same challenge appears in the project descriptions associated with CIDA's interim strategy where many projects that could easily include a gender equality focus (and most likely have profound results), such as projects fighting the spread of HIV/AIDS, fail to mention gender whatsoever.

In this domain, especially, we see the potential of a gender equality perspective to have profound positive impacts on creating a sustainable future for fragile states. As noted above, a development focus on women has profound effects on the people — male and female, young and old — that surround them. Neglecting a small investment in gender equality at these early stages in Haiti, as well as in other fragile states, could cost dearly in the future. Moreover, such neglect is hurting Haiti in the present, as a significant portion of its human resources — in terms of both physical labour and innovative thinking — are being underutilized. Harnessing that potential through programs that empower women and work to resolve gender inequalities can only serve Haiti positively in the long run.

While the cultural shift needed to see profound change will take time, simple steps could be taken immediately, such as affirmative action programs or leading by example through development projects. One concrete example could be in hiring and training women in non-traditional jobs. On a recent mission to Port-au-Prince, I was struck by how men and women are separated in their working roles. For example, the Haitian staff at my hotel were divided along gender lines: men could be waiters, maintenance or security staff, and work the front desk; the women I saw were entirely housekeeping staff, with the exception of one female administrator. Providing the opportunity to train and work in a non-gendered role through a development project could serve as the first step towards changing the norms that reinforce social inequalities. As a friend to Haiti, with a variety of interests in its sustainable development, Canada should be working proactively and visibly to promote gender equality in all of its programs and projects in that country.

Public Security

Apart from CIDA, the two arms of the Canadian government currently involved the most in Haiti are DFAIT and the RCMP.[37] DFAIT, as the lead department on diplomatic issues, and with responsibility for liaising with the United Nations, has contributed to the promotion of gender equality in a number of ways, particularly related to enhancing public security. At the UN in 2004, Canada contributed to ensuring that gender equality was included in the mandate of the UN Stabilization Mission in Haiti. As a result of this joint effort, "gender training" was included in MINUSTAH's mandate for reforming the Police Nationale d'Haïti (PNH).[38] Moreover, in the recent resolution extending MINUSTAH's mandate, gender equality was reinforced through an invocation of UN Security Council Resolution 1325 (on Women, Peace, and Security) in the following manner: "[The Security Council] … Welcomes MINUSTAH's policy to promote and protect the rights of women and to take into account gender considerations as set out in Security Council resolution 1325 as a cross-cutting issue throughout its mandate…"[39] Canada was among the states encouraging this language in the resolution.

Furthermore, in 2005 the DFAIT-sponsored Canadian Commission on Women, Peace, and Security (CCWPS) presented a case-study of Haiti as part of its annual conference. The report of this conference gives a thoughtful assessment of the challenges Canada faces in promoting GE in Haiti, and offers suggestions as to how those challenges can be met. As such, the report suggests that:

> "Given that gender considerations are still not a security priority in practice, it is important to be aware of and seize upon windows of opportunity. For example, when the UN decided to send an assessment mission to precede MINUSTAH, various actors, including Canada, pushed for there to be a human rights and a gender component in the assessment, as well as in the MINUSTAH mandate…"[40]

However, information available on the DFAIT Women, Peace, and Security webpage on these efforts and their relative success or failure has not been updated since mid-April 2006. Moreover, DFAIT confirms that a systematic review of its programming effectiveness in promoting GE in Haiti has not, as yet, been carried out. Haiti is not alone in this respect, as no review of GE promotion in any fragile state has taken place.[41] What therefore remains to be carried out is such a review with an eye to teasing out lessons learned for further engagement in Haiti and engagement in other fragile states.

As well, Canada is lagging behind other like-minded countries in the production of a National Action Plan on the implementation of UNSCR 1325, one of the key obligations of member states under the resolution. The CCWPS conference was an important part of the process of developing this plan, which was initiated just prior to the conference itself, in 2005 — five years after the resolution was confirmed.[42] As of summer 2007, nearly seven years post-resolution, the process has advanced considerably, but appears to be stalled within DFAIT. In order to meet this commitment under UNSCR 1325, and to provide strong and structured guidance to civil servants, especially those working in fragile states, the government should move forward to finalize and implement this policy without delay.

While DFAIT was involved in supporting the inclusion of GE principles in MINUSTAH's mandates, it was not involved in drafting the Police Nationale d'Haïti's reform plan in either 2005 or 2006 and thus could not promote a gender-sensitive approach. CIDA was poised to play a role in this process, but negotiations focused on the United Nations and the Haitian Government and resulted in a final document that is effectively gender-blind.[43] However, in practice, and through the work of CIDA and the RCMP as well as the UN, steps are being taken to remedy this absence. For instance, MINUSTAH has established a gender equality office that is currently in the process of conducting a small survey on the situation of women in the PNH.[44] While the survey is quite limited, the results will provide an important first assessment of how women are integrating into the PNH and where there is room for improvement.

MINUSTAH is also having modest success with respect to its efforts to reform and expand the PNH. According to United Nations Special Representative to the Secretary-General and Head of MINUSTAH, Edmond Mulet, the HNP is calling on more women to join its ranks. The class of recent recruits that will graduate in July 2007 includes 91 women (14 per cent). More importantly, President René Préval is calling for the new class to be composed of 50 per cent women, an extremely ambitious goal, but one that indicates the extent of the promotion of GE in HNP reform and that marks an improvement towards achieving gender parity in the police force compared with previous policies. As well, MINUSTAH is working with the HNP and Haitian civil society to combat violence against women in Haiti through media campaigns and education; the effectiveness of these campaigns may take some time to evaluate and no results are available at present.[45]

In addition to this, a CIDA-funded, RCMP-run project to support PNH reform through training and technical support exists.[46] Unfortunately, this project may also suffer from the possible reporting bias described above. While the CIDA Results Summary does identify key important results for this project, it does not disaggregate its data by gender, thus giving no insight into how many female police officers are being recruited or trained, nor is there any mention of gender-sensitivity training. At the very least, one can assume that some of the Canadian RCMP trainers are women: as of 2005, of the up-to-100 RCMP officers deployed to Haiti, 15 per cent were women. As well, the force was working to raise that percentage to 25 per cent.[47] However, UN statistics as of April 2007 show that Canada currently has only 62 police officers serving in Haiti.[48] Even at 25 per cent, that amounts to only fifteen or sixteen Canadian women serving with MINUSTAH's civilian police. In theory these female RCMP officers may be sensitive to issues of gender equality and certainly could act as positive role models for young Haitian women considering their career options. However, in the absence of systematic evaluations of gender-equality outcomes in this area, and especially given the small numbers present, it is dangerous to assume that the participation of female RCMP officers in Haiti has helped to promote GE within public security institutions. Indeed, as with DFAIT, stronger efforts should be made to assess and publicize the RCMP's work in promoting gender equality through its projects in this fragile state.

The question of RCMP officers working directly with Haitian police officers through a peace support operation brings us back to Canada's obligations under UNSCR 1325. The CCWPS conference report notes that DFAIT "will be conducting an assessment of the gender-related training provided to Canadian personnel involved in peace support operations."[49] In Haiti, this would apply to the RCMP. While the assessment has been completed, the report remains internal and it is unclear whether steps have been taken to identify the gaps in learning and reporting on gender issues that it identifies.[50]

Finally, Correctional Service Canada (CSC) has participated as part of Canada's engagement with Haiti in the past and could well play a key role in the future as reform of the justice sector becomes an increasingly pressing issue in Haiti. Unfortunately, despite CSC's assertion that its "international programs are consistent with Canada's international policy objectives..." it does not provide any discussion of how it addresses issues of gender equality through its work overseas.[51] This would seem a crucial gap, especially given that Canada plans to support a quick-impact project for prisons by funding the addition of a building for new and expectant mothers for the Haitian women's prison.[52] If Canada plans to draw on the expertise it has in its own government departments during the planning and implementation of such a project, every department that is involved should be robustly promoting gender equality as a cross-cutting theme. As with recommendations for other departments, much could be learned through a systematic review and assessment of the gender equality dimensions of previous CSC projects in Haiti and elsewhere.

Conclusions: Canada's Impact on State Fragility in Haiti — Realities and Recommendations

Canada has seen success in a number of venues regarding the promotion of gender equality. Positive change can be measured in the area of women's political participation. Limited success can be identified in the area of public security. A suspected reporting bias in the area of socio-economic development should be further investigated before concluding that Canada is not promoting gender equality in this key area. Many of these are steps forward that must be recognized and reinforced. However, Canada should also take further steps to promote gender equality in those development areas that are truly opened up through a whole-of-government approach, such as security, justice, and the political process. Most importantly, a comprehensive assessment/review of DFAIT and RCMP programming in fragile states should be conducted to provide insight into good practices and lessons learned, as well as providing a benchmark from which to measure progress in GE promotion.

Despite its many relative successes and its first steps towards whole-of-government programming of gender equality in fragile states, Canada will not have a significant and lasting impact on state fragility until it starts actively and consistently making the links in policy and programming between what are identified as priority issues for fragile states and those issues related to gender equality. Moreover, these links need to be made in policy and programming across government departments and agencies. Clearly, a disconnect exists within (and among) some government institutions regarding the links between GE issues and other programming in fragile states; this disconnect is reflected by the absence of these links in government reporting across the Canadian government, as seen in the SCFAID, Government Response, CIDA, DFAIT, and RCMP reports discussed above, as well as Canada's slow development of a national action plan to implement UNSCR 1325.

These links are not difficult to make if we focus on the principles behind both concepts, the promotion of GE and engagement with fragile states. Work in fragile states is aimed at creating strong, stable democracies that are able to provide for the needs of their poorest citizens. Yet how can democracies be truly robust without recognizing and practicing the equality of all their people, including equality between men and women? By not integrating all sectors of the population into the decision-making process as legitimate players whose voices are heard, we risk building nothing but a nominal democracy. By closing spaces for dialogue and ignoring those groups that have traditionally been excluded from power, we risk weakening the current situation, sowing the seeds for future state fragility, or at worst setting the stage for ultimate state failure. That said, change must take place at a pace that the society is able to tolerate; too much change imposed on a country by external forces can result in the opposite of the desired effect. Such a potential result highlights the importance of following good aid effectiveness guidelines and ensuring local ownership of any proposed project.

Yet how likely is Canada to adopt these policy prescriptions? This question raises further questions as to why Canada is so strongly implicated in Haiti: is it simply because we are a "good neighbour"? Does the Haitian-Canadian diaspora have such great influence? Are we engaged there at the request of a third party? Most likely, a confluence of these and other interests keep Canada engaged with Haiti. Another key question that is raised is whether or not gender equality really is a priority. It is clear that the promotion of GE has been adopted sporadically at best across government departments, despite the whole-of-government approach espoused by the OECD DAC which Canada is ostensibly following in Haiti. Moreover, Canada's uneven promotion of GE in Haiti throughout 2004–2006 was matched by relatively weak GE promotion by Haiti's transitional government. Taken together, these questions and historical experiences express a tension that exists in promoting GE in fragile states between national and international actors.[53] As well, as reflected in the SCFAID report and the Government response, parliamentarians — Canada's decision-makers — do not show an engagement with the theme, suggesting that the message has yet to reach the seats of power.

In the context of a fragile state, donor countries and organizations as well as national governments need to work together, along with civil society organizations, to realize the goal of building an equitable society. However, a panoply of issues make that process a difficult and tenuous one at best. In Haiti for example, these issues include: Canada's history of engagement in Haiti, especially during the questionable ouster of Aristide; the competing agendas of multi- and bilateral partners in Haiti and the region more broadly in the context of an ongoing fragile states discourse closely related to the "war on terror"; a national government that is increasingly asserting its sovereignty; and differing financial priorities among all stakeholders. As donors are increasingly following the lead of national governments in setting their priorities (following aid effectivness principles), the promotion of GE and the consolidation of an equitable society will only prosper if the Haitian government makes it a priority, and if Haitian civil society continues to push their elected officials to do so. This will not be an easy task, as international dimensions mix with tensions at the national level among those who have power and those who want it, all against the backdrop of an extremely politicized society, tinged with corruption and influenced daily by the presence of a multinational peacekeeping force.

If it chooses, Canada could rise to these challenges and break new and important ground by leading in the development of locally-owned, gender-sensitive, human-rights based programming in its priority countries. In the face of such complexity and power-bargaining, it would be easy to lose hope for an equitable Haitian society. However, despite the challenges they have faced over the past two centuries and the challenges they face today, Haitians have never lost hope and we must follow their example.

JENNIFER SALAHUB joined The North-South Institute in February, 2006 and is currently Program Assistant/Researcher with the Conflict Prevention Program. In that capacity, Jennifer is leading the Institute's continuing work on gender equality in fragile states, while supporting its work on security system reform. Jennifer holds a Master's degree in Political Science from McGill University.

Endnotes

1 Jennifer Salahub is Program Assistant/Researcher with the Conflict Prevention group at The North-South Institute. A previous version of this chapter was presented at the conference "Negotiating Women: Peace and Security in Fragile States" hosted by Carleton University, April 24, 2007.

2 For critical assessments of Canada's participation in Aristide's departure, see Anthony Fenton and Yves Engler, *Canada in Haiti: Waging War on the Poor Majority*, Black Point, NS: Fernwood Publishing, 2005; and, Coalition to Oppose the Arms Trade (COAT), "A Very Canadian Coup d'Etat in Haiti: The Top 10 Ways that Canada's Government Helped the 2004 Coup and its Reign of Terror," Press for Conversion! 60 (March 2007): 3–49.

3 For a discussion of the issues surrounding the term "fragile state," see Canadian Council for International Co-operation, *"Failed States" Canadian Action in Conflict-Affected States*, CCIC Discussion Papers, Ottawa: CCIC, 2007.

4 It is interesting to note the links of this definition of fragile states to the Responsibilty to Protect (R2P) doctrine, in which Canada was also greatly implicated. R2P also uses the concept of "unwilling or unable" to protect civilian populations as the basis for international intervention. See International Commission on Intervention and State Sovereignty, *The Responsibility to Protect*, Ottawa: IDRC, 2001.

5 Baranyi, Stephen and Kristiana Powell. "Fragile States, Gender Equality and Aid Effectiveness: A Review of Donor Perspectives," NSI working paper, Ottawa: The North-South Institute, 2005: 1–2.

6 See CIDA, *CIDA's Policy on Gender Equality*, Ottawa: Minister of Public Works and Government Services Canada, 1999.

7 United Nations, Security Council, *Resolution 1325 (2000)*, New York: United Nations, 2000.

8 Baranyi and Powell, "Fragile States, Gender Equality…"

9 Ibid: 1.

10 World Bank, *Global Monitoring Report 2007 Millennium Development Goals: Confronting the Challenges of Gender Equality and Fragile States*, Washington, DC: The International Bank for Reconstruction and Development / The World Bank, 2007.

11 By some measures, "strong" states could easily include strong authoritarian regimes that are able to provide services, but have few of the other characteristics of robust democracies. Part of the assumption is that the "strongest" states — those states most capable of providing services to the majority of the population, including vulnerable populations and most willing to provide those services — are robust democracies.

12 This follows the suggestion that states in transition from democracy are more likely to engage in conflict than consolidated democracies or nondemocracies. See the work of Edward Mansfield and Jack Snyder, such as *Electing to Fight: Why Emerging Democracies Go to War*, Cambridge, MA: MIT Press, 2005.

13 UN, SC, *Resolution 1325 (2000)*.

14 United Nations. *Report of the Fourth World Conference on Women*, New York: United Nations, 1995.

15 See, for example, Amartya Sen, *The Argumentative Indian*, London: Penguin, 2006, especially chapter 11.

16 World Bank. "Empowering Women, Boosting Economies," Online. Available: <http://web.worldbank.org/WBSITE/EXTERNAL/NEWS/0,,contentMDK:21079590~menuPK:34457~pagePK:34370~piPK:34424~theSitePK:4607,00.html>. Accessed: May 20, 2007.

17 Aristide, Jean Bertrand. "Haiti's Aristide Calls For His Restoration to Power," Interviewed by Democracy Now! [online news broadcast], April 21, 2005, Online. Available: <http://www.democracynow.org/article.pl?sid=05/04/21/1418214&mode=thread&tid=25>. Accessed: June 4, 2007.

18 See Fenton and Engler, and Coalition to Oppose the Arms Trade (COAT).

19 See Graham, Bill, Minister of Foreign Affairs, Interviewed by Jacquie Perrin for CBC Newsworld Feb 29, 2004, Online, Available: <http://www.cbc.ca/clips/rm-newsworld/perrin_graham0402291.rm>. Accessed: July 12, 2007; and Paul Knox, "International force deploys to Haiti as Aristide flees," *The Globe and Mail*, March 1, 2004: A1.

20 Canada. House of Commons, Standing Committee on Foreign Affairs and International Development, *Canada's International Policy Put to the Test in Haiti*, Ottawa: Communications Canada, 2006: 2.

21 Opinion expressed by UN SRSG Edmond Mulet. Edmond Mulet, "Haiti: The Journey Since the Deployment of MINUSTAH in June 2004 and the Main Upcoming Challenges," [Presentation], Canadian Institute of International Affairs Special Event, Ottawa, ON, June 1, 2007.

22 Elections Canada. "Elections Canada: International Activities," Online, Available: http://www.elections.ca/intro.asp?section=int&document=index&lang=e>. Accessed: June 4, 2007.

23 For an assessment of Canadian engagement in Haiti during the 2004–2006 period, see Stephen Baranyi, "Le Canada, Haïti et les dilemmes de l'intervention dans les 'États fragiles," paper presented at the Latin American Studies Association Annual Conference, Sept. 5–8, 2007, Montreal, Canada.

24 See Organisation for Economic Cooperation and Development, "Principles for Good International Engagement in Fragile States," Paris: OECD, 2005, and Organisation for Economic Cooperation and Development, "Whole of Government Approaches to Fragile States," Paris: OECD, 2006.

25 Canada. House of Commons, SCFAID: v.

26 The idea here is that with a group of witnesses with such diverse experiences, issues of gender equality and women's rights might get lost in the shuffle and that other, ostensibly more immediate, priorities would take precedence.

27 Canada. House of Commons, SCFAID: 20–21.

28 François, Lisa, Executive Director, Fanm Yo La, [Conversation with the author], March 28, 2007, Port-au-Prince.

29 Ibid. See also, CIDA, "Canada–Haiti Cooperation: Interim Cooperation Framework Result Summary (April 2004–March 2006) Final Report," Unpublished report, July 2006.

30 See CIDA, "Canada–Haiti Cooperation…"

31 CIDA, "Canada–Haiti Cooperation…": 7 (emphasis added).

32 DFAIT. "Canada's Commitment to Gender Equality and the Advancement of Women's Rights Internationally," Online. Available at: <http://www.dfait-maeci.gc.ca/foreign_policy/human-rights/lwe1-equal-en.asp>, Accessed: April 13, 2007.

33 CIDA, *CIDA's Policy on Gender Equality*: 8.

34 Schemmer, Darren, CIDA Haiti Program Director General, "Taking Stock: What Was Achieved in 2006–2007" [Presentation to CIDA's Canadian Cooperation partners], Ottawa, June 20, 2007.

35 Verret, Louis, CIDA Haiti Program Director, "Strategic Directions — Governance, Health and Education" [Presentation to CIDA's Canadian Cooperation partners], Ottawa, June 20, 2007.

36 Comeau, Louis Patrick, Plan Nagua, "Amélioration de l'éducation de base dans la région du nord et du nord-est d'Haïti" [Presentation to CIDA's Canadian Cooperation partners], Ottawa, June 20, 2007.

37 The Correctional Service of Canada has been active in Haiti in the past and may be again in the future. See below for further discussion.

38 United Nations, Security Council. *Resolution 1524 (2004)*, New York: United Nations, 2004.

39 United Nations, Security Council, *Resolution 1743 (2007)*, New York: United Nations, 2007.

40 DFAIT. *Towards a Canadian National Action Plan to Implement Security Council Resolution 1325 on Women, Peace and Security: Third Annual Symposium of the Canadian Committee on Women, Peace and Security*, Ottawa: DFAIT, 2005: 11 (emphasis in original).

41 DFAIT analyst B [Email correspondence with the author], May 10, 2007.

42 DFAIT, *Towards…*: 1.

43 For the 2006 Plan, see United Nations, Security Council, *Letter dated August 31, 2006 from the Secretary-General addressed to the President of the Security Council, S/2006/726*, New York: United Nations, 2006. The document contains no references to gender, women or girls, let alone the important issues associated with both integrating women into the police force and with combatting violence against women, among other issues.

44 Vital Metellus, Marie-Françoise, employee of MINUSTAH's Bureau de Parité [Conversation with the author], March 24, 2007, Port-au-Prince.

45 Mulet, Edmond. "Haiti…"

46 CIDA, "Canada–Haiti Cooperation…": 20.

47 DFAIT, *Towards…*: 11.

48 United Nations, Department of Peacekeeping Operations, *UN Mission's summary detailed by Country, Month of Report: 30-Apr-07*, Online, Available: <http://www.un.org/Depts/dpko/dko/contributors/2007/apr07_3.pdf>. Accessed: June 7, 2007. Note that these statistics from April 2007 conflict with the numbers provided in the Government response to the SCFAID Report. Presented to the House on April 17, 2007, the Government response (p. 8) states that 70 police are currently deployed to MINUSTAH. See Government of Canada. *Government Response to the Fourth Report of the Standing Committee on Foreign Affairs and International Development.* April 17, 2007. Online. Available: <http://cmte.parl.gc.ca/cmte/CommitteePublication.aspx?COM=10475&Lang=1&SourceId=201205>. Accessed April 17, 2007.

49 DFAIT, *Towards…*: 6.

50 DFAIT analyst B [Email correspondence with the author], June 26, 2007.

51 Correctional Service Canada, "CSC and the World," Online, Available: <http://www.csc-scc.gc.ca/text/intlform/index_e.shtml>. Accessed: June 7, 07.

52 DFAIT analyst A [Conversation with the author], November 24, 2006, Ottawa, ON. While the practice of imprisoning new and expectant mothers needs to be addressed philosophically, the fact remains that many Haitian women are currently imprisoned. Given this fact and the extreme state of disrepair of the Haitian penal and justice systems at the moment, any improvement of the penal infrastructure must be taken as a positive step. For an excellent analysis of Haiti's penal system, including Haiti's one women's prison, see International Crisis Group, "Haiti: Prison Reform and the Rule of Law," Online, available at: <http://www.crisisgroup.org/home/index.cfm?id=4809&l=1>. Accessed: 5 May 2007.

53 For example, the MCFDF received significantly less in actual funding than was proposed in their original budget for these years: on the order of 25 per cent of their provisional budget in the 2004–2005 was ultimately allocated by the government, and only 44 per cent was provided in 2005–2006. This forced the Ministry to turn directly to international aid agencies to increase its available resources. République d'Haïti, Ministère à la Condition Feminine et aux Droits des Femmes, *Bilan Mars 2004–Janvier 2006*, Port-au-Prince: MCFDF, 2006: 27–29. The *Bilan* also notes that Canada can take some credit for supporting the Ministry, despite its uneven support elsewhere, due to the fact that the Fonds Kore Famn was one of the principal sources of extra funding for the Ministry during these years, especially in building the Ministry's institutional capacity (p. 39).

Fragile Premises and Failed States: A Perspective from Latin America

Alejandro Bendaña

Fragile Premises and Failed States: A Perspective from Latin America

Alejandro Bendaña

> *"If you run away," says the mother, "I will run after you.*
> *For you are my little bunny"*
>
> — **The Runaway Bunny** *by Margaret Wise Brown*

State fragility or state failure are, in essence, the latest in a long history of ideological constructs created by powerful nations to legitimize interventions in weaker ones. Although perhaps less dismissive than the "rogue state" category invented by the Clinton Administration, "fragile" or "failing" purport to underscore the right claimed by the global superpower to revamp other nations — toppling governments, invading states, destabilization, and so on.

State weaknesses, fragility, or "failure" are pretexts for empire-building. In many places, the US is increasingly perceived as a power in search of an empire but its determination to employ military means necessitates new justifications or rationalizations, particularly with a view to recruiting allies.

Given the term's origins, it is no surprise the characterizations of failing states usually ignore causes of "failure" or "fragility," often rooted in the global economy structure, neo-liberal economic policies pushed by international financial institutions (IFIs), or Northern governments, alongside the absence of effective democracy and domestic accountability within the country.

The Bush Administration, its European and NATO allies, and Bretton Woods institutions, have now proclaimed themselves the global arbiters of what constitutes good governance and acceptable states, and what and who does not. Not that a great deal of high-minded discussion goes on before invading: lower level policy-makers and policy-watchers are left, usually *ex post facto*, to problematize the role of donors and states in the post 9/11 security-first global order.

Revisiting the State

Before examining what is a failed or weak state, analysts would do well to address the question of what are the expectations, duties, responsibilities, and rights of states. Who are the legitimate parties to make such a determination? Domestic constituencies, of course, have varying public policy expectations and demands — as varied as the sectors that compose civil society along with the business sector. Differences notwithstanding there is a larger principle involved, which is the principle of democratic self-determination. In a world of sovereign states, governments may influence each other but, again in principle, it is individual nations alone that must decide with or on behalf of the citizenry.

Dominant hegemonic powers are not particularly keen on respect for sovereignty, save for their own. There are, of course, legal international responsibilities and agreements that require observation and monitoring. But over and above those norms, power and wealth considerations enter into the picture, and with it the imposition of particular "national" interests and corresponding "interpretations" over collective ones. At issue is the state, its purpose and the pressure for change, from within and outside national boundaries. From a normative perspective, a state fails when it cannot effectively ensure the delivery of physical security, economic opportunity and fundamental services to its citizenry, or at least a large majority thereof.

A case by case approach would be necessary to determine whether a state is functional or dysfunctional, but hopefully carried out in an objective fashion that ensures full respect for democracy, accountability, and legitimacy. Only then could one arrive at broader formulas for determining state efficacy or its absence, and just what specifically state-building should entail. Subsequently one would ask, and not simply assume, that donors and international bodies assist with such a process. Which, in turn, leads to the central question of whether the state "reform" or "reconstruction" process driven from a market-oriented or a security-oriented perspective coincides with a domestic alignment of forces, or mostly to an external induction by powers suffering from delusional control issues.

Fragility and failure, in this context, may be more in the eyes of the beholder, conducive to the export of ideology and mechanisms ("reform," "good governance," "anti-terrorism") defined by the hegemonic state and demanded by its requirement for a "global" environment conducive to its own economic and security concerns. Failed or fragile states cannot be full members of the new global order, nor can they enjoy the same rights as other countries — they are assigned a second class legal status, not fully worthy of independence and obliged to receive external tutelage and intervention. This new white man's burden requires conceptual and eventual legal enshrinement contrary, in many basic senses, to the evolution of international law and the hard-won principles of non-intervention and national self-determination.

As with genocide, a politics of naming comes into play. Some states will win the designation of "failed" and others, engaged in much the same practices, will not. There is no mathematical formula derived from the application of indicators. The logic is political not scientific having more to do with the real world of power projections and the definition of new codes of international behaviour from which the powerful are somehow exempt. Targeting is selectively guided by the existence of resources or strategic geographical locations (Afghanistan yes, Somalia no).[1]

Unfortunately, the more the categorization is propagated, the more interventions gain in legitimacy. A new generation of donor darlings and aid effectiveness criteria is born and the older generation of donor orphans is sent packing. Historical, systemic and global structural causes of state weaknesses are not acknowledged let alone tackled. The pre-determined prescription (intervention) requires a pre-determined diagnosis (state failure). Neither the prescription nor the diagnosis take sovereignty into account, let alone the alternative economic and security perspectives being proposed by a nation's citizens. Democracy is mentioned but not the facts that independence is its prerequisite, that democracy cannot be exported, or that external tutorials seldom make an enduring contribution.

If the rather meddlesome issue of democracy is sacrificed in the name of state or international security, then the picture, at least analytically, becomes clearer. It becomes a matter of "stabilization," or "pacification" driven from the outside. A genuine peacebuilding and democracy building as bottom-up processes. Just if and how the lively-fiction called the "international community" can assist a true democratic endeavour is open to question, particularly if the subject being "helped" has its own ideas of what that help should be. Stakeholders before rights-holders?

State failure per se is not a social problem. In fact, a state collapse may be welcome news when it puts an end to a repressive or undemocratic regime. But tears may be shed on the part of that regime's external partners. Nor is fragility a problem if it entails the logical, slow, and complicated process of perfecting democracy and building citizenship-centred public institutions, a process that can involve decades and, in many senses, is never ending for rich and poor countries alike.

The crux of the issue is the social and economic character of the state and its capacity to protect and promote democratic transformation, not to contain it. Granted the notions of state modern-ization or state-building have their problems, but this is not to trade-in processes for quick-fix solutions in which the technical experts take over from the internal beneficiaries. Nor is there much qualitative difference between "state-building," public sector development and democratization in fragile states as opposed to other poor developing countries, save for the unfortunate intrusion of the "anti-terrorist" criteria that is leading to the "securitization" of ODA and the emergence of "triple D" criteria (diplomacy, development, defence).

The problem has more to do with politics and power than with policy. In the name of rescuing or even preventing failed states, the United States and some of its allies have deliberately ignored international law and multilateral leaderships. In the absence of genuine multilateral decision-making, NATO determines what constitutes failure or fragility, and what states or even regions lack the capacity to ensure certain standards and what countries or multilateral institutions should step in for the reconversion and reconstruction. Governments would then organize "consultations" and commission research around good practices, the "how," "when," and "who," sidelining the "whether."

An insistence on "practical," "policy-oriented," "operative results" reinforces the dominant donor-defined framework. State fragility or failure become simplistic misnomers for what could be a more legitimate discussion around institution building and democratization — two interlocked propositions whose separation is responsible for more than one failure. We witness thereupon a regression to the era of trusteeships with entire nations held as wards of the so-called international community. That may be the easy way out given the complexities of state-building in the context of historical specificities and normative principles. The critical principal here is national sovereignty as observers, particularly from the South, continue to reject concepts and practices that, in effect, signify a recolonization with the reversion of the hard-won principle of national self-determination.

What we require is a greater understanding of how the proposition of the state is intimately linked to national democratization, the failure of one is the failure of the other. But failure or fragility is also linked to the absence of global democratic governance, which makes any national democratic state-building process all the more difficult. The Latin American state, and states elsewhere, are caught in between the pressures from below (democratic) and the pressures from the outside (colonialist). Nonetheless, as Mariano Aguirre has argued, Latin America's search for new models of governance can benefit from an understanding of how its fragile states encourage violence and block democracy. Indeed, extending these concepts to Latin America may help better illuminate the problems posed by changing political and social dynamics.[2] From this standpoint, a deeper understanding and definition of fragility and failure is warranted.

Failed National States or Failed Global Systems?

The stepping stone for the World Bank's entry into the fragile states foray was its "Low Income Countries Under Stress" initiative also known as LICUS. Not until January 2006 did the World Bank sign on to the new terminology.[3] Multi-donor trust funds or reconstruction fund mechanisms managed by the World Bank gave this institution enormous power to complement its already sizeable influence over national economic policy-making. Unfortunately, donor fragility concerns are translating into yet another mission sweep by the World Bank as it is granted authority to enhance its already deep involvement in domestic policy-making.[4]

And there is no direct relation between IFI involvement on the one hand and macro-stabilization on the other. A recent study by William Easterly, a former World Bank official, found a disturbing correlation between IMF interventions and state fragility pointing to eight cases of state failure in the 1990s where each of these countries had an average of 55 IMF programs, as opposed to the average of 20 for all developing countries between 1970 and 1990.[5] Statistically, claims the author, "spending a lot of time under an IMF program is associated with a higher risk of state collapse… At best, the IMF doing a program in these countries was like recommending heart-healthy calisthenics every morning for patients with broken limbs. …the planner's mentality in which the IMF applies the same type of program to all countries is ill matched to such ill societies… People in the country receiving the IMF loan," he adds, "often blame the IMF when the government does those things, and they take to the streets to protest IMF-enforced austerity. One big trouble in IMF stabilization plans is their disturbance of domestic politics."[6]

Genuine democratic development itself is a destabilizing proposition as it inevitably challenges the role and power of the IFIs. Economic fragility has political repercussions; a drop in revenue can strain or even provoke the collapse of basic services, including elementary physical protection. Fragility and non-performance, in a social context, are also linked to years of failed donor-imposed structural adjustment conflicts resulting in violent conflicts, at worst or massive violations of economic and social rights. Structural Adjustment Programs and the contemporary spinoffs are responsible for the dismantled state and public sector structures, for accentuating inter-elite conflicts over the spoils of office and policy, and for generating social unrest. Trade liberalization can aggravate internal contradictions and provoke the emergence of new elites and external corporate control that is resented by distinct sectors of national producers, increasing poverty and unemployment. Migration and remittances may attenuate conflict and offer an escape valve, but it raises reactions in the rich countries bordering on hysteria.

In Latin America, we witness new evidence of an old phenomenon with a new name: state failure and fragility that take the form of government incapacity to help guarantee basic rights and services. Fragility and failure are also the result of the pressure placed on governments attempting to shift economic power away from the traditional elites and their corporate multinational partners. For their part, the IFIs and "donors" will insist on economic and governance "reform" packages in which the government is told to constrain public sector budgets, and promote privatization and liberalization. Washington seems obsessed with Venezuela, but this is a distraction from the real issues around state-restructuring in Latin America. Former Chief World Bank Economist Joseph Stiglitz believes that, "The mistake, from my point of view, is trying to figure out Chávez. What you've got to figure out is why the market economic model has not worked to include the majority from Mexico down to Tierra del Fuego."[7]

The global power structure in both its military and economic manifestations can (and is sometimes intended to) induce destabilizations among Southern governments. Models of state transformation that do not respond to the needs of the global political economy, or the global war on terror (GWOT), will hardly be the subject of "assistance" save for that provided to internal forces bent on regime change. Domestic processes develop with external constraints, and with sharply reduced spaces for policy discussion and democratic accountability.

Until recently, Latin American governments did not feel sufficiently empowered to explore development and security options different from those defined in Washington. Intervention and external expectations can overload the state, and this may well be the greatest source of failure or weakness, far more than the corruption and lack of good governance as fashionable donor wisdom argues. The problem, the North insists, is not the "advice" but the unwillingness of the countries to adopt it.

The Pentagon and the GWOT in Latin America

The events of 9/11 convinced the US governing elite that the normal mechanisms for dealing with perceived security threats were insufficient. Individual freedoms and the democratic process may be taking second place to counter-terrorism, weakening democratic institutions in the process. If this is already reflected within the US and some of its allies, then it is that much more intense when operating abroad. In parts of Latin America it could entail the return of features of the Cold War anti-communist national security state.

In Latin America and the Caribbean, the Pentagon demands a "new architecture of hemispheric security" to integrate the region's security forces more tightly into the US military's command structure and global policy. An immediate need was to secure broader Latin American participation for the occupation of Haiti and Iraq. By 2006, however, only El Salvador continued to ship soldiers to Iraq. Washington continued to press Latin American armies to do more domestic policing and establish control over what it called "ungoverned spaces", ranging from shantytowns to coastlines to rural areas where the civil state has a limited role. Root causes of statelessness are overlooked as the public security dimension is given priority, dangerously blurring the lines between military and police functions while weakening civil control.[8]

That is not the only line being blurred. Over the course of the past decade, economic suffering has led to peaceful organized social protests. Social movements are now warning that legitimate protest is being "criminalized" and dealt with as a security threat. "Terrorists, drug traffickers, hostage takers, and criminal gangs," Donald Rumsfeld told the 2004 meeting of the Defence Ministers of the Americas, "form an anti-social combination that increasingly seeks to destabilize civil societies." James Hill, the head of the Pentagon's Southern Command was more explicit: "Legal boundaries don't make sense anymore given the current threat."[9] The Pentagon pushed Latin American and Caribbean armed forces to become more involved in the various fronts of the war on terror, the occupation of Haiti, containing the Colombian guerrillas, playing a greater role in disaster relief, integrating military commands in Central America, and making bases and forward operation facilities available to US forces.

In response to Rumsfeld, the Chilean defence minister reminded the defence ministers' meeting in Quito in 2004 that the United Nations was the "only forum with international legitimacy to act globally on security issues". The Argentine minister said that he and his colleagues could take care of their own borders and that "terrorism is a concern but not a top priority". A former head of Ecuador's armed forces, General René Vargas, claimed Rumsfeld's proposal was an attempt to "consolidate control" over his country's oil and water: "In Latin America there are no terrorists, only hunger and unemployment and delinquents who turn to crime. What are we going to do, hit you with a banana?"[10] At the October 2006 defence ministers' meeting in Managua, the US again insisted on lining up the hemisphere's armies in the GWOT, not only in the region but elsewhere. According to an October 2 report by Reuters, "The United States is pressing some Latin American countries to send troops to Afghanistan and Iraq not so much for combat purposes but for the war-to-reconstruction transition envisioned by the Pentagon."[11]

Canadian journalist Naomi Klein argues correctly "that the real war on terror is being waged by Latin America's social movements — Brazil's landless rural activists, Argentina's unemployed, Ecuadorian indigenous confederations, Bolivian coca leaf growers, and many others — are actually waging the real war on terrorism — not with law and order but by providing alternatives to the fundamentalist tendencies that exist wherever there is true desperation."[12]

Weak government has been endemic to much of Latin America, assuming indeed that lapses into authoritarianism are indicators of neither "fragility" nor strength. The reasons are many, including institutional crisis, narrow governing elite interests, and of course largely non-violent popular uprisings that have forced the removal of government leaders and, increasingly, of political systems. Ecuador, Bolivia, and Venezuela spring to mind, although each has its own characteristics.

Strange as it sounds, Washington now has a problem with the absence of sovereignty in parts of the region. Pentagon doctrine calls for helping fragile states achieve "effective sovereignty" in territories that supposedly are, or could be, operating grounds for terrorist organizations. While the extension of effective political and civic sovereignty to remote regions would be welcome in terms of enhancing access to public services, what the Pentagon has in mind is something different, demanding that the local militaries take up that occupation, guided by security considerations. As a result, the military and security apparatus acquire an enhanced political influence and leeway in their operations. This does not happen by chance: US policy, according to Adam Isaacson, "seeks to direct military aid to the lawless areas, and to erase the dividing lines between the roles of military and police forces in these areas, giving the military a new role in the domestic politics of the region's countries."[13]

Is insecurity primarily the product of poverty, unemployment, and institutional weakness, meriting a political and state overhaul? Or is it the other way around, as is claimed by the United States, requiring big increases in the security forces? What each course entails is illustrated by the cases Colombia and Ecuador.

Addressing State Fragility in Latin America: Counterinsurgency in Colombia

With one of the world's highest rates of economic inequality, Colombia is also the largest recipient of US aid outside the Middle East and Afghanistan. It receives one-third of all US assistance to Latin America, and 80 per cent of that "assistance" is military.[14] Anti-terrorism means counterinsurgency, and the main emphasis of US support is precisely on the military, with economic and social assistance lagging considerably behind.

Washington's simplistic anti-terrorism policy reduces the possibility of finding a political solution to the three-decade-old violent conflict between the government and the armed extreme left. A conflict that is further complicated by the activities of paramilitary right-wing groups, drug traffickers and criminal groups.

Following his election in May 2002, President Álvaro Uribe unleashed a massive heavy-handed assault on the guerrillas and the drug trade. He pushed for constitutional changes to allow him to run for a second term, winning a strong mandate in May 2006. By the end of the year, however, there came embarrassing revelations of paramilitaries connected to his own party, government, and even cabinet members. The US-backed strategy generated a new state crisis as manifested in the degree to which drug cartels and paramilitaries had "infiltrated" the government, making Colombia, said critics, a narco-state or "para-state". As of April 2007, eight pro-Uribe congressmen, a governor, and the president's former top intelligence chief had been arrested. Nearly 20 other current or former members of Congress, most of them allies of the president, were being investigated by the Supreme Court and the attorney-general's office. That some branches of government took on the investigations only underscores the extent of governmental incoherence.

Uribe claims he is fighting all of Colombia's illegal armed groups, denying links to paramilitaries, including those responsible for imposing a reign of terror in certain parts of the country. It is a fact, however, that tens of thousands of "paras" were the creation not only of drug-traffickers and landowners, but also of the army and some politicians, ostensibly to fight the guerrillas but also profiting from extortion and criminal activities. Uribe's critics claim he seeks a return to the legalized, centralized, authoritarian governance practices of the past, also known as the national security state.

While trends toward the recentralization of power also appear in Ecuador, Bolivia, and Venezuela, these are driven by another logic altogether and are the product of an electoral mandate free from the influence of the elite and the armed forces. Unsurprisingly, the US government supports state centralization in Colombia, but attacks it in Venezuela, Ecuador, and Bolivia. This probably has much to do with the fact that the Colombian government is eager to sign a Free Trade Agreement with the US, something rejected by its three neighbours who are also in the process of challenging foreign-owned oil and gas companies while Colombia puts out the welcome mat. According to William Drennan of Exxon Mobil, Colombia now offers "among the best fiscal terms in the world".[15]

State reconfiguration in Colombia seeks to place the government and its armed forces in a better position to battle the FARC (Fuerzas Armadas Revolucionarias de Colombia / Revolutionary Armed Forces of Colombia), even at the expense of an already deteriorated human rights situation. Uribe and the military leaders are making the most of the GWOT to secure material resources and political legitimacy for the counterinsurgency plan and to maintain the traditional elite in power. Notwithstanding inherent limitations of a strategy based on external support, President Uribe has echoed US rhetoric, aligning his national and foreign policies with the US, to the detriment of relations with some of Columbia's neighbours.

A new US-Colombian drive known as *Plan Patriota* is intended to redress state "fragility" by providing massive military assistance to the Colombian government to fight the guerrillas, and to a lesser degree the drug cartels and criminals. However, that framework is facilitated by the absence of civil and political control over the security bodies — something that should, in fact, be an indicator of a failing state. There is moreover a danger that a new US-protected security-first regime in Colombia will become aggressive toward Ecuador and Venezuela.

Addressing State Fragility in Latin America: Reinventing the State in Ecuador

In Latin America there are two sources of state power: one stems from US economic and military favours, while the second emerges from a mobilized electorate demanding greater self-respect and social sensitivity from elected officials. Serving either master is difficult enough and can generate fragility; trying to serve both is a recipe for failure.

In Ecuador, as in Bolivia, the elections were clean and the platforms clear as to the intention to push radical state and socio-economic transformation. There are numerous ambiguities and tensions in such a process, beginning with the fact that the traditional ruling elites, and the United States, do not take kindly to the process and throw obstacles in its path. Governments also face the temptation to deal with opponents (and their press organs) in a high-handed manner. Nonetheless, defenders of the state-transformation process believe that a new concentration of power may be necessary in order to effect constitutional change that will institutionalize state and societal overhaul, legalizing new forms of popular participation in decision-making and government.

Mandates and majorities are built, to no small degree, on the basis of failed US and donor policies, from the social cost of Washington Consensus programs to the presence of the US military. In Ecuador this included a general dislike for the presence of foreign oil companies and the US Forward Operation Location (FOL) base in Manta, as well as memories of the ten thousand peasants who, in September 2001, filed a lawsuit against DynCorp for indiscriminate fumigation with untested chemicals, which ruined their food harvest, poisoned adults, and killed children and livestock.[16] The goal is to throw out the policies and mentalities that sustained injustice in Ecuador, kept it from diminishing its poverty rate, kept it from asserting greater governmental control over its resources and territory, and forced it to tolerate a foreign military presence. In and of themselves these are not necessarily anti-US steps; European, Canadian, and even Brazilian resource extraction corporations are also being questioned. But in the larger hemispheric context, there is no question that the US is the principal country being affected by the recuperation of state authority over national resources, along with the country's self-respect.

In different ways and to different degrees, governments in Venezuela, Bolivia, and Ecuador are gearing the state to be more attuned to the aspirations of the majority of the people. Elected in November 2006, Ecuadorian President Rafael Correa is no wild-eyed demagogue but a serious politician; a US-educated economist and former minister of finance who ran on a platform of ending traditional politics characterized by subservience to foreign corporations, the IFIs, and the Pentagon. As with Morales in Bolivia and to a lesser extent Chávez in Venezuela, Correa embodies a social demand for the overhaul and further democratization of the entire state apparatus.

Three policy shifts underscore the determination of the Ecuadorian government to strengthen the role of the state in a democratic, legal, and accountable manner. And having sufficient political support and clout, there is no need to appeal to populism or political overkill.

The first is the announcement, upon taking office, that the government would not renew a 1999 bilateral agreement with the US that allowed for the presence of US military forces at the Manta air base on Ecuador's Southern coast. In a remarkable example of previous state fragility, the agreement had circumvented congressional approval, yet few officials challenged its legality. Humiliation grew after the US Navy took to detaining and even destroying local fishing vessels in the name of anti-drug trafficking and anti-terrorism. The new government brought a new security perspective: "There can be no sustained security policy if there is not full sovereignty at all levels. The public position of the government is not to renew the Manta base agreement," said the defence minister on March 5, 2007.[17]

Broad consensus in favour of closure had existed for years, to a large degree shared by the military and state authorities inasmuch as the Manta base hosted US operations against the Colombian guerrillas and, ostensibly, against the illegal drug traffic. US support for the military and police became conditional on the maintenance of base rights and this too caused resentment. US officials insist that Ecuador's best interests are met through the continuation of the anti-drug effort. Correa's government, in contrast, perceives that national security is at risk by the possibility of becoming involved in the Colombian war.

Second, the new government is making good on its pledge to define a people-oriented development model in open contravention of the IMF neo-liberal parameters. Between 1960 and 2000, Ecuador received 16 standby loans from the IMF and had suffered considerably, including the decision to abandon its own currency in favour of the US dollar. Beginning in 2002, loan conditions included the forced reduction of teacher salaries and big increases in fuel and electricity prices. On January 22 of that year protestors from the indigenous communities occupied the Congress as thousands stood vigil and demonstrated outside. When President Jami Mahaud ordered 35,000 troops and police to confront the demonstrators, the leaders of the armed forces and the congressional opposition forced the resignation of the president in favour of vice-president Gustavo Noboa.

Bowing to US and banker pressure, Noboa decided he would "stay the course" with IMF reforms. In May teachers again went on strike to protest salary reductions and the government sent in the riot police. Defiant organizations then called a general strike and government employees, doctors, oil workers, and unions joined in. Two more confrontations followed. The army was summoned but the dispatched unit, under Colonel Lucío Gutiérrez, took sides with the indigenous protesters and attempted an unsuccessful coup. Gutiérrez became a hero and, in November 2002, was elected President. However, by February 2004 the indigenous confederation was back on the streets demonstrating against the "traitor" Gutiérrez who by then was embracing the IMF and the US. On April 20, 2005, it was Gutierrez's turn to flee the protests and go into exile. "Whatever respite it now enjoys, Ecuador's democracy is deeply discredited," said the *Economist* following the April 2005 "street coup".[18]

Rafael Correa won the election in November 2006. His inaugural speech called for an opening to the "new twenty-first century socialism," earlier proclaimed by Hugo Chávez. He declared the need to end "the perverse system that has destroyed our democracy, our economy, and our society". Having refused to field parliamentary candidates, Correa pushed through with his promise to reinvent the state, then still dominated by what he and his followers regarded as a corrupt pro-US and pro-free trade political and economic oligarchy.

Correa's election and his state "reinvention" program is rooted in a militant mass movement that has long demanded an end to the political oligarchy and economic inequality. Referred to as the "*partidocracia,*" the Ecuadorian political system has been run by splintering political parties dominated by a small corrupt elite that controls much of Congress, the Supreme Court, as well as the presidency, until Correa's election. Even Michel Camdessus, the former IMF chief, once commented that Ecuador was characterized "by an incestuous relation between bankers, political-financial pressure groups, and corrupt government officials."[19] The goal is to end the dysfunctional state, reinvent not only the state but the country as a plurinational participatory democracy, reasserting Ecuadorian sovereignty and mandating the state to advance social and economic policies that benefit the majorities, regardless of what the old elite and the IMF would say.

In stark contrast to the conservative IMF-dictated fiscal policy of his predecessors, Correa ordered more government spending on social programs instead of repaying parts of the foreign debt he denounced as illegitimate. Until then some 90 per cent of all oil revenue (the chief source of revenue) was assigned to debt repayment. He also made good on the campaign promise to end negotiations with the United States for a Free Trade Agreement. Elected authorities and the social movements believe that an FTA, however beneficial for big capital and exporters, would prove disastrous for the small producer. Ecuador and Bolivia instead have asked the US to maintain the preferential trade agreement tied to the anti-drug trafficking concerns.

As with Bolivia, Ecuador is fortunate to have the support of Venezuela, which in no small degree is deflecting US attention away from the rest of the "pink tide". A new regional network may be able to provide markets and capital, through a Bank of the South, which, in some degree, would make the country less dependent on the usual providers.[20] Joining the regional trend toward increased state control over natural resources, Correa ratified the previous government's cancellation of a contract with the US oil giant Occidental and announced that the Manta base agreement would not be renewed. Trade unions and the indigenous movement claimed their year-long mobilization had yielded victory.

The third innovation is the decision to call a referendum on the election of a Constituent Assembly to write a new Constitution. Ecuador's "institutions have collapsed," he said, "after overcoming neo-liberal dogma" a new constitution was needed to "prepare the country for the 21ˢᵗ century…. To overcome the political and social impasse in which the country is bogged down." When a group of legislators attempted to block the referendum, a broad civil society coalition joined together to back Correa and to prepare for the constitutional discussions around the creation of new political, legal, and economic structures in Ecuador. Social movement leaders are insisting that the upholding of sovereignty, the nationalization of natural resources, the defence of biodiversity, and promoting agrarian revolution all become part of the new Constitution. Correa for his part said he would consider resigning if the initiative was rejected by the voters.

On April 15, 2007, the referendum approved the proposal by a landslide victory with 78.1 per cent of voters in favour. The Constituent Assembly will be installed in mid-November following the election of its 130 members. That same week Correa announced the country had paid off its entire debt to the IMF and would henceforth sever ties with the financial institution: "We don't want to hear anything more from that international bureaucracy."[21] The World Bank representative was told to pack his bags and leave.

Reclaiming National Sovereignty and Public Sector Responsibility

If it drew on the positive changes in Latin America, the state failure/fragility debate could acquire greater legitimacy than it now enjoys. State strengthening could be addressed in terms of mass mobilization, new forms of democratic participation, and sovereign re-nationalization of basic resources and public services.

But globalization in its economic and military components — with its own version of state failure and state weakness — continues to manifest in practice (and often in theory) a deep-seated aversion to both democracy and sovereignty. Debt conditions have allowed the US, the IFIs, corporations, and "donors" to liberalize economic activity to the point of losing control over foreign investors who are usually in complicity with local elites. To which we now add the security demands posed by the GWOT, but also the war on drugs and against the Colombian insurgents. Small wonder that states become fragile and even collapse in the face of such pressures, or simply step up repressive tendencies in order to survive.

Although unlikely, local militaries could take over in light of state breakdowns. Before that happens, however, some international preventive action would be contemplated. Where mass human rights violations are the case, should some external liberal intervention be mounted? The trouble with this argument, aside from the implicit double standard (Venezuela yes, Israel no) is that it might still prove counterproductive. Susan Woodward points out: "If outsiders do take political positions, as occurs in the labelling of their favoured politicians and parties as 'moderates,' 'reformers,' and pro-Westerners [or fragile states], this tends actually to worsen the asymmetry by substituting local legitimacy with international legitimacy and making them an easy target of nationalism or frustration with international demands at home."[22]

In short, notions of state failure and state fragility are of little analytical and political utility, if not understood in terms of what a majority of a country's citizens expects of its government. Labelling is risky, particularly where, as argued, radically different expectations of the state confront each other. New majorities in Bolivia, Ecuador, and Venezuela gave elected leaders a mandate for state restructuring — yet the democratic mandate and its implementation is cause for alarm in imperialist quarters, still very much linked to the old regimes and the protection of their "minority" rights. But the GWOT cannot demand that democratic expectations be placed on hold, lest they provoke the US or be subsumed under the terrorist label. States can and must undergo profound change, sometimes, by definition, upsetting the old institutionalism and international relationships. Democracies must either deepen or decay.

Take for example the obligation of the state to ensure minimal public services to its citizens. In many places, people and governments come to the conclusion that the free market and the private sector have not guaranteed quality and accessible services — the state of public infrastructure in Latin America, as in Africa, so testifies. Public Services International defines public services as "those which are universally provided to the public and available equally to all; they affect life, safety and the public welfare and are vital to commercial and economic development; they involve regulatory or policy-making functions; the service is incompatible with the profit motive or cannot be effectively or efficiently delivered through market mechanisms ... and to promote quality public services as essential in building fair and inclusive societies, where all people have equal access and opportunity."[23] A violation of "economic freedom" and "common sense economics"?

Failure to secure the adequate provision of minimal resources should be considered a form of state failure, rather than an invitation for foreign corporations to step in, deregulate, and privatize left and right. The goal is to take back the public commons and, where warranted, revert privatizations that are inimical to the public interest.

The New Imperialism and Sub-sovereignty

One government in particular is disproportionately responsible for the sorry state of global affairs: the United States, invoking a war against terror, has embarked on a new cycle of global warfare and expansion. Such is the central reality of contemporary international politics. Michael Ignatieff, formerly of the Kennedy School of Government at Harvard University, summed it up: "This new imperialism... is humanitarian in theory but imperial in practice; it creates 'sub-sovereignty,' in which states possess independence in theory but not in fact. The reasons the Americans are in Afghanistan, or the Balkans, after all is to maintain imperial order in zones essential to the interest of the United States. They are there to maintain order against a barbarian threat."[24]

But the barbarian threat hiding within fragile states is yet another ideological construct. Does refusal to follow the free market model and cater to US security demands constitute barbarism and merit sub-sovereignty? Is a nation refusing to follow that model a threat to Western civilization and doomed to "failure" — and therefore subject to regime change? Such is the logic of the War on Terror but also of the expansion of capitalist colonialism bent on securing more markets, more access to cheap labour, more raw materials, and more investment markets. Must states, economies, and even societies be structured so as to better take their global place in the era of US supremacy?

In the final analysis, the question is whether states and electorates in the South and elsewhere will be denied the right to determine the future of their own countries and be trusted to exercise that right in a responsible and legitimate manner, nationally and internationally. As long as there is no respect for this right, then trauma and disorder will continue affecting not only a few states but the entire international system. And it is the system — imperialism — which must give way, not democracy.

State-building prescriptions are not a matter of taste, judgment, or of adopting the latest business model requiring World Bank-driven re-engineering. The issue is much deeper, societal, and global. Where is the "international community's" concern for state failure and legal indecency in the United States? How can one change behaviour that is not the result of a temporary lapse of rational thinking, or a cognitive wrong turn in the road, or even an "understandable response" to the blow of 9/11? If we are going to engage in a discussion of failed states, we should not limit it to the South.

Many US citizens are the first to demand that US "allies" not reinforce Washington's self-conception as a state economy that easily corrects itself and eventually will. The idea that the world can talk the US out of its behavioural disorder is not satisfactory. It disrespects human beings in nations suffering the daily cruelty of intervention. There are factors at work that go beyond elections. Corporations and bankers cannot abandon the bottom line and will not promote justice by force of will or reason any more than a leopard can change its spots. One can always hope that there is a small, still rational part of the brain of the social polity that will recognize there is a state, or community of states, suffering from serious control issues, and that the current obsession with consumption and security are but its symptoms and not its cause. Force-feeding is not an option, but neither is the continued appeal to good intentions while maintaining a shocking disregard for the human beings concerned.

States, Sovereignty, and Democracy

Although a necessary step, a diagnosis is not the same as treatment. But good science depends on focusing the research in the right direction and in collecting the pertinent data. If liberated from its captors in the Security Council, the UN can still play a healthy role in a nation's reconstruction and development, particularly if it can help deliver what is most needed — resources and not rationalizations.

A check needs to be placed on patronizing explanations of state disorder that feature societal dysfunction or plain native ignorance as causes. Also unwelcome are political therapists from the North promising to expunge the traumas, inner needs, and attachment disorders of the South. States are told they are too lean in security terms and must be force-fed, or too fat in social spending and require being starved for a while. To see through this deception one must remember that it is not simply a matter of countries needing to be "fixed" or people being occasionally "consulted" or "included," but that people are at the centre of the entire equation — it is *their* nation and *their* people. Countries in the South should not be testing grounds for other people's ideologies or research hypotheses.

By the same token, societies in the South cannot simply heap all blame on external factors. Although an often convenient hook on which to hang the misery of day-to-day life, blaming the outsider is no substitute for confronting the internal factors that generate a dysfunctional state in human security terms. When rich nations are failing in so many respects as functional democratic states, there is a danger that illegitimate and illicit security-first clandestine coping methods will be exported to the rest of the world, North and South.

From a Latin American perspective, US behavioural flaws were not substantially greater in the days after 9/11 than they were the day or decades before. Countries in trouble have the right to get support, long before they need hospitalization, but the choices should not be between being treated like children or dealt with as rogue elements, infantilized and criminalized in equal and patronizing measure. "Surgeons" from abroad must also be held accountable, principally to the "patients" enduring their intervention. State-building support is for the purpose of protecting the state *for* and not *from* the people.

Are there "lessons" Latin America can offer policy makers? Two issues should be acknowledged from the outset. First, many of us in this region have trouble, and will continue to have trouble, distinguishing between the United States and the rest of the "donor" community (Europe, Canada, and Japan). The overwhelming historical, political, and commercial weight of that country in our region is the principal reason. One might detect different tactics, but there is a common bottom line around what constitutes "good governance" and a belief in the superiority of the capitalist, investor-privileging model of economic growth.

Second a Latin American visualization of what constitutes a failed state is considerably different from the pictures emerging from Central Asia, the Middle East, or Sub-Saharan Africa. There may be disagreements as to definitions, but these should not blind Latin Americans to the need to contribute more intelligent and pragmatic responses to failure where it affects human beings, whatever the causes. Nor can our region be insensitive to real or credibly impending human rights disasters, including the use of a state's territory for proven (as opposed to suspected) terrorist operations.

A formidable Latin American contribution could be to demand clearer answers to questions about the criteria of intervention, who judges and how, and who responds and how. Based on our region's considerable history of endured interventions, we would highlight the importance of legal (UN yes, NATO or OAS no) collective decision-making mechanisms and collective responses characterized by a strong preferential option for political means with regional involvement.

So, for example, the fact that none of Sudan's neighbouring governments favours Northern military "humanitarian" responses makes it difficult for non-African states in the South to support intervention unauthorized not simply by the African Union but by the UNSC. The arrogant and illegal military overthrow and removal of the Aristide government has not been forgotten. Unlike their governments, key social movements and churches in Latin America support the demand of their Haitian counterparts in denouncing the UN occupation of that country. After all, non-intervention as an international legal norm was born in Latin America — coming up with a list of exceptions will be hard, particularly when someone powerful seems restive.

It should go without saying, that NATO war planes or soldiers killing innocent civilians, as in Afghanistan, thoroughly discredits concurrent state-building initiatives. It is shocking that some believe they can do development as usual in an occupied country. What much of the population in Afghanistan, along with many in the South, witnesses is merely the civilian wing of an ongoing military counterinsurgency effort. Under these circumstances, Washington's partners should not ask for the benefit of the doubt, particularly if the UN Security Council is bypassed.

Alternatives to intervention or alternatives to US modalities of intervention? Many in the North will lean toward the latter — and refraining from following the Pentagon is always commendable. But people's movements and many Southern governments will focus on the first question, inviting their Northern associates, within and outside the US, to do so also. Policy and political discussions may need to be differentiated, and colleagues in the South should at least be sympathetic to the complexities faced by Northern counterparts forced to deal with both worlds and deal with their own government's multi-faceted intervention. All intervention areas need to be scrutinized, but the growing fragile state industry is by and large operating within "safe" parameters. Other colleagues believe that genuine peacebuilding requires a clear denunciation of military intervention and rejection of the current script whereby US military steps in, gets bogged-down, and then dumps the problem in the laps of its allies or the UN, while, of course, retaining strategic and operational control.

Externally-driven state-building exercises capable of generating inclusive and participatory governance? External military interventions that incorporate genuine peacebuilding (as opposed to pacification and stabilization) and gender awareness? Democracy in an occupied country? Perhaps easier to fit a square peg into a round hole.

Finally, beyond the contextual issues, and in order to better analyze them, it is important to review the roles of ideology and paradigm. One can give credit to the challenge, within and outside the US, to Washington's increasingly discredited position and pretension to act unilaterally whenever or wherever it decides. But there is a larger proposition. Does unfettered capitalism and corporate-friendly "good governance" produce freedom, democracy, and state stability? By definition perhaps, policy-making circles will not easily recognize the constraint, let alone tackle it. Those outside the bureaucracies may simply take a pass on this question. But that is an unaffordable luxury for many in the South because, as events in Ecuador, Bolivia, and Venezuela are showing, the failure of the capitalist neo-liberal state to deliver basic necessities can be taken as a failure not simply of the state, but of democracy itself.

Linking neo-liberal capitalism to democracy is a precondition for either the deepening or the discarding of democracy altogether. In the short run, however, the capitalism/democracy confusion, often openly propagated by Northern democracy assistance programs and our own Southern elites, creates a contradiction in people's minds that can have disastrous consequences for democracy (and security). If the failed/fragile states discussion chooses not to deal with the dichotomy then it will follow the course of the international mainstream debate on governance and development, becoming reduced to simplistic, undemocratic, and insensitive propositions of what kind of government and policies are needed to fit into the global market.

The same can be said about a "hard power" response to bringing about "democratic states" but which fuel a backlash against democracy (and democracy promotion work). Although the terminology is not helpful, failed/failing states demand a different international response: one that strengthens the principles and values of democracy and helps make the state newly relevant to people; democracy you can feel; a state that belongs to you. Responses to failed states that continue to exclude those previously excluded from decision-making will get us nowhere. The real question will then be how to promote sovereign, participatory, self-determined, democratic processes in the face of globalization's military and economic onslaught.

ALEJANDRO BENDAÑA is Director of the Center for International Studies, Managua, Nicaragua. During the 1980s, he served as Nicaragua's Ambassador to the UN. He has a Ph.D. in history from Harvard University. He is the author of various publications on international relations, peacebuilding, development and history. He has worked as an consultant on demobilization and reintegration issues in Central America, Mozambique, Sri Lanka, Somalia and Indonesia.

References

Articles and Newspapers

Bendaña, Alejandro. "From Peace-Building to State-Building: One Step Forward and Two Backwards?" Presentation "Nation-Building, State-Building and International Intervention: Between 'Liberation' and Symptom Relief, CERI, Paris, October 15, 2004 and Centro de Estudios Internacionales, Managua, 2006.

Birns, Larry. Hemispheric Echoes: The Reverberations of Latin American Populism June 22, 2007, *Harvard International Review*, http://hir.harvard.edu/articles/1592/.

Duffield, Mark. "Globalization and War Economies: Promoting Order or the Return of History?" *Fletcher Forum of World Affairs*, Vol. 23, No. 2, 1999.

Frechette, Myles. Rethinking Latin America, A New Approach in US Foreign Policy Academy and Policy, *Vol. 28 (2) — Summer 2006* http://hir.harvard.edu/articles/1547/.

Ignatieff, Michael. "The Challenges of American Imperial Power," *Naval War College Review*.

Isaacson, Adam. "United States Security Cooperation Policy in Latin America," *The Reality of Aid 2006*.

Klein, Naomi. "The Daily War," *Guardian*, March 17, 2003.

Levitsky, Steven. "Not the Populism of Yesteryear, An interview with Professor Steven," June 22, 2007, *Harvard International Review*, http://hir.harvard.edu/articles/1591/.

Moore, David. Leveling the Playing Fields & Embedded Illusions: 'Post Conflict' Discourse & Neoliberal 'Development' in War-torn Africa. *Review of African Political Economy*, March 2000, Vol. 27, No. 93.

Whittington, Less. "PM sees payoff in adding Americas to foreign agenda," *Toronto Star*, June 22, 2007.

Woodward, Susan. "Institutionally Fragile States, Prevention and Post Conflict: Recommendations," FRIDE (Madrid), *Failing States or Failed States? The Role of Development Models*, Working Paper 19 (February 2006).

Publications

Bendaña, Alejandro. *Constructing Alternatives* (Managua: Centro de Estudios Internacionales , 2006).

Bricmont, Jean. *Using Human Rights to Sell War* (New York: Monthly Review Press, 2006).

Centro de Estudios Internacionales, E*xpansionismo Económico y Militar de Estados Unidos en América Latina y el Caribe* (Managua: Centro de Estudios Internacionales, 2007).

Grandin, Greg. *Empire's Workshop, Latin America, the United States and the Rise of the New Imperialism* (New York: Henry Holt, 2007).

Easterly, William. *The White Man's Burden, Why the West's efforts to aid the rest have done so much ill and so little good* (Penguin Press: New York, 2006).

Foster, John Bellamy. *Naked Imperialism* (New York: Monthly Review Press, 2006)

Katz, Mauricio. "Security, Cooperation for Development and Conflict: Elements for Analysis of the Colombian Case, *The Reality of Aid 2006: Focus on Conflict, Security and Development Cooperation* (Manila: Ibon Books, 2006).

Koonings, Kees & Dirk Krujit (eds.,) *Armed Actors: Organized Violence and State Failure in Latin America* (London: Zed Press, 2005).

Reality of Aid, The. *The Reality of Aid 2006: Focus on Conflict, Security and Development Cooperation* (Manila: Ibon Books, 2006).

Rotberg, Richard. *When States Fail: Causes and Consequences of State Failure* (Princeton, NJ: Princeton University Press, 2002).

Vanaik, Achin. (ed.) *Selling US Wars* (New York: Interlink, 2007).

World Bank Group, The Independent Evaluation Group, *Engaging with Fragile States* (Washington, 2005).

Fernández Terán, Fernando. *FMI, Banco Mundial y Estado Colonial: Poder supranacional en Bolivia* (La Paz: May 2003)

Web Articles

Aguirre, Mariano. Failed states or weak democracies? The state in Latin America *OpenDemocracy.net, 17 January 2006, Transnational Institute*, http://www.tni.org/detail_page.phtml?act_id=420&username=guest@tni.org&password=9999&publish=Y.

Baranyi, Stephen. "Fragile States and Sustainable Peacebuilding," *NSI Policy Brief*, http://www.nsi-ins.ca/english/pdf/fragile_states.pdf.

Bendaña, Alejandro. "Lecciones aprendidas de donantes en situaciones de posconflicto: instrumentos, políticas, estrategias y mecanismos a emplear," *Informe de Conferencia*, 24 de octubre, 2006. (FRIDE, Madrid), http://www.fride.org/File/ViewLinkFile.aspx?FileId=1203.

"Blurring the lines," Washington Office on Latin America, http://www.wola.org/index.php?option=com_content&task=view&id=64&Itemid=2.

Burbach, Roger. "Ecuador's Nascent Leftist Government Victorious in Confrontation with the Right," *ZNET*, March 25, 2007, http://www.zmag.org/content/showarticle.cfm?ItemID=12412.

Council on Hemispheric Affairs, "Morales Does the Unthinkable — He Carries out his Campaign Pledge," Press Release, May 4, 2006, http://www.coha.org/2006/05/04/morales-does-the-unthinkable-%e2%80%93-he-carries-out-his-campaign-pledge/.

Council on Hemispheric Affairs, Ecuador Finds the Courage to "Just Say No," January 16th, 2007, http://www.coha.org/2007/01/16/ecuador-finds-the-courage-to-%e2%80%9cjust-say-no%e2%80%9d/.

Council on Hemispheric Affairs, "COHA to Ecuador's Rafael Correa: Tread carefully so your detractors don't have an easy target," Press release, May 29, 2007, http://www.coha.org/2007/05/29/coha-to-ecuador%e2%80%99s-rafael-correa-tread-carefully-so-your-detractors-do-not-have-an-easy-target/.

Edwards, Sandra. "The US FOL in Manta: The Ecuadorian Perspective," Washington Office on Latin America, March 30, 2007. www.wola.org.

OECD/DAC, Principles for Good International Engagement in Fragile States & Situations (Paris: 2007), www.oecd.org/fragilestates.

Public Services International, *Focus on the public services*, Vol. 8 No. 4, 2001, http://www.world-psi.org/TemplateEn.cfm?Section=English.

Kyriakou, Niko. "Chavez's Market Vision," http://www.tompaine.com/articles/2006/12/14/chavezs_market_vision.php.

"How to boost the coca crop," *The Economist*, May 22, 2007, https://www.economist.com/displayStory.cfm?story_id=8888847.

"Oil in Colombia," *The Economist*, February 1, 2007. https://www.economist.com/displayStory.cfm?story_id=8633187.

"A coup by Congress and the street," *The Economist*, April 26, 2005, https://www.economist.com/agenda/displaystory.cfm?story_id=E1_PRJPSPT

Endnotes

1 A variation on the theme is Canada's announced "re-engagement" with Latin America in the form of diplomatic support for countries that are outside the Venezuelan sphere of influence: "There are questions about whether Harper is mainly trying to help Bush, whose last visit to Latin America sparked widespread protests, and lend encouragement to free-market governments in the face of Venezuelan President Hugo Chavez's push for a new leftist, anti-capitalist consensus in the region." Whittington, Less. "PM sees payoff in adding Americas to foreign agenda," *Toronto Star*, June 22, 2007, p. A14.

2 Mariano Aguirre, "Failed states or weak democracies? The State in Latin America," January 17, 2006, http://www.opendemocracy.net/democracy-protest/state_violence_3187.jsp, accessed June 2007; Kees Koonings & Dirk Kruijt's (eds.,) *Armed Actors: Organized Violence and State Failure in Latin America* (London: Zed Press, 2005).

3 World Bank Group, The Independent Evaluation Group, *Engaging with Fragile States* (Washington, 2005). http://www.worldbank.org/ieg/licus/download.html. Accessed June 2007.

4 The Reality of Aid, *The Reality of Aid 2006: Focus on Conflict, Security and Development Cooperation* (Manila: Ibon Books, 2006) p. 9. http://www.realityofaid.org/roa.php?id=34. Accessed June 2007.

5 Easterly, William. *The White Man's Burden, Why the West's efforts to aid the rest have done so much ill and so little good* (Penguin Press: New York, 2006), p. 218, drawing on state failure data in Richard Rotberg, *When States Fail: Causes and Consequences of State Failure* (Princeton, NJ: Princeton University Press, 2002).

6 Easterly, *The White Man's Burden*, pp. 216–217.

7 Quoted by Kyriakou, Niko. "Chavez's Market Vision," http://www.tompaine.com/articles/2006/12/14/chavezs_market_vision.php. Accessed June 2007.

8 "Blurring the lines," Washington Office on Latin America, http://www.wola.org/index.php?option=com_content&task=view&id=64&Itemid=2.

9 Grandin, Greg. *Empire's Workshop, Latin America, the United States and the Rise of the New Imperialism* (New York: Henry Holt, 2007), pp. 214–215.

10 *Ibid.*, p. 215.

11 Quoted in Centro de Estudios Internacionales, *Expansionismo Económico y Militar de Estados Unidos en América Latina y el Caribe* (Managua: Centro de Estudios Internacionales, 2007), p. 36.

12 Klein, Naomi. "The Daily War," *Guardian*, March 17, 2003.

13 Isaacson, Adam. "United States Security Cooperation Policy in Latin America," *The Reality of Aid*, p. 165.

14 "How to boost the coca crop," *The Economist*, May 22, 2007, https://www.economist.com/displayStory.cfm?story_id=8888847. Accessed June 2007.

15 "Oil in Colombia," *The Economist*, February 1, 2007, https://www.economist.com/displayStory.cfm?story_id=8633187. Accessed June 2007.

16 Grandin, *Empire's Workshop*, p. 221.

17 Cited in Edwards, Sandra. "The US FOL in Manta: The Ecuadorian Perspective," Washington Office on Latin America, March 30, 2007. www.wola.org.

18 "A coup by Congress and the street," *The Economist*, April 26, 2005, https://www.economist.com/agenda/displaystory.cfm?story_id=E1_PRJPSPT. Accessed June 2007.

19 Burbach, Roger. "Ecuador's Nascent Leftist Government Victorious in Confrontation with the Right," *ZNET*, March 25, 2007, http://www.zmag.org/content/showarticle.cfm?ItemID=12412.

20 Council on Hemispheric Affairs, "COHA to Ecuador's Rafael Correa: Tread carefully so your detractors don't have an easy target," Press release, May 29, 2007, www.coha.org/2007/05/09.

21 Associated Press, April 16, 2007.

22 Woodward, Susan. "Institutionally Fragile States, Prevention and Post Conflict: Recommendations," FRIDE (Madrid), *Failing States or Failed States? The Role of Development Models*, Working Paper 19 (February, 2006), p. 21.

23 Public Services International, *Focus on the public services*; Vol. 8 No. 4, 2001.

24 Ignatieff, Michael. "The Challenges of American Imperial Power," *Naval War College Review*, cited in John Bellamy Foster, *Naked Imperialism* (New York: Monthly Review Press, 2006), p. 12.

Statistical Annex 2008

Marcelo Saavedra-Vargas

Layout and design: **Marcelo Saavedra-Vargas**

Table of contents

Progress Toward the Millenium Development Goals

Canada's Relations with Developing Countries

Progress Toward the Millenium Development Goals

Table A: Sub-Saharan Africa (2006)

Goal 1: People living on less than $1 a day (%)

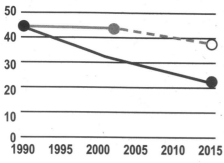

Goal 2: Primary completion rate total (%)

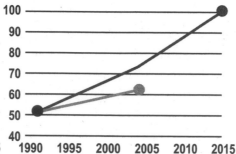

Goal 3: Ratio of girls to boys in primary and secondary education (%)

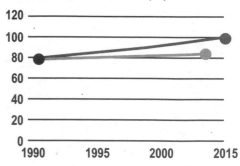

Goal 4: Under 5 mortality (deaths per 1,000)

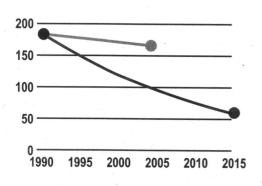

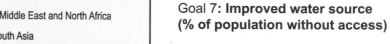

— progress needed to achieve the goal
— progress made
-- projected

● benchmark
● most recent
● goal
○ projected

EAP — East Asia and the Pacific
ECA - Eastern Europe and Central Asia
LAC — Latin America and the Caribbean
MNA — Middle East and North Africa
SA — South Asia
SSA — Sub-Saharan Africa

Goal 5: Maternal mortality ratio, (modeled estimate, per 100,000 births, 2000)

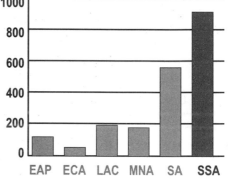

Goal 6: Prevalence of HIV, (% of population ages 15-49, 2003)

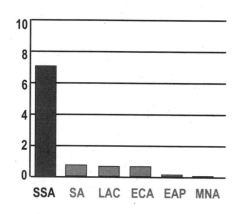

Goal 7: Improved water source (% of population without access)

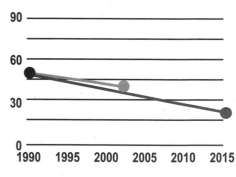

Source: **World Bank, World Development Indicators, 2006.** http://ddp-ext.worldbank.org/ext/GMIS/gdmis.do?siteId=2&menuId=LNAV01.

Table B: Latin America and the Caribbean (2006)

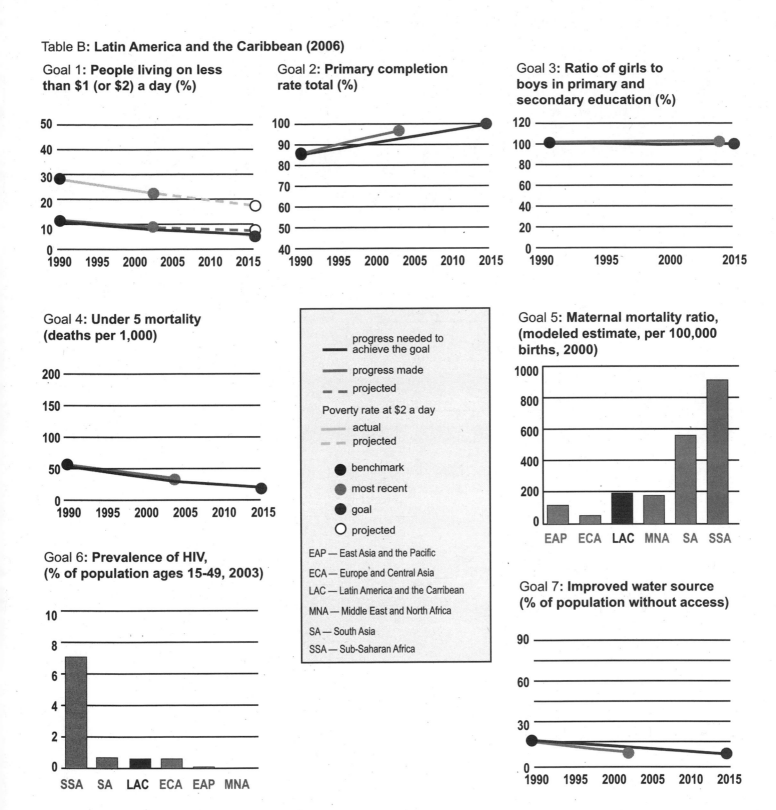

Goal 1: People living on less than $1 (or $2) a day (%)

Goal 2: Primary completion rate total (%)

Goal 3: Ratio of girls to boys in primary and secondary education (%)

Goal 4: Under 5 mortality (deaths per 1,000)

Goal 5: Maternal mortality ratio, (modeled estimate, per 100,000 births, 2000)

Goal 6: Prevalence of HIV, (% of population ages 15-49, 2003)

Goal 7: Improved water source (% of population without access)

Legend:
- progress needed to achieve the goal
- progress made
- projected

Poverty rate at $2 a day
- actual
- projected

- ● benchmark
- ● most recent
- ● goal
- ○ projected

EAP — East Asia and the Pacific
ECA — Europe and Central Asia
LAC — Latin America and the Carribean
MNA — Middle East and North Africa
SA — South Asia
SSA — Sub-Saharan Africa

Source: *World Bank, World Development Indicators, 2006.* http://ddp-ext.worldbank.org/ext/GMIS/gdmis.do?siteId=2&menuId=LNAV01.

Canada's Relations with Developing Countries

Chart 1.1: Net ODA as Percentage of GNI of the DAC Members (2005)

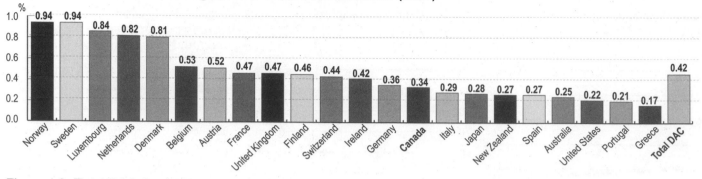

Norway 0.94 | Sweden 0.94 | Luxembourg 0.84 | Netherlands 0.82 | Denmark 0.81 | Belgium 0.53 | Austria 0.52 | France 0.47 | United Kingdom 0.47 | Finland 0.46 | Switzerland 0.44 | Ireland 0.42 | Germany 0.36 | **Canada 0.34** | Italy 0.29 | Japan 0.28 | New Zealand 0.27 | Spain 0.27 | Australia 0.25 | United States 0.22 | Portugal 0.21 | Greece 0.17 | **Total DAC 0.42**

Figure 1.2: Total DAC Countries

Gross Bilateral ODA, 2004-05 average, unless otherwise shown

Net ODA	2004	2005	Change 2004-05
Current (USD m)	79,410	106,777	34.5%
Constant (2004 USD m)	79,410	104,835	32.0%
Bilateral ODA/GNI	0.26%	0.33%	
Bilateral share of total ODA	68%	77%	

Top Ten Recipients of Gross ODA/OA

		(USD million)
1	Iraq	12,924
2	Nigeria	3,160
3	China	2,682
4	Afghanistan	1,946
5	Indonesia	1,867
6	India	1,785
7	Ghana	1,394
8	Egyp	1,319
9	Viet Nam	1,312
10	Sudan	1,163

By Region
(USD m)

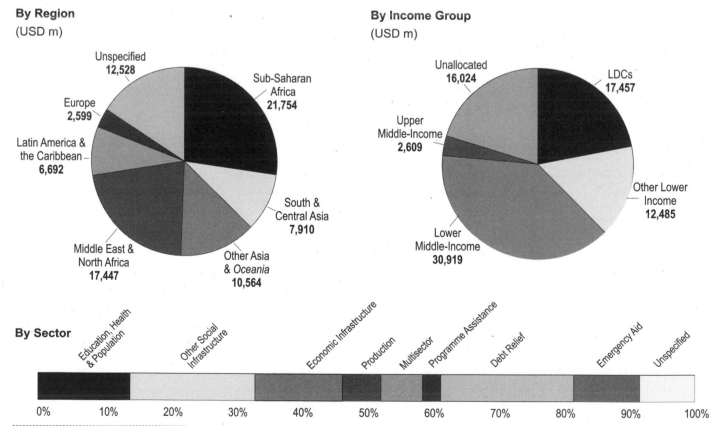

Unspecified 12,528 | Sub-Saharan Africa 21,754 | Europe 2,599 | Latin America & the Caribbean 6,692 | Middle East & North Africa 17,447 | Other Asia & *Oceania* 10,564 | South & Central Asia 7,910

By Income Group
(USD m)

Unallocated 16,024 | LDCs 17,457 | Upper Middle-Income 2,609 | Other Lower Income 12,485 | Lower Middle-Income 30,919

By Sector

Education, Health & Population | Other Social Infrastructure | Economic Infrastructure | Production | Multisector | Programme Assistance | Debt Relief | Emergency Aid | Unspecified

0% | 10% | 20% | 30% | 40% | 50% | 60% | 70% | 80% | 90% | 100%

Source: **OECD, Development Assistance Committee (DAC), The DAC Journal: Development Co-operation Report 2005.**

Table 1: **Canada and Other High Human Development Economies (2004 and 2005)**

Selected indicators of relations with developing countries

Table 1.1: **High Income OECD Countries**

Countries	UNDP Human Development Index 2004	UNDP Gender-Related Development Index 2004	GNI Per Capita (PPP$) 2005	Total Net ODA (US$ millions) 2005	% Change Over Previous Year (real terms) 2005	ODA/GNI Ratio (%) 2005	ODA/GNI Rank Among DAC Countries 2004-05	Multi-lateral Share as % of Net ODA 2005	Grant Share as % of Total ODA 2005	% Share of Net ODA to Low Income Countries 2005	% Share of Total Exports to Developing Countries 2005	% Share of Total Imports from Developing Countries 2005	Net Private Financial Flows to Developing Countries (long-term) (US$ millions) 2005
	1	2	3	4	5	6	7	8	9	10	11	12	13
Canada	0.950	0.947	32,220	3,756	31.2	0.34	14	24.6	100.0	63.3	7.2	24.3	9,178
Australia	0.957	0.956	30,610	1,680	6.7	0.25	19	13.8	100.0	65.7	52.8	46.2	2,780
Austria	0.944	0.937	33,140	1,573	127.1	0.52	7	21.7	100.0	33.5	26.4	21.5	2,192
Belgium	0.945	0.943	32,640	1,963	31.5	0.53	6	33.4	98.5	65.9	15.5	18.8	538
Denmark	0.943	0.940	33,570	2,109	1.9	0.81	5	35.6	98.7	74.5	16.7	20.9	33
Finland	0.947	0.943	31,170	902	29.9	0.46	10	33.8	99.1	52.4	37.6	31.3	723
France	0.942	0.940	30,540	10,026	16.8	0.47	8	27.8	85.4	63.5	25.5	23.6	7,107
Germany	0.932	0.928	29,210	10,082	32.9	0.36	13	26.1	80.2	53.2	28.0	33.0	11,352
Greece	0.921	0.917	23,620	384	15.9	0.17	22	46.3	100.0	31.2	44.9	38.6	325
Iceland	0.960	0.958	34,760	..	..	..	..	..	..	..	10.8	20.2	..
Ireland	0.956	0.951	34,720	719	15.7	0.42	12	32.9	100.0	80.0	10.1	13.9	..
Italy	0.940	0.934	28,840	5,091	101.4	0.29	15	55.4	88.8	57.3	29.5	36.1	44
Japan	0.949	0.942	31,410	13,147	51.7	0.28	16	20.8	48.8	41.4	58.7	68.0	12,197
Korea, Rep.	0.912	0.905	21,850	..	..	..	..	..	..	..	59.5	53.6	..
Luxembourg	0.945	0.949	65,340	256	5.4	0.84	3	27.1	100.0	69.9	9.0	20.4	..
Netherlands	0.947	0.945	32,480	5,115	19.8	0.82	4	28.0	100.0	67.0	16.0	37.8	17,565
New Zealand	0.936	0.932	23,030	274	18.5	0.27	17	18.2	100.0	57.0	35.3	36.3	26
Norway	0.965	0.962	40,420	2,786	13.5	0.94	1	27.0	72.7	69.5	8.9	23.2	..
Portugal	0.904	0.902	19,730	377	- 64.1	0.21	21	42.1	93.9	87.9	13.0	19.5	728
Spain	0.938	0.933	25,820	3,018	19.5	0.27	18	38.3	87.3	49.3	21.0	30.4	3,716
Sweden	0.951	0.949	31,420	3,362	24.1	0.94	2	32.9	99.8	68.6	21.0	20.1	159
Switzerland	0.947	0.944	37,080	1,767	13.7	0.44	11	20.8	98.0	61.8	23.0	13.7	6,098
United Kingdom	0.940	0.938	32,690	10,767	35.0	0.47	9	24.2	96.5	73.2	22.7	28.7	34,924
United States	0.948	0.946	41,950	27,622	36.5	0.22	20	8.5	100.0	38.7	46.8	55.3	68,952
Average or Total	0.942	0.939	33,616	106,777	32.0	0.42		23.1	93.1	54.3	26.7	30.6	178,643

Sources: *UNDP, Human Development Report 2006, Statistical Annex.*
The World Bank Group, WDI Online.
OECD, Development Assistance Committee (DAC), The DAC Journal: Development Co-operation Report 2005.
IMF, Direction of Trade Statistics Yearbook 2006.

Table 1 *(continues)* ▶

Chart 1.3: DAC Members' ODA: 1990-2005 and Simulations to 2010

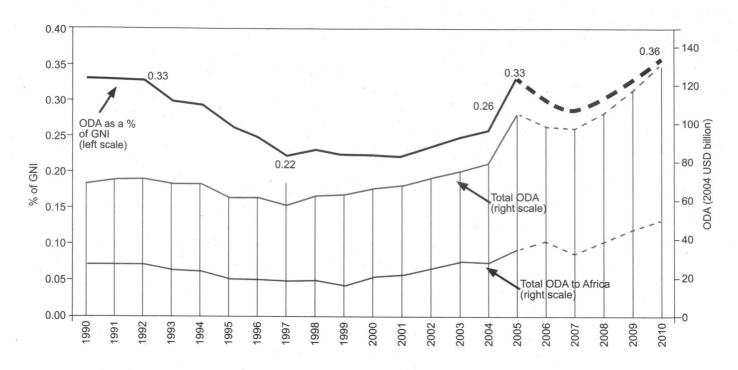

Source: *OECD, Statistical Annex of the 2006 Development Co-operation Report.* http://www.oecd.org/dataoecd/57/30/35320618.pdf

Map 1.1: UNDP Human Development Index by Region (2005)

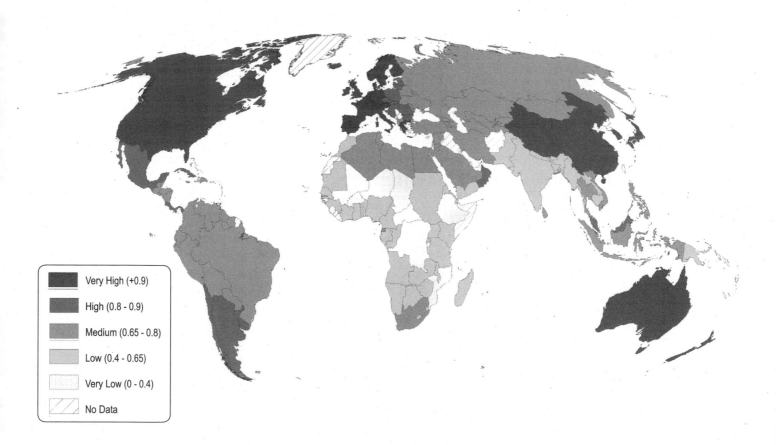

Legend:
- Very High (+0.9)
- High (0.8 - 0.9)
- Medium (0.65 - 0.8)
- Low (0.4 - 0.65)
- Very Low (0 - 0.4)
- No Data

Source: *OECD, Statistical Annex of the 2006 Development Co-operation Report.*

▶ Table 1 *(continued)*

Table 1.2: **Other High Income Countries (2004 and 2005)**

Countries	UNDP Human Development Index 2004	UNDP Gender-Related Development Index 2004	GNI Per Capita (PPP$) 2005	% Share of Total Exports to Developing Countries 2005	% Share of Total Imports from Developing Countries 2005
	1	2	3	4	5
Antigua and Barbuda	0.957	..	11,700	..	..
Bahamas	0.947	..	..	23.9	55.4
Bahrain	0.947	0.849	21,290	22.9	61.4
Barbados	0.945	..	..	62.0	38.5
Brunci	0.932	..	..	42.1	77.9
Cyprus	0.869	0.900	22,230	20.2	27.3
Hong Kong, China	0.809	..	34,670	61.6	74.0
Israel	..	0.925	25,280	27.2	25.2
Kuwait	0.790	0.864	24,010	57.1	38.6
Malta	0.767	0.869	18,960	32.4	16.2
Qatar	0.724	..	..	46.7	34.8
Singapore	0.692	..	29,780	67.4	63.3
Slovenia	0.683	0.908	22,160	37.1	26.6
United Arab Emirates	0.527	0.829	24,090	47.1	49.3
Average or Total	**0.815**	**0.886**	**23,490**	**42.1**	**45.3**

Sources: *UNDP, The 2006 Human Development Report.*
World Bank, World Development Indicators database 2006.
OECD, Development Database on Aid from DAC Members. (DAC online: http://www.oecd.org*).*
IMF, Direction of Trade Statistics Yearbook 2006.

Chart 2.1: **UNDP Human Development Index (2005)**

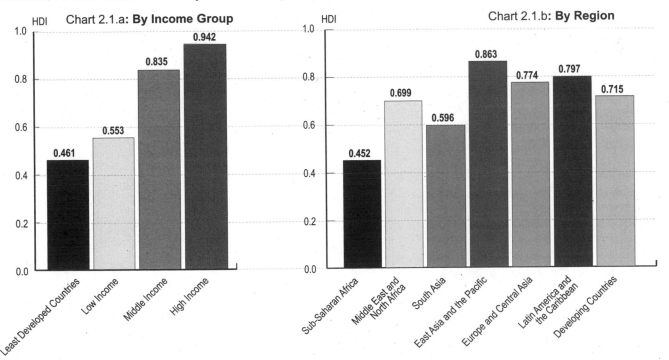

Chart 2.1.a: **By Income Group**

Chart 2.1.b: **By Region**

Source: *OECD, Statistical Annex of the 2006 Development Co-operation Report.* http://www.oecd.org/dataoecd/57/30/35320618.pdf.

Chart 2.2: **Social and Economic Indicators (2005)**

Chart 2.2.a: **GNI per Capita by Income Group**

Chart 2.2.b: **GNI per Capita by Region**

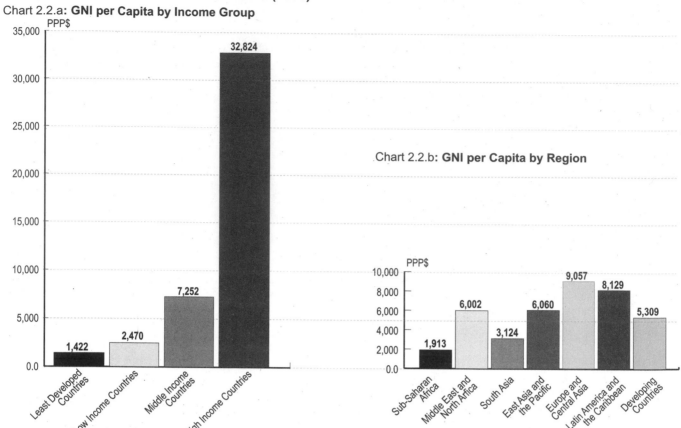

Chart 2.3: **Total Debt Service (TDS) and Aid as Percentage of GNI (2005)**

Chart 2.3.a: **TDS/GNI and Aid/GNI by Income Group**

Chart 2.3.b: **TDS/GNI and Aid/GNI by Region**

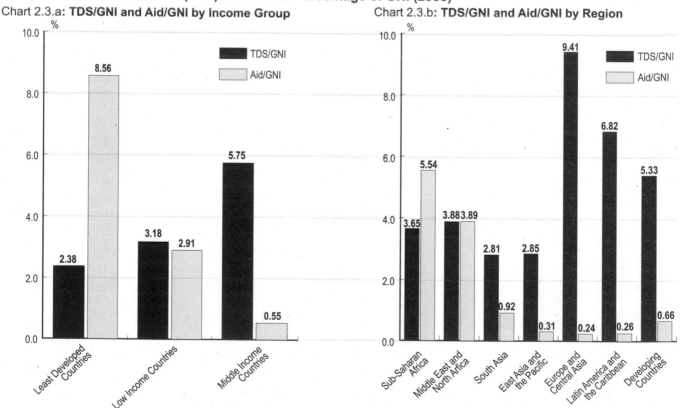

Source: *OECD, Statistical Annex of the 2006 Development Co-operation Report.* http://www.oecd.org/dataoecd/57/30/35320618.pdf.

Table 2: The Developing Countries: Selected Social and Economic Indicators (2004-05)

Regions and Countries	UNDP Human Development Index 2004	UNDP Gender-Related Development Index 2004	GNI Per Capita (PPP$) 2005	GDP (US$ millions) 2005	GDP Per Capita Growth (annual %) 2005	Population (millions) 2005	Adult Literacy Rate (%) 2006	Under-5 Years Mortality Rate (per 1,000 live births) 2005	External Debt/GNI (%) 2005	Present Value of Debt/GNI (%) 2005	Total Debt Service/GNI (%) 2005	Aid/GNI (%) 2005
	1	2	3	4	5	6	7	8	9	10	11	12
SUB-SAHARAN AFRICA												
Angola	0.439	0.431	2,040	32,811	17.2	15.9	67.4	260	74.0	59.0	7.8	1.5
Benin	0.428	0.412	1,130	4,287	0.7	8.4	34.7	150	56.0	22.7	1.6	8.2
Botswana	0.570	0.555	11,510	10,317	6.4	1.8	81.2	120	8.0	4.7	0.5	0.7
Burkina Faso	0.342	0.335	1,210	5,171	1.6	13.2	21.8	191	48.0	22.5	0.9	12.8
Burundi	0.384	0.380	680	800	-2.6	7.5	59.3	190	227.0	130.9	5.0	46.8
Cameroon	0.506	0.497	2,240	16,875	0.3	16.3	67.9	149	81.0	14.5	4.9	2.5
Cape Verde	0.722	0.714	5,610	983	3.4	0.5	..	35	67.0	43.4	3.5	16.9
Central African Republic	0.353	0.336	1,220	1,369	0.9	4.0	48.6	193	91.0	67.0	0.4	7.0
Chad	0.368	0.350	1,160	5,469	2.3	9.7	25.7	208	73.0	30.9	1.4	8.6
Comoros	0.556	0.550	1,980	387	2.1	0.6	..	71	99.0	56.2	1.0	6.6
Congo, Dem. Rep.	0.391	0.378	680	7,103	3.4	57.5	67.2	205	208.0	123.0	3.1	26.9
Congo, Rep.	0.520	0.519	980	5,091	6.0	4.0	..	108	214.0	155.8	3.0	36.8
Côte d'Ivoire	0.421	0.401	1,570	16,344	0.2	18.2	48.7	195	91.0	69.4	3.0	0.8
Equatorial Guinea	0.653	0.639	..	3,231	..	0.5	87.0	205	..	..	..	..
Eritrea	0.454	..	1,100	970	-3.4	4.4	56.7	78	90.0	57.1	2.1	36.9
Ethiopia	0.371	..	1,050	11,174	6.8	71.3	41.5	127	97.0	20.6	0.8	17.4
Gabon	0.633	..	6,280	8,055	0.6	1.4	71.0	91	80.0	63.1	1.5	0.7
Gambia	0.479	..	1,860	461	2.3	1.5	37.8	137	186.0	98.5	6.5	13.0
Ghana	0.532	0.528	2,450	10,720	3.8	22.1	57.9	112	95.0	26.1	2.7	10.6
Guinea	0.445	0.434	2,280	3,289	0.8	9.4	29.5	160	100.0	34.9	5.0	5.6
Guinea-Bissau	0.349	..	790	301	0.5	1.6	39.6	200	331.0	289.8	11.3	27.4
Kenya	0.491	0.487	1,230	18,730	3.4	34.3	73.6	120	47.0	28.5	1.3	4.1
Lesotho	0.494	0.486	4,080	1,450	1.4	1.8	82.2	132	60.0	32.2	3.1	3.9
Liberia	..	..	..	548	3.9	3.3	43.0	235	674.0	1,086.8	0.2	54.1
Madagascar	0.509	0.507	910	5,040	1.8	18.6	70.7	119	74.0	36.9	1.6	18.7
Malawi	0.400	0.394	650	2,072	0.4	12.9	64.1	125	188.0	57.8	4.7	28.4
Mali	0.338	0.329	990	5,305	3.0	13.5	19.0	218	83.0	29.8	1.7	13.6
Mauritania	0.486	0.478	2,310	1,850	2.4	3.1	51.2	125	161.0	116.8	3.5	9.9
Mauritius	0.800	0.792	12,700	6,290	3.7	1.2	84.4	15	44.0	36.5	4.5	0.5
Mozambique	0.390	0.387	1,160	6,636	5.7	19.8	46.5	145	98.0	28.5	1.5	20.7
Namibia	0.626	0.622	7,690	6,126	2.4	2.0	85.0	62	..	..	..	2.0
Niger	0.311	0.443	780	3,405	1.1	14.0	28.7	256	74.0	25.1	1.1	15.2
Nigeria	0.448	0.443	990	98,951	4.7	131.5	66.8	194	72.0	33.5	10.2	7.4
Rwanda	0.450	0.449	1,190	2,153	4.2	9.0	64.9	203	96.0	18.3	1.1	27.1
São Tomé and Principe	0.607	..	2,090	71	0.9	0.2	83.1	118	666.0	175.3	14.4	47.1
Senegal	0.460	0.451	1,760	8,238	2.7	11.7	39.3	119	60.0	34.1	2.4	8.5
Seychelles	0.842	..	15,250	694	-3.3	0.1	91.8	13	94.0	105.5	8.4	2.9
Sierra Leone	0.335	0.317	780	1,193	3.8	5.5	35.1	282	177.0	40.5	2.1	29.6
Somalia	..	..	..	..	..	8.2	..	225	..	..	..	..
South Africa	0.653	0.646	10,880	239,543	3.7	46.9	82.4	68	18.0	14.1	2.0	0.3
Sudan	0.516	0.492	1,940	27,542	5.9	36.2	60.9	90	116.0	87.5	1.5	7.1
Swaziland	0.500	0.479	4,870	2,731	0.8	1.1	79.6	160	26.0	24.2	1.6	1.7
Tanzania	0.430	0.426	740	12,111	5.0	38.3	69.4	122	76.0	22.3	1.1	12.5
Togo	0.495	0.476	1,480	2,203	0.2	6.1	53.2	139	106.0	74.1	0.8	4.0
Uganda	0.502	0.498	1,430	8,724	2.9	28.8	66.8	136	78.0	29.0	2.0	14.0
Zambia	0.407	0.396	960	7,270	3.5	11.7	68.0	182	170.0	29.3	3.5	13.9
Zimbabwe	0.491	0.483	1,950	3,372	-7.0	13.0	90.0	132	33.0	85.4	7.0	11.0
Total Sub-Saharan Africa	**0.452**	**0.455**	**1,913**	**621,879**	**3.4**	**742.9**	**61.1**	**163**	**57.4**	**31.9**	**3.6**	**5.5**
MIDDLE EAST and NORTH AFRICA												
Algeria	0.728	0.713	6,720	102,256	3.7	32.9	69.9	39	33.0	20.9	6.1	0.4
Djibouti	0.494	..	2,380	709	1.4	0.8	65.5	133	65.0	42.5	2.3	12.1
Egypt	0.702	..	4,330	89,369	3.0	74.0	71.4	33	36.0	35.8	2.8	1.9
Iran	0.746	0.736	7,850	189,784	2.9	68.3	77.0	36	10.0	12.8	1.3	0.1
Iraq	..	..	2,170	..	..	28.9	74.1	..	..	..	..	..

Table 2 (continues) ▶

Regions and Countries	UNDP Human Development Index 2004	UNDP Gender-Related Development Index 2004	GNI Per Capita (PPP$) 2005	GDP (US$ millions) 2005	GDP/Capita Growth Average Over Previous Year (%) 2005	Population (millions) 2005	Adult Literacy Rate (%) 2006	Under-5 Years Mortality Rate (per 1,000 live births) 2005	External Debt/GNI (%) 2005	Present Value of Debt/GNI (%) 2005	Total Debt Service/GNI (%) 2005	Aid/GNI (%) 2005
	1	2	3	4	5	6	7	8	9	10	11	12
Jordan	0.760	0.747	5,690	12,712	4.9	5.5	89.9	26	77.0	64.6	4.7	5.0
Lebanon	0.774	..	5,450	21,944	..	3.6	86.5	30	116.0	113.6	16.5	1.3
Libya	0.798	..	..	38,756	1.5	5.9	81.7	19	..	..	..	..
Morocco	0.640	0.615	4,530	51,621	0.6	30.2	52.3	40	41.0	34.2	5.3	1.4
Oman	0.810	0.785	14,680	..	..	2.6	81.4	12	18.0	14.1	..	0.2
Saudi Arabia	0.777	0.744	15,730	309,779	3.8	23.1	79.4	26	..	..	..	..
Syria	0.716	0.702	3,680	26,320	2.5	19.0	79.6	15	102.0	27.4	0.8	0.5
Tunisia	0.760	0.744	7,930	28,683	3.2	10.0	74.3	24	79.0	69.0	7.6	1.2
West Bank and Gaza	..	..	..	4,014	2.8	3.6	92.4	23	..	..	..	..
Yemen	0.492	..	830	15,066	-0.6	21.0	49.0	102	53.0	32.4	1.6	2.1
Total Middle East and North Africa	**0.699**	**0.712**	**6,002**	**625,311**	**2.4**	**329.3**	**71.3**	**53**	**36.9**	**29.8**	**3.9**	**3.9**
SOUTH ASIA												
Afghanistan	..	..	..	7,308	..	..	28.1	..	..	..	..	38.0
Bangladesh	0.530	0.524	2,160	60,034	4.0	141.8	..	73	37.0	22.4	1.3	2.4
Bhutan	0.538	..	..	844	2.6	0.6	59.5	75	99.0	95.2	0.8	13.2
India	0.611	0.591	3,430	805,714	7.8	1,094.6	61.0	74	21.0	15.9	3.0	0.1
Maldives	0.739	..	..	766	-7.5	0.3	96.3	42	52.0	43.4	4.6	2.6
Nepal	0.527	0.513	1,560	7,391	0.7	27.1	48.6	74	56.0	33.8	1.6	6.4
Pakistan	0.539	0.513	2,320	110,732	5.2	155.8	49.9	99	44.0	30.0	2.3	1.5
Sri Lanka	0.755	0.749	4,540	23,479	4.4	19.6	90.7	14	61.0	48.4	1.9	2.7
Total South Asia	**0.596**	**0.577**	**3,124**	**1,016,267**	**6.9**	**1,439.9**	**57.8**	**83**	**25.8**	**18.8**	**2.8**	**0.9**
EAST ASIA and the PACIFIC												
Cambodia	0.583	0.578	2,620	6,187	11.2	14.1	73.6	87	80.0	57.9	0.5	10.3
China	0.927	0.765	6,790	2,234,297	9.5	1,304.5	90.9	27	15.0	14.2	1.2	0.1
Indonesia	0.711	0.704	3,720	287,217	4.2	220.6	90.4	36	63.0	55.2	6.5	..
Korea, Dem. Rep.	..	..	24,090	..	..	22.5	..	55	..	..	..	..
Laos	0.553	0.545	1,850	2,875	4.6	5.9	68.7	79	..	..	6.6	11.4
Malaysia	0.805	0.795	10,360	130,326	3.3	25.3	88.7	12	52.0	46.0	7.6	0.3
Mongolia	0.691	0.685	2,050	1,880	4.6	2.6	97.8	49	114.0	62.7	2.5	16.4
Myanmar	0.581	..	..	..	3.9	50.5	89.9	105	..	..	..	..
Papua New Guinea	0.523	0.521	2,370	4,945	1.3	5.9	57.3	74	72.0	55.4	..	7.6
Philippines	0.763	0.761	5,570	99,029	3.2	83.1	92.6	33	71.0	67.3	9.2	0.5
Thailand	0.784	0.781	8,470	176,634	3.6	64.2	92.6	21	36.0	32.4	11.3	..
Timor-Leste	0.512	..	..	349	-2.8	1.0	58.6	61	..	..	..	47.9
Vietnam	0.709	0.708	3,000	52,408	7.2	83.1	90.3	19	45.0	38.0	1.9	4.1
Oceania	0.709	0.000	5,106	..	1.5	2.1	87.4	..	70.4	..	..	26.2
Total East Asia and the Pacific	**0.863**	**0.752**	**6,060**	**3,039,976**	**8.0**	**1,885.3**	**90.8**	**33**	**25.0**	**22.9**	**2.9**	**0.3**
EUROPE and CENTRAL ASIA												
Albania	0.784	0.780	5,410	8,380	5.3	3.1	98.7	18	25.0	19.0	1.0	4.7
Armenia	0.768	0.765	4,990	4,903	10.9	3.0	99.4	29	43.0	36.2	2.8	8.1
Azerbaijan	0.736	0.733	4,380	12,561	9.2	8.4	98.8	89	29.0	17.7	2.2	2.2
Belarus	0.794	0.793	7,920	29,566	12.0	9.8	99.6	12	20.0	20.1	2.3	0.2
Bosnia and Herzegovina	0.800	..	7,790	9,949	6.4	3.9	96.7	15	44.0	51.8	2.6	7.7
Bulgaria	0.816	0.814	9,140	26,648	6.5	7.7	98.2	15	81.0	68.5	21.5	2.6
Croatia	0.846	0.844	12,620	38,506	3.8	4.4	98.1	7	113.0	88.8	13.2	0.4
Czech Republic	0.885	0.881	19,560	124,365	4.5	10.2	..	4	53.0	..	5.0	0.3
Estonia	0.858	0.856	14,660	13,101	8.2	1.3	99.8	7	116.0	101.6	12.8	1.3
Georgia	0.743	..	3,410	6,395	7.0	4.5	99.9	45	49.0	27.5	2.9	6.0
Hungary	0.869	0.867	16,780	109,239	4.9	10.1	..	8	80.0	69.1	22.9	0.3
Kazakhstan	0.774	0.772	7,120	57,124	8.8	15.1	99.5	73	107.0	106.2	25.5	0.7
Kyrgyzstan	0.705	0.701	1,860	2,441	5.9	5.1	98.7	67	114.0	53.9	5.4	12.2
Latvia	0.845	0.843	13,490	15,826	9.1	2.3	99.7	11	112.0	103.7	19.8	1.2
Lithuania	0.857	0.856	14,140	25,625	7.6	3.4	99.6	9	53.0	52.5	10.3	1.2
Macedonia, FYR	0.796	0.791	7,130	5,766	3.9	2.0	96.1	17	45.0	39.7	4.2	4.7
Moldova	0.694	0.692	2,360	2,917	7.6	4.2	98.4	16	81.0	70.1	7.6	4.0

Table 2 (continues) ▶

Regions and Countries	UNDP Human Development Index 2004	UNDP Gender-Related Development Index 2004	GNI Per Capita (PPP$) 2005	GDP (US$ millions) 2005	GDP/Capita Growth Average Over Previous Year (%) 2005	Population (millions) 2005	Adult Literacy Rate (%) 2006	Under-5 Years Mortality Rate (per 1,000 live births) 2005	External Debt/GNI (%) 2005	Present Value of Debt/GNI (%) 2005	Total Debt Service/GNI (%) 2005	Aid/GNI (%) 2005
	1	2	3	4	5	6	7	8	9	10	11	12
Poland	0.862	0.859	13,370	303,229	5.3	38.2	99.7	7	47.0	38.7	11.6	0.6
Romania	0.805	0.804	8,980	98,565	8.7	21.6	97.3	19	52.0	51.4	7.1	1.3
Russia	0.797	0.795	10,580	763,720	7.7	143.1	99.4	18	45.0	39.7	5.6	0.2
Serbia and Montenegro	0.000	..	..	26,215	8.9	8.1	96.4	15	80.0	68.9	4.9	4.9
Slovak Republic	0.856	0.853	15,200	46,412	5.4	5.4	99.6	8	68.0	61.0	13.2	0.6
Tajikistan	0.652	0.648	1,300	2,312	9.4	6.5	99.5	71	58.0	40.7	3.5	12.1
Turkey	0.757	0.745	8,390	362,502	7.4	72.1	87.4	29	67.0	59.1	11.6	0.1
Turkmenistan	0.724	..	..	8,067	..	4.8	98.8	104	..	15.8	4.1	0.6
Ukraine	0.774	0.771	6,770	82,876	13.0	47.1	99.4	17	42.0	53.1	7.2	0.6
Uzbekistan	0.696	0.694	2,060	13,951	6.1	26.2	..	68	4.0	34.3	5.7	2.1
Total Europe and Central Asia	**0.774**	**0.770**	**9,057**	**2,201,159**	**5.9**	**471.8**	**97.4**	**32**	**55.7**	**49.9**	**9.4**	**0.2**
LATIN AMERICA and the CARIBBEAN												
Argentina	0.863	0.859	13,800	183,193	8.1	38.7	97.2	18	141.0	73.1	6.0	0.1
Belize	0.751	..	6,390	1,105	-0.2	0.3	76.9	17	99.0	116.1	23.0	1.3
Bolivia	0.692	0.687	2,710	9,334	2.1	9.2	86.7	65	77.0	38.3	5.9	9.1
Brazil	0.792	0.789	8,140	796,055	0.9	186.4	88.6	33	44.0	34.1	8.1	..
Chile	0.859	0.850	10,920	115,248	5.2	16.3	95.7	10	58.0	51.7	7.3	0.1
Colombia	0.790	0.787	6,970	122,309	3.5	45.6	92.8	21	45.0	42.9	8.7	0.5
Costa Rica	0.841	0.831	9,860	20,021	3.5	4.3	94.9	12	34.0	35.8	3.1	0.1
Cuba	0.826	..	..	..	..	11.3	99.8	7	..	..	..	..
Dominica	0.793	..	5,560	284	..	0.1	88.0	15	93.0	86.4	6.6	0.5
Dominican Republic	0.751	0.745	7,710	29,502	7.7	8.9	87.0	31	39.0	37.2	3.2	0.5
Ecuador	0.765	..	4,110	36,489	3.3	13.2	91.0	25	65.0	60.0	12.0	0.6
El Salvador	0.729	0.725	5,080	16,974	1.0	6.9	79.7	27	50.0	47.6	4.0	1.4
Grenada	0.762	..	7,260	474	..	0.1	96.0	21	115.0	103.1	..	3.0
Guatemala	0.673	0.659	4,510	31,717	0.8	12.6	69.1	43	22.0	20.2	1.5	0.8
Guyana	0.725	..	4,230	787	-2.4	0.8	96.5	63	189.0	84.3	4.4	12.4
Haiti	0.482	..	1,660	4,268	0.5	8.5	51.9	120	37.0	24.4	1.4	6.7
Honduras	0.683	0.676	3,290	8,291	1.8	7.2	80.0	40	95.0	36.7	4.8	9.1
Jamaica	0.724	0.721	4,010	9,574	1.3	2.7	79.9	20	79.0	93.2	10.8	0.9
Mexico	0.821	0.812	10,560	768,438	1.9	103.1	91.0	27	22.0	26.1	5.8	..
Nicaragua	0.698	0.684	3,580	4,911	3.4	5.2	76.7	37	127.0	46.2	3.6	28.3
Panama	0.809	0.806	7,050	15,467	4.5	3.2	91.9	24	77.0	89.8	14.5	0.3
Paraguay	0.757	..	4,650	7,328	1.0	5.9	91.6	23	54.0	54.3	6.7	..
Peru	0.767	0.759	5,650	79,379	4.9	28.0	87.7	27	52.0	49.1	7.5	0.7
St. Kitts and Nevis	0.825	..	12,500	453	..	..	97.8	20	96.0	83.4	12.2	..
St. Lucia	0.790	..	5,980	825	..	0.2	90.1	14	64.0	58.2	4.2	2.3
St. Vincent and the Grenadines	0.759	..	6,100	430	1.7	0.1	88.1	20	71.0	70.6	6.0	1.8
Suriname	0.759	..	6,690	1,342	4.5	0.5	89.6	39	..	..	..	0.9
Trinidad and Tobago	0.809	0.805	13,960	14,358	6.7	1.3	99.9	19	29.0	24.2	2.8	..
Uruguay	0.851	0.847	9,620	16,791	5.8	3.5	97.7	15	104.0	116.2	13.7	0.2
Venezuela	0.784	0.780	6,540	140,192	7.5	26.6	93.0	21	3.0	48.2	4.0	..
Total Latin America and the Caribbean	**0.797**	**0.761**	**8,129**	**2,460,991**	**3.1**	**550.5**	**89.7**	**31**	**43.9**	**38.6**	**6.8**	**0.3**
Total Developing Countries	**0.715**	**0.665**	**5,310**	**9,965,583**	**6.3**	**5,419.7**	**78.0**	**66**	**39.7**	**32.8**	**5.4**	**0.7**
Of which:												
LDCs	**0.461**	**0.476**	**1,422**	**306,214**	**4.3**	**751.5**	**53.8**	**148**	**80.4**	**44.0**	**2.4**	**8.6**
Low Income Countries	**0.553**	**0.540**	**2,470**	**1,416,212**	**6.1**	**2,352.4**	**60.9**	**114**	**44.8**	**30.6**	**3.2**	**2.9**
Middle Income Countries	**0.835**	**0.746**	**7,252**	**8,553,720**	**5.5**	**3,074.5**	**89.9**	**37**	**37.2**	**32.9**	**5.8**	**0.6**
High Income Countries	**0.942**	**0.939**	**33,902**	**33,137,010**	**4.2**	**928.1**	**99.0**	**6**	**..**	**..**	**..**	**..**

Note: Bold-italicized countries are not ODA eligible (see Technical Notes) but Official Assistance (OA) to these countries was used in constructing Column 11. Data for External Debt/GNI (%) included in Column 9 represents an average for the year 2001-2005.

Sources: *Human Development Report 2006, Statistical Annex.*
World Bank, World Development Indicators 2006.
World Bank, Global Development Finance 2006 and World Development Indicators Online (WDI).

Figure 3.1: Top 10 Recipients of Total Canadian Allocated ODA (2004-05)

	Countries	C$ millions	%	Region
1	Haiti	104.62	5.59	Latin America and the Caribbean
2	Afghanistan	103.72	5.54	South Asia
3	Indonesia	89.36	4.77	East Asia and the Pacific
4	Ethiopia	82.04	4.38	Sub-Saharan Africa
5	Bangladesh	65.38	3.49	South Asia
6	Mozambique	59.47	3.18	Sub-Saharan Africa
7	Mali	58.48	3.12	Sub-Saharan Africa
8	Ghana	52.04	2.78	Sub-Saharan Africa
9	Sri Lanka	50.63	2.15	South Asia
10	Tanzania	46.84	2.50	Sub-Saharan Africa
	Top 10 Total	**712.58**	**38.06**	
	Total Canadian ODA Allocated	**1,872.23**		

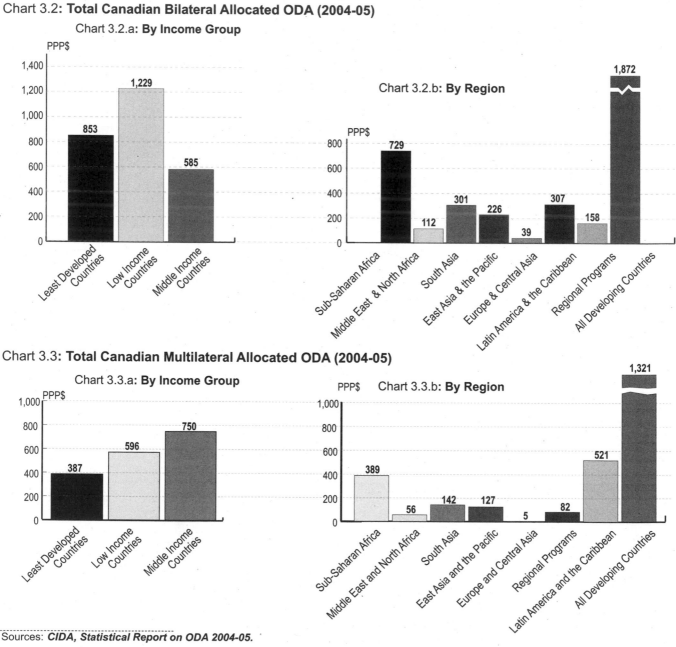

Chart 3.2: Total Canadian Bilateral Allocated ODA (2004-05)

Chart 3.2.a: By Income Group

Chart 3.2.b: By Region

Chart 3.3: Total Canadian Multilateral Allocated ODA (2004-05)

Chart 3.3.a: By Income Group

Chart 3.3.b: By Region

Sources: *CIDA, Statistical Report on ODA 2004-05.*

Table 3: Canadian Official Development Assistance: Basic Data (2004-05) *(In millions of Canadian dollars)*

Regions and Countries	Total Bilateral 2004-05	Total Bilateral 1994-95 (2004 prices)	Real Percent Change Per Year 1994-2004	Rank of Canada Among DAC Bilateral Donors in Recipient Country 2004	Total Multilateral (all agencies) 2004-05	Total Canadian Aid (all sources) 2004-05	Rank of Recipient Country for Total Canadian Aid (including multilateral) (if in top 50) 2004-05
	1	2	3	4	5	6	7
SUB-SAHARAN AFRICA							
Angola	2.96	11.49	-12.68	14	6.32	9.28	
Benin	11.27	8.86	2.44	8	6.44	17.71	42
Botswana	1.95	2.58	-2.75	4	3.18	5.13	
Burkina Faso	17.52	13.64	2.54	8	11.04	28.56	26
Burundi	6.22	6.06	0.26	10	8.69	14.91	50
Cameroon	39.55	25.31	4.57	2	8.05	47.60	36
Cape Verde	0.64	0.82	-2.43	10	3.53	4.17	
Central African Republic	0.80	0.53	4.29	4	5.13	5.93	
Chad	6.72	0.61	27.10	5	8.53	15.25	49
Comoros	0.18	0.12	3.95	2	3.33	3.51	
Congo, Dem. Rep.	28.29	11.12	9.79	8	20.18	48.47	17
Congo, Rep.	0.57	0.24	8.84	5	4.48	5.05	
Côte d'Ivoire	5.89	12.57	-7.30	4	7.71	13.60	
Equatorial Guinea	0.42	0.13	12.07	3	3.16	3.58	
Eritrea	4.17	7.91	-6.20	7	4.89	9.06	
Ethiopia	82.04	34.75	8.97	5	26.34	108.38	3
Gabon	2.29	2.53	-0.99	3	3.19	5.48	
Gambia	1.86	1.26	3.98	2	4.39	6.25	
Ghana	52.04	37.27	3.39	6	15.35	67.39	11
Guinea	12.78	10.02	2.46	5	6.11	18.89	37
Guinea-Bissau	1.29	1.17	0.95	5	4.76	6.05	
Kenya	23.51	13.70	5.55	8	9.86	33.37	22
Lesotho	1.02	0.90	1.21	5	4.31	5.33	
Liberia	2.04	3.54	-5.37	9	5.04	7.08	
Madagascar	23.10	2.38	25.50	11	14.42	37.52	45
Malawi	19.04	15.97	1.77	8	9.18	28.22	24
Mali	58.48	31.87	6.26	4	10.19	68.67	10
Mauritania	3.71	2.73	3.13	7	5.33	9.04	
Mauritius	0.87	0.42	7.67	3	3.23	4.10	
Mozambique	59.47	28.47	7.64	7	14.97	74.44	8
namibia	1.15	2.97	-9.05	11	3.60	4.75	
Niger	11.98	14.36	-1.79	5	8.97	20.95	34
Nigeria	25.61	2.30	27.27	10	17.12	42.73	20
Rwanda	11.00	37.74	-11.60	8	10.11	21.11	40
São Tomé and Principe	0.35	0.26	3.15	4	3.15	3.50	
Senegal	38.26	25.89	3.98	6	10.86	49.12	19
Seychelles	0.26	0.37	-3.38	3	3.16	3.42	
Sierra Leone	6.61	0.35	33.99	5	7.09	13.70	
Somalia	4.76	0.37	29.22	7	5.45	10.21	
South Africa	17.33	10.78	4.86	11	4.70	22.03	35
Sudan	26.99	10.28	10.14	9	10.56	37.55	21
Swaziland	0.97	1.92	-6.59	2	3.31	4.28	
Tanzania	46.84	20.04	8.86	10	22.86	69.70	9
Togo	3.37	0.76	16.10	4	4.01	7.38	
Uganda	16.07	7.03	8.62	11	17.44	33.51	23
Zambia	34.50	17.80	6.84	6	10.70	45.20	28
Zimbabwe	11.76	23.36	-6.63	6	4.18	15.94	48
Total Sub-Saharan Africa	**728.50**	**465.55**	**4.58**		**388.60**	**1,117.10**	
MIDDLE EAST and NORTH AFRICA							
Algeria	0.75	2.53	-11.45	7	3.56	4.31	
Djibouti	0.51	0.18	10.77	4	3.66	4.17	
Egypt	18.45	33.62	-5.82	6	6.64	25.09	30
Iran	0.00	0.49	-100.00	...	1.71	1.71	
Iraq	45.16	2.97	31.28	8	3.58	48.74	16
Jordan	9.26	12.77	-3.16	5	4.23	13.49	
Lebanon	3.09	2.60	1.73	5	4.07	7.16	
Libya	..	...	...	...	..	...	

Table 3 *(continues)* ▶

Regions and Countries	BILATERAL						
	Total Bilateral 2004-05	Total Bilateral 1994-95 (2004 prices)	Real Percent Change Per Year 1994-2004	Rank of Canada Among DAC Bilateral Donors in Recipient Country 2004	Total Multilateral (all agencies) 2004-05	Total Canadian Aid (all sources) 2004-05	Rank of Recipient Country for Total Canadian Aid (including multilateral) (if in top 50) 2004-05
	1	2	3	4	5	6	7
Morocco	5.69	0.12	46.83	6	4.49	10.18	
Oman	..	...	...	...	..	...	
Saudi Arabia	0.00	0.00	...	...	0.06	0.06	
Syria	2.27	0.22	26.29	5	3.50	5.77	25
Tunisia	-0.26	3.84	...	7	3.28	3.02	
West Bank and Gaza	26.01	2.82	24.87	...	9.66	35.67	1
Yemen	1.35	1.25	0.80	9	7.66	9.01	
Total Middle East and North Africa	**112.28**	**62.32**	**6.06**		**56.10**	**168.38**	
SOUTH ASIA							
Afghanistan	103.72	8.07	29.10	4	11.50	115.22	2
Bangladesh	65.38	70.95	-0.81	3	30.25	95.63	6
Bhutan	1.32	0.70	6.60	7	2.88	4.20	
India	43.16	36.07	1.81	5	49.58	92.74	7
Maldives	6.86	0.04	68.74	2	2.71	9.57	
Nepal	10.64	7.34	3.78	9	8.65	19.29	38
Pakistan	19.07	13.82	3.27	5	30.71	49.78	14
Sri Lanka	50.63	7.63	20.84	7	5.66	56.29	18
Total South Asia	**300.78**	**142.13**	**7.78**		**141.94**	**442.72**	
EAST ASIA and the PACIFIC							
Cambodia	9.48	6.40	4.00	10	7.20	16.68	46
China	37.15	112.88	-10.52	6	19.99	57.14	12
Indonesia	89.36	37.04	9.21	6	10.23	99.59	5
Korea, Dem. Rep.	4.86	...	...	8	2.47	7.33	
Laos	4.04	0.95	15.54	9	4.87	8.91	
Malaysia	1.33	10.09	-18.35	4	2.46	3.79	
Mongolia	1.57	0.09	33.77	11	3.86	5.43	
Myanmar	0.47	0.67	-3.51	15	5.15	5.62	
Papua New Guinea	0.64	...	...	7	3.25	3.89	
Philippines	20.93	37.93	-5.77	6	4.72	25.65	27
Thailand	9.12	24.50	-9.41	6	2.64	11.76	
Timor-Leste	4.07	...	...	...	2.77	6.84	
Vietnam	38.04	11.76	12.46	9	17.87	55.91	13
Oceania	5.37	5.34	0.06	...	39.91	45.28	15
Total East Asia and the Pacific	**226.43**	**243.48**	**-0.72**		**127.39**	**353.82**	
EUROPE and CENTRAL ASIA							
Albania	0.87	0.06	30.42	17	4.78	5.65	
Armenia	1.43	0.42	13.16	13	0.00	1.43	
Azerbaijan	2.04	0.42	17.25	8	0.00	2.04	
Belarus	0.16	...	...	11	0.00	0.16	
Bosnia and Herzegovina	10.18	...	...	11	0.00	10.18	39
Bulgaria	1.76	...	...	...	0.00	1.76	
Croatia	0.55	...	...	10	0.00	0.55	
Czech Republic	0.78	...	...	...	0.00	0.78	
Estonia	0.61	...	...	...	0.00	0.61	
Georgia	4.10	0.42	25.73	10	0.00	4.10	
Hungary	0.80	...	...	...	0.00	0.80	
Kazakhstan	1.31	0.81	4.97	8	0.00	1.31	
Kyrgyzstan	..	0.24	...	12	..	...	
Latvia	0.42	...	...	...	0.00	0.42	
Lithuania	0.45	...	...	...	0.00	0.45	
Macedonia, FYR	0.42	...	...	16	0.00	0.42	
Moldova	0.84	...	...	13	0.00	0.84	
Poland	0.75	...	...	...	0.00	0.75	
Romania	2.56	...	...	...	0.00	2.56	
Russia	21.42	...	...	...	0.00	21.42	31
Serbia and Montenegro	9.78	...	...	14	0.00	9.78	44
Slovenia	0.16	...	...	...	0.00	0.16	
Slovakia	1.37	...	...	...	0.00	1.37	

Table 3 *(continues)* ▶

Regions and Countries	Total Bilateral 2004-05	Total Bilateral 1994-95 (2004 prices)	BILATERAL Real Percent Change Per Year 1994-2004	Rank of Canada Among DAC Bilateral Donors in Recipient Country 2004	Total Multilateral (all agencies) 2004-05	Total Canadian Aid (all sources) 2004-05	Rank of Recipient Country for Total Canadian Aid (including multilateral) (if in top 50) 2004-05
	1	2	3	4	5	6	7
Tajikistan	5.70	...	...	5	0.00	5.70	
Turkey	0.53	-1.16	~	14	0.00	0.53	
Turkmenistan	0.09	...	...	4	0.00	0.09	
Ukraine	24.62	...	...	...	0.00	24.62	29
Uzbekistan	1.46	...	...	7	0.00	1.46	
Total Europe and Central Asia	**39.30**	**1.20**	**41.78**		**4.78**	**44.08**	
LATIN AMERICA and the CARIBBEAN							
Argentina	3.57	2.15	5.20	6	1.89	5.46	
Belize	0.81	0.66	2.07	4	1.86	2.67	
Bolivia	15.40	18.39	-1.76	10	6.48	21.88	33
Brazil	12.82	7.54	5.45	6	4.71	17.53	47
Chile	5.04	4.63	0.85	5	2.17	7.21	
Colombia	11.09	6.56	5.39	7	2.86	13.95	
Costa Rica	3.77	4.52	-1.80	7	2.03	5.80	
Cuba	10.46	1.50	21.41	4	1.71	12.17	
Dominica	1.99	2.22	-1.11	1	2.17	4.16	
Dominican Republic	3.51	0.62	18.87	5	1.73	5.24	
Ecuador	8.32	9.65	-1.48	8	3.15	11.47	
El Salvador	5.14	1.60	12.37	8	1.97	7.11	
Grenada	10.82	0.07	64.78	2	1.66	12.48	
Guatemala	10.37	6.71	4.45	8	2.34	12.71	
Guyana	9.82	10.19	-0.37	3	2.70	12.52	
Haiti	104.62	41.38	9.72	3	4.64	109.26	4
Honduras	23.75	13.06	6.16	5	6.40	30.15	41
Jamaica	12.47	19.05	-4.15	3	2.00	14.47	
Mexico	6.14	8.57	-3.28	5	3.87	10.01	
Nicaragua	10.18	16.99	-4.99	14	7.28	17.46	43
Panama	1.30	0.65	7.22	4	1.94	3.24	
Paraguay	3.42	0.42	23.47	4	1.59	5.01	
Peru	18.76	37.50	-6.69	6	3.51	22.27	32
St. Kitts and Nevis	1.82	...	...	1	1.54	3.36	
St. Lucia	2.33	10.03	-13.58	2	2.09	4.42	
St. Vincent and the Grenadines	2.14	0.16	29.70	2	1.59	3.73	
Suriname	1.26	...	...	5	1.09	2.35	
Trinidad and Tobago	2.10	0.98	7.95	2	1.68	3.78	
Uruguay	2.31	1.72	2.98	4	1.48	3.79	
Venezuela	1.72	1.67	0.27	5	1.60	3.32	
Total Latin America and the Caribbean	**307.25**	**229.21**	**2.97**		**81.73**	**388.98**	
Regional Programs	**157.69**	**175.16**	**-1.05**		**520.83**	**678.52**	
Total ODA Allocated	**1,872.23**	**1,326.86**	**3.50**		**1,321.37**	**3,193.60**	
Of which:							
LDCs	**853.14**	**467.16**	**6.21**		**386.65**	**1,239.79**	
Low Income Countries	**1,229.15**	**697.54**	**5.83**		**571.52**	**1,800.67**	
Middle Income Countries	**585.29**	**629.32**	**-0.72**		**749.85**	**1,392.93**	
Countries not Specified	**97.43**	**370.36**	**-12.50**		**309.75**	**407.18**	
Unallocable by Country	**618.48**	**866.09**	**-3.31**		**441.37**	**1,059.85**	
Total ODA	**2,588.14**	**2,592.56**	**-0.02**		**1,549.14**	**4,660.63**	

Sources: ***CIDA, Statistical Report on ODA 2004-05.***
CIDA, Statistical Report on ODA 1994-95.

Figure 4.1: Top 3 Recipients of Canadian Bilateral ODA in Each Region (2004-05)

Regions and Countries	C$ millions	% Participation Regionally	% Participation Globally
Sub-Saharan Africa			
1 Ethiopia	81.19	12.92	5.20
2 Mozambique	58.87	9.37	3.77
3 Mali	57.74	9.19	3.70
Middle East and North Africa			
1 Iraq	45.12	40.83	2.89
2 West Bank and Gaza	24.08	21.79	1.54
3 Egypt	17.76	16.07	1.14
South Asia			
1 Afghanistan	103.20	36.25	6.61
2 Bangladesh	64.46	22.64	4.13
3 Sri Lanka	40.59	14.26	2.60
East Asia and the Pacific			
1 Indonesia	91.18	40.83	5.84
2 China	39.48	17.68	2.53
3 Vietnam	37.31	16.71	2.39
Europe and Central Asia			
1 Ukraine	24.62	61.14	1.58
2 Russia	21.42	53.19	1.37
3 Bosnia and Herzegovina	10.18	25.28	0.65
Latin America and the Caribbean			
1 Haiti	98.91	35.99	6.33
2 Peru	17.46	6.35	1.12
3 Bolivia	14.46	5.26	0.93

Chart 4.2: Cumulative Evolution of Canadian ODA (1950 to 2005)

Chart 4.3: Canadian Evolution of the ODA/GNI Index (1950 to 2005)

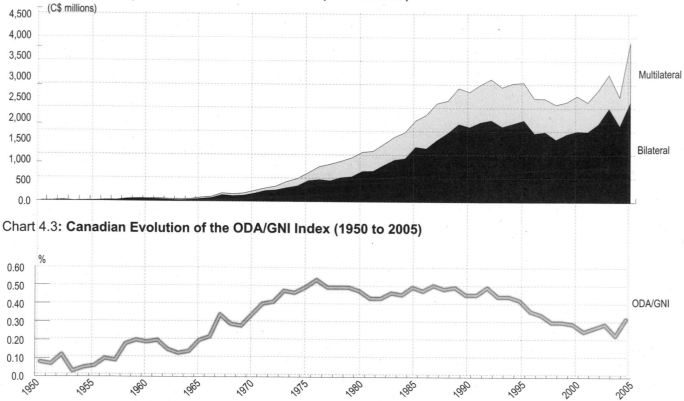

Sources: *CIDA, Statistical Report on ODA 2004-05.*

Table 4: Canadian Bilateral Official Development Assistance by Channel and by Country (2004-05)
(In millions of Canadian dollars)

Regions and Countries	Government-to-Government Aid	Voluntary Sector and Others	Private Sector	International Humanitarian Assistance (IHA)	CIDA and Commonwealth Scholarships	Bilateral Food Aid	Official Bilateral Debt Relief	International Development Research Centre (IDRC)	Int'l Centre for Human Rights and Democratic Development (ICHRDD)	Total Bilateral	Rank of Recipient Country (if in top 30)
	1	2	3	4	5	6	7	8	9	10	11
SUB-SAHARAN AFRICA											
Angola	0.56	0.51	0.01	0.37	0	1.24	0	0.22	0	2.96	
Benin	7.43	2.39	0.20	0	0.51	0	0	0.27	0	11.27	
Botswana	0.44	1.35	0.04	0	0	0	0	0.05	0	1.95	
Burkina Faso	10.48	5.54	0.11	0	0	0	0	0.89	0	17.52	30
Burundi	2.08	0.70	0.16	2.39	0	0.81	0	0	0	6.22	
Cameroon	9.56	1.33	0.03	0	0.51	0	27.97	0	0	39.55	12
Cape Verde	0.47	0.06	0	0.11	0	0	0	0	0	0.64	
Central African Republic	0.56	0.08	0.01	0	0	0	0	0.14	0	0.80	
Chad	0.79	0.29	0.21	4.44	0	1.00	0	0	0	6.72	
Comoros	0.13	0.05	0	0	0	0	0	0	0	0.18	
Congo, Dem. Rep.	13.41	1.70	0.48	6.12	0	4.66	1.56	0	0.12	28.29	18
Congo, Rep.	0.34	0.20	0	0	0	0	0	0.02	0	0.57	
Côte d'Ivoire	2.54	0.52	0.04	2.23	0.51	0	0	0.01	0.01	5.89	
Equatorial Guinea	0.33	0.04	0.04	0	0	0	0	0	0	0.42	
Eritrea	0.22	0.16	0	1.20	0	2.50	0	0	0	4.17	
Ethiopia	38.85	3.79	0.14	0.31	0.02	38.08	0.39	0.40	0	82.04	4
Gabon	1.65	0.14	0.49	0	0	0	0	0	0	2.29	
Gambia	0.37	0.79	0	0.11	0.51	0.06	0	0	0	1.86	
Ghana	41.32	4.65	0.17	0	0.57	0.69	4.26	0.17	0	52.04	8
Guinea	10.09	1.17	0.28	0.81	0.01	0.36	0	0.07	0	12.78	
Guinea-Bissau	0.71	0.33	0.01	0.24	0	0	0	0	0	1.29	
Kenya	13.35	4.77	0.02	0.67	0.60	2.80	0	1.01	0	23.51	23
Lesotho	0.32	0.44	0.01	0	0	0.20	0	0.01	0	1.02	
Liberia	0.23	0.26	0	0.98	0	0.58	0	0	0	2.04	
Madagascar	0.56	1.05	0	0	0	0	21.47	0	0	23.10	24
Malawi	13.05	3.54	0	0	0	2.25	0	0.14	0	19.04	27
Mali	39.75	5.43	0.60	1.30	0.50	10.17	0	0.06	0	58.48	7
Mauritania	0.67	0.73	0.13	1.61	0.51	0	0	0.04	0	3.71	
Mauritius	0.17	0.12	0.01	0	0.50	0	0	0	0	0.87	
Mozambique	42.36	3.02	0.03	0.78	0	12.68	0	0.58	0	59.47	6
Namibia	0.26	0.89	0	0	0	0	0	0	0	1.15	
Niger	7.82	2.78	0.02	1.30	0	0	0	0	0	11.98	
Nigeria	23.81	1.39	0.03	0	0.03	0.02	0	0.02	0.05	25.61	21
Rwanda	4.93	1.17	0.17	0.50	0.02	0.78	3.22	0.06	0	11.00	
São Tomé and Principe	0.28	0.07	0	0	0	0	0	0	0	0.35	
Senegal	17.13	3.53	1.04	1.78	0.51	8.58	3.97	1.56	0	38.26	14
Seychelles	0.17	0.08	0	0	0	0	0	0	0	0.26	
Sierra Leone	1.06	1.54	0.01	2.65	0.51	0.36	0	0.05	0	6.61	
Somalia	0.91	0.19	0.01	1.14	0	2.50	0	0	0	4.76	
South Africa	11.21	3.34	0.50	0	0	0	0	2.06	0	17.33	
Sudan	3.21	0.30	0	14.26	0	8.95	0	0.02	0.01	26.99	19
Swaziland	0.28	0.42	0	0	0	0.20	0	0.01	0	0.97	
Tanzania	34.02	4.35	0.01	0.50	0.54	5.86	0	1.44	0	46.84	10
Togo	1.67	1.33	0.11	0	0	0.13	0	0.07	0.01	3.37	
Uganda	3.40	3.56	0.36	3.68	0.50	2.33	0	2.05	0	16.07	
Zambia	10.15	1.89	0.12	0	0.02	2.27	20.00	0.01	0	34.50	17
Zimbabwe	8.78	1.91	0	0.25	0.51	0.04	0	0.17	0	11.76	
Total Sub-Saharan Africa	381.88	73.92	5.60	49.73	7.39	110.10	82.84	11.60	0.20	728.50	
MIDDLE EAST and NORTH AFRICA											
Algeria	2.79	0.07	0.85	0	0	0	0	0.09	0.02	0.75	
Djibouti	0.40	0.04	0.06	0	0	0	0	0	0	0.51	
Egypt	16.57	0.83	1.49	0	0	0	0	1.02	0	18.45	29
Iran	0.00	0	0	0	0	0	0	0	0	0	
Iraq	45.05	0.07	0	0	0	0	0	0	0	45.16	11

Table 4 *(continues)* ▶

Regions and Countries	Canadian International Development Agency (CIDA)						Other Government Department (OGD) / Other Official Canadian Source				
	Government-to-Government Aid	Voluntary Sector and Others	Private Sector	International Humanitarian Assistance (IHA)	CIDA and Commonwealth Scholarships	Bilateral Food Aid	Official Bilateral Debt Relief	International Development Research Centre (IDRC)	Int'l Centre for Human Rights and Democratic Development (ICHRDD)	Total Bilateral	Rank of Recipient Country (if in top 30)
	1	2	3	4	5	6	7	8	9	10	11
Jordan	7.34	0.45	0.62	0.22	0	0	0	0.37	0	9.26	
Lebanon	1.89	0.71	0.05	0	0	0	0	0.42	0	3.09	
Libya	0.00	0	0	0	0	0	0	0	0	0	
Morocco	6.56	1.44	0.42	0	0	0	0	0.18	0.06	5.69	
Oman	0.00	0	0	0	0	0	0	0	0	0	
Saudi Arabia	0.00	0	0	0	0	0	0	0	0	0	
Syria	2.25	0.02	0	0	0	0	0	0	0	2.27	
Tunisia	3.43	0.33	0.67	0	0	0	0	0.03	0	-0.26	
West Bank and Gaza	19.75	1.89	0.13	2.30	0	0	0	1.39	0.01	26.01	20
Yemen	0.93	0.09	0.15	0.15	0	0	0	0	0	1.35	
Total Middle East and North Africa	**106.96**	**5.94**	**4.44**	**2.67**	**0**	**0**	**0**	**3.50**	**0.09**	**112.28**	
SOUTH ASIA											
Afghanistan	95.20	0.54	0.13	0.22	0	7.10	0	0.25	0.05	103.72	2
Bangladesh	50.30	2.35	0.49	0.51	0.04	10.77	0	0.26	0	65.38	5
Bhutan	0.75	0.22	0	0	0	0	0	0.35	0	1.32	
India	19.16	8.56	4.39	4.77	0.06	3.25	0	2.27	0	43.16	11
Maldives	0.22	0.01	0.02	6.52	0	0	0	0	0	6.86	
Nepal	5.66	2.55	0.04	0.99	0.02	0.67	0	0.65	0	10.64	
Pakistan	18.04	0.61	0	0	0	0	0	0.30	0	19.07	26
Sri Lanka	4.87	2.62	0.32	35.01	0.01	0	0	0.29	0	50.63	9
Total South Asia	**194.20**	**17.46**	**5.39**	**48.02**	**0.13**	**21.79**	**0**	**4.37**	**0.05**	**300.78**	
EAST ASIA and the PACIFIC											
Cambodia	4.20	1.44	0.29	2.20	0	0.70	0	0.52	0	9.48	
China	29.93	4.63	4.75	0	0.06	0.10	0	0.73	0.02	37.15	16
Indonesia	17.16	2.35	0.98	64.73	0	10.14	0	0.22	0.01	89.36	3
Korea, Dem. Rep.	0.24	0.02	0	0.50	0	4.08	0	0.03	0	4.86	
Laos	1.79	1.10	0.23	0.62	0	0	0	0.30	0	4.04	
Malaysia	0.71	0.21	0.34	0.21	0	0	0	0.04	0	1.33	
Mongolia	0.80	0.44	0.14	0	0	0	0	0.21	0	1.57	
Myanmar	0.04	0.01	0	0.33	0	0	0	0	0.09	0.47	
Papua New Guinea	0.00	0.59	0	0	0	0	0	0.01	0	0.64	
Philippines	15.03	2.97	1.43	0.56	0.13	0.40	0	0.45	0	20.93	25
Thailand	3.63	1.90	1.62	3.01	0	0.62	0	0.11	0.01	9.12	
Timor-Leste	2.70	0.47	0	0.82	0	0	0	0	0	4.07	
Vietnam	28.57	7.35	0.98	0.39	0.02	0	0	0.71	0	38.04	15
Oceania	4.18	1.64	0	0	0.02	0	0	0.01	0	6.01	
Total East Asia and the Pacific	**108.98**	**25.12**	**10.76**	**73.37**	**0.23**	**16.04**	**0**	**3.34**	**0.13**	**227.07**	
EUROPE and CENTRAL ASIA											
Albania	0.76	0.02	0	0	0	0	0	0	0	0.87	
Armenia	1.34	0.09	0	0	0	0	0	0	0	1.44	
Azerbaijan	2.03	0.02	0	0	0	0	0	0	0	2.05	
Belarus	0.15	0.01	0	0	0	0	0	0.07	0	0.50	
Bosnia and Herzegovina	7.33	0.02	0.04	2.79	0	0	0	0	0	10.91	
Bulgaria	1.71	0.06	0	0	0	0	0	0	0	1.76	
Croatia	0.37	0.02	0.15	0	0	0	0	0	0	0.55	
Czech Republic	0.77	0	0	0	0	0	0	0	0	0.78	
Estonia	0.59	0.01	0	0	0	0	0	0	0	0.61	
Georgia	4.07	0.03	0.01	0	0	0	0	0	0	4.10	
Hungary	0.78	0.02	0	0	0	0	0	0	0	0.80	
Kazakhstan	1.19	0.12	0	0	0	0	0	0	0	1.31	
Kyrgyzstan	0.91	0.06	0	0	0	0	0	0	0	0.98	
Latvia	0.41	0	0	0	0	0	0	0	0	0.42	
Lithuania	0.43	0.01	0	0	0	0	0	0	0	0.46	
Macedonia, FYR	0.41	0.01	0	0	0	0	0	0	0	0.42	
Moldova	0.82	0.02	0	0	0	0	0	0	0	0.84	

Table 4 *(continues)* ►

Regions and Countries	Canadian International Development Agency (CIDA)						Other Government Department (OGD) / Other Official Canadian Source				
	Government-to-Government Aid	Voluntary Sector and Others	Private Sector	International Humanitarian Assistance (IHA)	CIDA and Commonwealth Scholarships	Bilateral Food Aid	Official Bilateral Debt Relief	International Development Research Centre (IDRC)	Int'l Centre for Human Rights and Democratic Development (ICHRDD)	Total Bilateral	Rank of Recipient Country (if in top 30)
	1	2	3	4	5	6	7	8	9	10	11
Poland	0.69	0.02	0.05	0	0	0	60.66	0	0	61.41	
Romania	2.46	0.03	0.06	0	0	0	0	0	0	2.56	
Russia	21.09	0.27	0.06	0	0	0	0	0.07	0	21.64	
Serbia and Montenegro	9.51	0.22	0.05	0	0	0	0	0	0	10.53	
Slovakia	1.34	0	0.03	0	0	0	0	0	0	1.37	
Tajikistan	5.58	0.12	0	0	0	0	0	0	0	5.76	
Turkey	0.33	0.02	0.39	0	0	0	0	0	0	-2.90	
Turkmenistan	0.08	0.01	0	0	0	0	0	0	0	0.09	
Ukraine	23.34	1.22	0.07	0	0	0	0	0.07	0	24.72	
Uzbekistan	1.42	0.04	0	0	0	0	0	0	0	1.46	
Total Europe and Central Asia	36.15	0.82	0.64	2.79	0	0	0	0	0	38.41	
LATIN AMERICA and the CARIBBEAN											
Argentina	2.86	0.47	0.01	0	0	0	0	0.23	0.02	3.57	
Belize	0.54	0.26	0.01	0	0	0	0	0	0	0.81	
Bolivia	8.09	6.04	0.37	0	0	0	0	0.74	0	15.40	
Brazil	6.53	3.27	1.39	0	0.02	0.02	0	1.48	0	12.82	
Chile	1.85	2.03	1.02	0	0.02	0	0	0.14	0	5.04	
Colombia	6.32	1.47	0.30	2.13	0.05	0	0	0.39	0.02	11.09	
Costa Rica	1.19	2.09	0.29	0	0	0	0	0.12	0	3.77	
Cuba	5.44	3.72	0.47	0.20	0.06	0	0	0.25	0	10.46	
Dominica	1.81	0.15	0	0	0	0	0	0	0	1.99	
Dominican Republic	1.81	0.68	0.71	0.20	0	0	0	0	0	3.51	
Ecuador	4.97	2.14	0.35	0.05	0	0	0	0.74	0	8.32	
El Salvador	2.65	2.24	0.11	0.03	0	0	0	0.12	0	5.14	
Grenada	10.19	0.19	0.04	0.37	0	0	0	0	0	10.82	
Guatemala	5.92	3.42	0.19	0	0	0	0	0.64	0.04	10.37	
Guyana	7.06	0.52	0	0.10	0	0	1.87	0	0	9.82	
Haiti	78.97	4.59	0	3.35	0	12.00	0	0	0.01	104.62	1
Honduras	6.89	3.91	0.32	0	0	0	11.08	1.27	0	23.75	22
Jamaica	10.72	1.24	0.10	0.32	0.04	0	0	0.16	0	12.47	
Mexico	0.96	3.49	1.26	0	0.02	0	0	0.21	0.04	6.14	
Nicaragua	4.93	4.13	0.51	0	0	0	0	0.12	0	10.18	
Panama	0.68	0.39	0.01	0.05	0.01	0	0	0.03	0.05	1.30	
Paraguay	2.44	0.65	0.14	0	0	0	0	0.15	0	3.42	
Peru	12.54	4.30	0.47	0.15	0	0	0	0.77	0.01	18.76	28
St. Kitts and Nevis	1.77	0.03	0	0	0	0	0	0	0	1.82	
St. Lucia	2.05	0.13	0.08	0	0.02	0	0	0	0	2.33	
St. Vincent and the Grenadines	1.77	0.31	0	0	0	0	0	0	0	2.14	
Suriname	0.73	0.24	0	0	0	0	0	0.14	0	1.26	
Trinidad and Tobago	1.20	0.47	0.33	0	0.03	0	0	0	0	2.10	
Uruguay	1.45	0.54	0.09	0	0.01	0	0	0.21	0	2.31	
Venezuela	1.30	0.04	0.30	0	0	0	0	0.01	0	1.72	
Total Latin America and the Caribbean	195.63	53.15	8.87	6.95	0.28	12.02	12.95	7.92	0.19	307.25	
Regional Programs	59.15	26.35	0.21	10.95	0	5.01	0	38.31	0.46	157.69	
Total ODA Allocated to Developing Countries	1,082.95	202.76	35.91	194.48	8.03	164.96	95.79	69.04	1.12	1,871.98	
Of which:											
LDCs	509.16	66.22	5.68	62.29	4.22	137.59	50.61	10.41	0.29	857.21	
Low Income Countries	712.30	105.66	13.04	129.20	7.03	158.61	82.84	15.89	0.36	1,231.77	
Middle Income Countries	354.82	70.68	23.07	54.23	0.98	1.34	71.74	15.25	0.30	585.29	
Countries not Specified	38.07	0	0	6.85	0	5.01	0	28.97	0.45	97.43	
Unallocable by Country	0.00	0	0	0	0	0	0	24.87	0.64	618.48	
Total ODA	1,121.02	202.76	35.91	201.33	8.03	169.97	95.79	122.88	2.21	2,587.89	

Note: Bold-italicized countries are not included in Canadian ODA totals (see Technical Notes).

Sources: **CIDA, *Statistical Report on ODA 2004-05.***

Chart 5.1: Comparative Net Canadian Disbursements Across Category of Recipients (2002 to 2005)

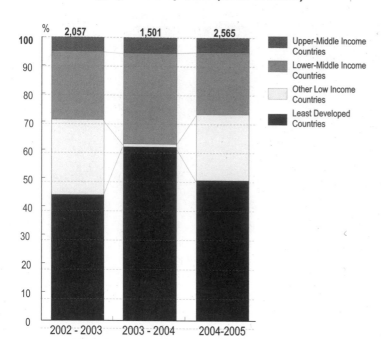

Legend:
- Upper-Middle Income Countries
- Lower-Middle Income Countries
- Other Low Income Countries
- Least Developed Countries

Values above bars: 2,057 (2002-2003); 1,501 (2003-2004); 2,565 (2004-2005)

Chart 5.2: Canadian Bilateral ODA Allocated by Sector and Grouped by Channel (2004-05)

(C$ millions)

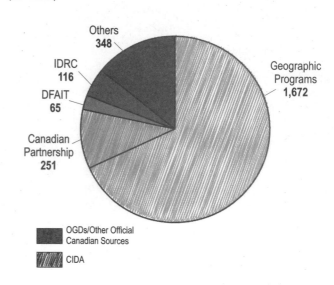

- Others 348
- IDRC 116
- DFAIT 65
- Canadian Partnership 251
- Geographic Programs 1,672

Legend:
- OGDs/Other Official Canadian Sources
- CIDA

Chart 5.3: Cumulative Canadian Bilateral ODA by Channel (2004-05)

(C$ millions)

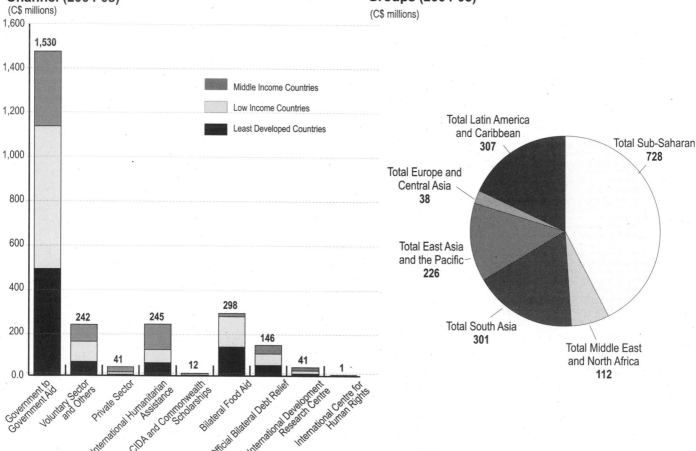

Legend:
- Middle Income Countries
- Low Income Countries
- Least Developed Countries

Bar values: Government to Government Aid 1,530; Voluntary Sector and Others 242; Private Sector 41; International Humanitarian Assistance 245; CIDA and Commonwealth Scholarships 12; Bilateral Food Aid 298; Official Bilateral Debt Relief 146; International Development Research Centre 41; International Centre for Human Rights 1

Chart 5.4: Canadian Bilateral ODA by Regional Groups (2004-05)

(C$ millions)

- Total Latin America and Caribbean 307
- Total Europe and Central Asia 38
- Total East Asia and the Pacific 226
- Total South Asia 301
- Total Middle East and North Africa 112
- Total Sub-Saharan 728

Sources: *CIDA, Statistical Report on ODA 2004-05.*

Table 5: Canadian Bilateral Official Development Assistance by Sector (2004-05)

(In millions of Canadian dollars)

Sector	CIDA Geographic Programs $	CIDA Canadian Partnership $	SUBTOTAL $	SUBTOTAL %	DFAIT $	ICHRDD $	IDRC $	Others $	SUBTOTAL $	SUBTOTAL %	TOTAL Country to Country $	TOTAL Country to Country %
SOCIAL INFRASTRUCTURE / SERVICES												
Education	170.13	48.85	218.99	11.39	0.03	0.00	3.50	0.00	3.53	0.66	222.52	9.07
Education Level Unspecified	73.78	21.82	95.60	4.97			2.80		2.80	0.53	98.40	4.01
Basic Education	73.96	11.62	85.59	4.45			0.15		0.15	0.03	85.74	3.49
Secondary Education	15.85	3.80	19.62	1.02			0.02		0.02	0.00	19.65	0.80
Post -Secondary Education	6.57	11.61	18.18	0.95	0.03	0.00	0.53		0.56	0.11	18.73	0.76
Health	77.58	22.44	100.20	5.21	0.02	0.00	10.22	0.00	10.24	1.93	110.27	4.49
Health, General	19.38	8.49	27.87	1.45	0.02	0.00	7.98		8.00	1.51	35.87	1.46
Basic Health	58.21	13.95	12.16	0.63	0.00	0.00	2.24		2.24	0.42	74.40	3.03
Population Policies/ Programs and Reproductive Health (incl. HIV/AIDS)	76.54	26.96	103.50	5.38		0.00	2.75		2.75	0.52	106.26	4.33
Water Supply and Sanitation	54.61	8.86	63.47	3.30		0.00	2.80		2.80	0.53	56.25	2.29
Government and Civil Society	356.37	50.00	406.37	21.13	9.28	0.95	19.55	0.00	29.78	5.61	436.15	17.77
Government and Civil Society, General	292.90	48.06	340.96	17.73	2.56	0.80	15.13		18.49	3.48	359.45	14.65
Conflict Prevention and Resolution, Peace and Security	63.47	1.93	65.40	3.40	6.73	0.15	4.42		11.29	2.13	76.69	3.12
Other Social Infrastructure and Services	32.33	6.44	38.76	2.02	0.72	0.00	1.43		2.15	0.40	40.92	1.67
Subtotal	767.56	163.55	931.11	48.41	10.06	0.95	40.25	0.00	51.26	9.65	982.37	40.03
ECONOMIC INFRASTRUCTURE / SERVICES												
Transport and Storage	1.34	3.31	4.65	0.24	0.05	0.00	0.00		0.05	0.01	4.69	0.19
Communications	7.36	2.49	9.85	0.51	0.00	0.16	15.92		16.08	3.03	25.94	1.06
Energy Generation and Supply	14.29	3.49	17.78	0.92	0.00	0.00	0.05		0.05	0.01	17.82	0.73
Banking and Financial Services	18.94	7.47	26.42	1.37	0.00	0.00	0.26		0.26	0.05	26.68	1.09
Business and Other Services	15.00	3.60	18.60	0.97	0.00	0.00	0.53		0.53	0.10	19.14	0.78
Sub-Total	56.94	20.36	77.30	4.02	0.05	0.16	16.77	0.00	16.98	3.20	94.27	3.84
PRODUCTION SECTORS												
Agriculture	67.85	21.29	89.14	4.64	0.00	0.00	7.15		7.15	1.35	96.29	3.92
Forestry	4.68	2.51	7.19	0.37	0.00	0.00	2.30		2.30	0.43	9.49	0.39
Fishing	1.09	0.69	1.77	0.09	0.00	0.00	0.45		0.45	0.08	2.22	0.09
Industry	25.48	11.14	36.62	1.90	0.00	0.00	2.59		3.16	0.60	39.78	1.62
Mineral Resources and Mining	4.41	1.40	5.81	0.30	0.57	0.00	1.38		1.38	0.26	7.19	0.29
Construction	0.33	1.24	1.58	0.08	0.00	0.00	0.00		0.00	0.00	1.58	0.06
Trade Policy and Regulations	8.01	1.16	9.21	0.48	0.00	0.00	4.30		4.51	0.85	13.72	0.56
Tourism	0.15	0.49	0.64	0.03	0.21	0.00	0.00		0.00	0.00	0.64	0.03
Sub-Total	112.01	39.94	151.95	7.90	0.00	0.00	18.17	0.00	18.96	3.57	170.91	6.96
MULTISECTOR / CROSSCUTTING												
General Environment Protection	45.63	8.78	54.41	2.83	0.00	0.00	5.49		5.49	1.03	59.90	2.44
Women in Development	0.00	0.00	0.00	0.00	0.15	0.41	3.09		3.65	0.69	3.65	0.15
Other Multisector	49.02	5.41	54.43	2.83	3.57	0.00	5.84	25.43	34.84	6.56	89.27	3.64
Sub-Total	94.65	14.18	108.84	5.66	3.72	0.41	14.42	25.43	43.99	8.28	152.82	6.23
COMMODITY AID AND GENERAL PROGRAM ASSISTANCE												
General Budget Support	28.13	0.01	28.14	1.46	0.00	0.00	0.00	0.00	0.00	0.00	1.18	0.05
Developmental Food Aid /Food Security Assistance	1.04	0.14	1.18	0.06	0.00	0.00	0.00	0.00	0.00	0.00	0.08	0.00
Other Commodity Assistance	0.06	0.01	0.08	0.00	0.00	0.00	0.00	0.00	0.00	0.00	29.40	1.20
Sub-Total	29.23	0.17	29.40	1.53	0.00	0.00	0.00	0.00	0.00	0.00	111.51	4.54
ACTION RELATING TO DEBT	15.80	0.01	15.81	0.82	0.00	0.00	0.00	95.80	95.80	18.04	607.06	24.73
EMERGENCY ASSISTANCE AND RECONSTRUCTION	379.92	0.38	380.00	19.76	0.38	0.00	0.06	226.31	223.76	42.13	182.01	7.42
Emergency Food Aid	182.01	0.00	182.01	9.46	0.00	0.00	0.00	0.00	0.00	0.00	414.11	16.87
Other Emergency and Distress Relief	187.16	0.25	187.41	9.74	0.38	0.00	0.01	226.31	226.70	42.68	0.00	0.00
Reconstruction Relief	10.75	0.13	10.88	0.57	0.00	0.00	0.06	0.00	0.06	0.01	0.00	0.00
ADMINISTRATIVE COSTS OF DONORS	210.70	0.37	211.06	10.97	49.02	0.64	25.52	0.00	75.18	14.16	286.25	11.66
SUPPORT TO NON-GOVERNMENTAL ORGANIZATIONS (NGOs)	5.29	12.13	17.42	0.91	0.84	0.33	1.03	0.00	2.20	0.41	19.62	0.80
ALLOCABLE BY SECTOR	1,672.11	251.10	1,923.20	100.00	64.86	2.50	116.23	347.54	531.12	100.00	2,454.33	100.00

Sources: **CIDA, Statistical Report on ODA 2004-05.**

Chart 6.1: Experts on Assignment Abroad by Expertise and Gender (2004-05)

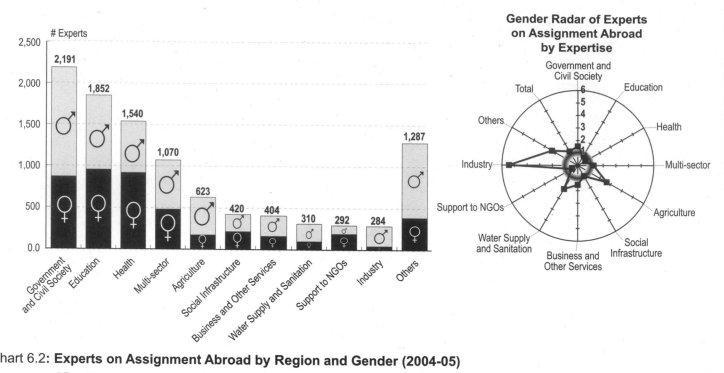

Chart 6.2: Experts on Assignment Abroad by Region and Gender (2004-05)

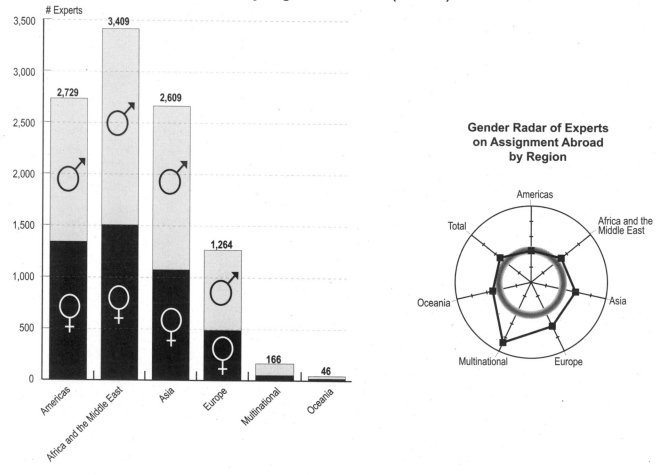

Sources: *CIDA, Statistical Report on ODA 2004-05.*

Table 6: Canadian Technical Assistance to Developing Countries (1999 - 2004)
Table 6.1.a: Experts on Assignment Abroad by Area of Expertise, Duration and Gender

Area of Expertise	Total Experts 2004			
	♀	♂	Total	Ratio ♂/♀
Government and Civil Society	866	1,325	2,191	1.53
Education	953	899	1,852	0.94
Health	916	624	1,540	0.68
Multi-sector *	476	594	1,070	1.25
Agriculture	171	452	623	2.64
Social Infrastructure and Services	213	207	420	0.97
Business and Other Services	159	245	404	1.54
Water Supply and Sanitation	98	212	310	2.16
Support to NGOs **	189	103	292	0.55
Industry	44	240	284	5.45
Banking and Financial Services	72	150	222	2.08
Energy	26	196	222	7.54
Communications	75	94	169	1.25
Tourism	21	92	113	4.38
Trade	33	47	80	1.42
Population Policies	49	30	79	0.61
Transportation	15	61	76	4.07
Forestry	23	48	71	2.09
Construction	9	53	62	5.89
Fisheries	22	38	60	1.73
Mineral Resources and Mining	13	44	57	3.38
Unallocated / Unspecified	10	35	45	3.50
Commodity Aid/Gen, Prog. Assistance	10	4	14	0.40
Emergency Assistance and Reconstruction	2	9	11	4.50
Administration Costs to Donors	5	1	6	0.20
Total	**4,470**	**5,803**	**10,273**	**1.30**

Area of Expertise	Total Experts 1999 **			
	♀	♂	Total	Ratio ♂/♀
Education	1,190	1,367	2,557	1.15
Government and Civil Society	618	1,601	2,219	2.59
Multi-sector *	512	705	1,217	1.38
Agriculture	164	458	622	2.79
Industry	94	488	582	5.19
Health	311	264	575	0.85
Population Policies	242	266	508	1.10
Communications	155	281	436	1.81
Energy	54	373	427	6.91
Water Supply and Sanitation	55	157	212	2.85
Transportation	30	152	182	5.07
Forestry	24	148	172	6.17
Mineral Resources and Mining	14	104	118	7.43
Fisheries	21	77	98	3.67
Social Infrastructure and Services	8	51	59	6.38
Commodity Aid/Gen, Prog. Assistance	8	12	20	1.50
Business and Other Services	1	3	4	3.00
Total	**3,501**	**6,507**	**10,008**	**1.86**

Table 6.1.b: Experts on Assignment Abroad by Region of Assignment, Duration and Gender

Region of Assignment	Total Experts 2004			
	♀	♂	Total	Ratio ♂/♀
Americas	1,339	1,390	2,729	1.04
Africa and Middle East	1,502	1,907	3,409	1.27
Asia	1,070	1,589	2,659	1.49
Europe	487	777	1,264	1.60
Multinational	52	114	166	2.19
Oceania	20	26	46	1.30
Total	**4,470**	**5,803**	**10,273**	**1.30**

Region of Assignment	Total Experts 1999 **			
	♀	♂	Total	Ratio ♂/♀
Americas	1,105	1,727	2,832	1.56
Africa and Middle East	900	1,533	2,433	1.70
Asia	972	1,953	2,925	2.01
Europe	490	1,182	1,672	2.41
Multinational	16	23	39	1.44
Oceania	20	17	37	0.85
Total	**3,503**	**6,435**	**9,938**	**1.84**

Notes: * Technical Cooperation personnel, either fully or partially supported by CIDA, working for CIDA directly, or through private firms, institutions, associations, and non-governmental organizations.
Tables 6.1a and 6.1b for 2004 include a total of 2,903 technical cooperation personnel are from developing countries; 800 are sent to non-ODA countries in Central and Eastern Europe, as well as, 9 are sent to non-ODA more advanced developing countries.

** Tables 6.1a and 6.1b for 1999 include 974 experts from developing countries.

Sources: *CIDA, Statistical Report on ODA 2004-05.*

Chart 6.3: Canadian Technical Assistance to Developing Countries (2004-05)

(# Experts)

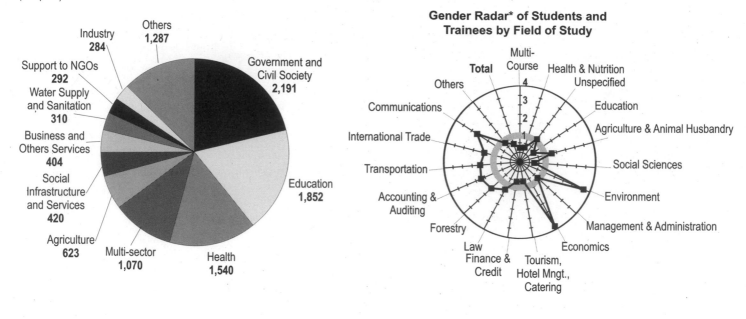

Gender Radar* of Students and Trainees by Field of Study

* See "Technical Notes"

Chart 6.4: Total Students and Trainees by Location of Study (2004-05)

Students and Trainees

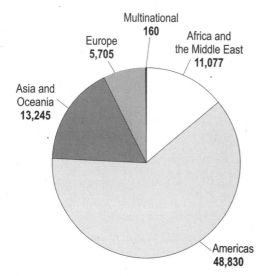

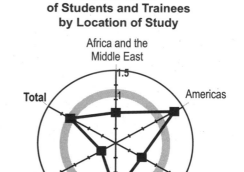

Gender Radar of Students and Trainees by Location of Study

Sources: *CIDA, Statistical Report on ODA 2004-05.*

Table 6.2.a: CIDA's Investment in Training and Education by Field of Study and Gender

Field of Study	Total Students and Trainees 2004			Ratio ♂/♀
	♀	♂	Total	
Multi-Course	21,089	15,603	36,692	0.74
Health and Nutrition	4,401	3,475	7,876	0.79
Unspecified	2,782	4,158	6,940	1.49
Education	2,983	2,558	5,541	0.86
Agriculture, Animal Husbandry	1,635	2,857	4,492	1.75
Social Sciences	1,471	1,107	2,578	0.75
Environment	528	1,936	2,464	3.67
Management and Administration	1,053	1,318	2,371	1.25
Economics	363	1,395	1,758	3.84
Tourism, Hotel Mngt, Catering	729	754	1,483	1.03
Finance and Credit	688	720	1,408	1.05
Law	437	718	1,155	1.64
Forestry	366	748	1,114	2.04
Accounting and Auditing	152	336	488	2.21
Transportation	151	315	466	2.09
International Trade	139	267	406	1.92
Communications	88	235	323	2.67
Human Settlements, Urban Dev.	124	187	311	1.51
Engineering and Technology	67	145	212	2.16
Computer Science	91	87	178	0.96
Languages and Linguistics	71	89	160	1.25
Energy	31	94	125	3.03
Geology, Mining, Metallurgy	35	90	125	2.57
Arts and Humanities	93	3	96	0.03
Natural Sciences	71	22	93	0.31
Fisheries	26	49	75	1.88
Mathematics and Statistics	18	9	27	0.50
Secretariat and Clerical	10	5	15	0.50
Geography	5	7	12	1.40
Surveying	6	6	12	1.00
Architecture	1	10	11	10.00
Customs and Excise	1	9	10	9.00
Total	**39,705**	**39,312**	**79,017**	**0.99**

Field of Study	Total Students and Trainees 1999			Ratio ♂/♀
	♀	♂	Total	
Environment	1,037	3,135	4,172	3.0
Management and Administration	976	1,987	2,963	2.0
Health and Nutrition	703	564	1,267	0.8
Education	586	581	1,167	1.0
Human Settlements, Urban Dev.	267	883	1,150	3.3
Social Sciences	499	453	952	0.9
Communications	265	519	784	2.0
Law	285	443	728	1.6
Engineering and Technology	98	378	476	3.9
Agriculture, Animal Husbandry	113	353	466	3.1
Economics	170	205	375	1.2
Energy	45	302	347	6.7
International Trade	80	221	301	2.8
Mathematics and Statistics	85	116	201	1.4
Transportation	36	124	160	3.4
Finance and Credit	67	73	140	1.1
Computer Science	37	101	138	2.7
Forestry	30	93	123	3.1
Geology, Mining, Metallurgy	20	92	112	4.6
Natural Sciences	39	59	98	1.5
Accounting and Auditing	30	55	85	1.8
Arts and Humanities	29	22	51	0.8
Fisheries	18	33	51	1.8
Languages and Linguistics	25	13	38	0.5
Architecture	9	11	20	1.2
Tourism, Hotel Mngt, Catering	10	10	20	1.0
Surveying	5	14	19	2.8
Geography	4	13	17	3.3
Customs and Excise	1	4	5	4.0
Secretariat and Clerical	0	1	1	...
Total	**5,569**	**10,858**	**16,427**	**1.95**

Table 6.2.b: CIDA's Investment in Training and Education by Region of Origin, Location of Study and Gender

Location of Study	Total Students and Trainees 2004					
	Africa and Middle East	Americas	Asia and Oceania	Europe	Multi-national	Total
Country of Origin	7,853	47,710	10,692	4,236	0	**70,491**
Canada	1,439	728	1,556	877	160	**4,760**
Third Country	1,785	392	997	592	0	**3,766**
Total	**11,077**	**48,830**	**13,245**	**5,705**	**160**	**79,017**
Of which:						
Women (♀)	6,805	21,174	8,389	2,823	121	**39,312**
Men (♂)	4,272	27,656	4,856	2,882	39	**39,705**
Gender ratio (♂/♀)	0.63	1.31	0.58	1.02	0.32	**1.01**

Location of Study	Total Students and Trainees 1999				
	Africa and Middle East	Americas	Asia and Oceania	Europe	Total
Country of Origin	927	1,099	6,301	970	**9,297**
Canada	1,357	1,720	1,785	1,190	**6,052**
Third Country	167	310	211	390	**1,078**
Total	**2,451**	**3,129**	**8,297**	**2,550**	**16,427**
Of which:					
Women (♀)	775	1,330	2,337	1,127	**5,569**
Men (♂)	1,676	1,799	5,960	1,423	**10,858**
Gender ratio (♂/♀)	2.16	1.35	2.55	1.26	**1.95**

Sources: ***CIDA, Statistical Report on ODA 2004-05.***

Chart 7.1: Canadian Bilateral and Multilateral Growth Rates (1950 to 2005)

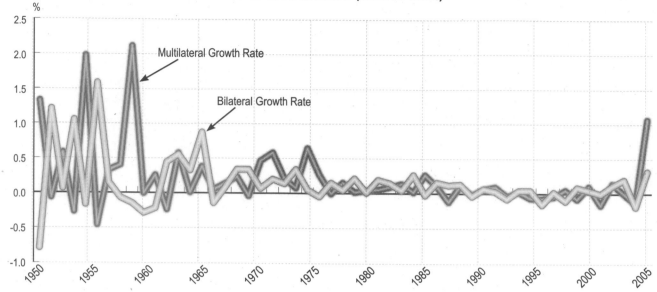

Multilateral Growth Rate

Bilateral Growth Rate

Chart 7.2: Canadian Multilateral ODA by Income Group and Region (2004-05)

(Estimated in C$ millions)

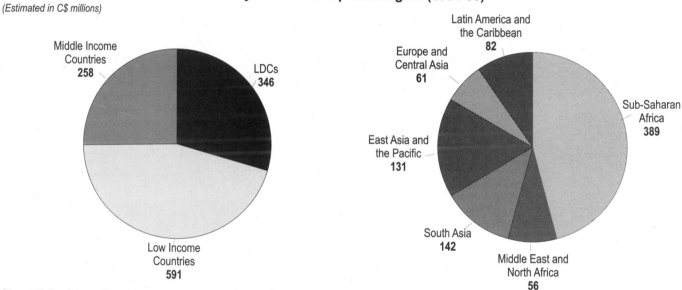

Middle Income Countries **258**

LDCs **346**

Low Income Countries **591**

Latin America and the Caribbean **82**

Europe and Central Asia **61**

Sub-Saharan Africa **389**

East Asia and the Pacific **131**

South Asia **142**

Middle East and North Africa **56**

Chart 7.3: Canadian Multilateral ODA by Channel, Income and Region (2004-05)

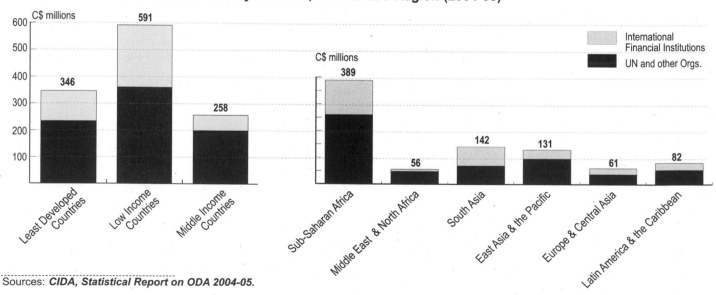

C$ millions

346

591

258

International Financial Institutions

UN and other Orgs.

Least Developed Countries

Low Income Countries

Middle Income Countries

C$ millions

389

56

142

131

61

82

Sub-Saharan Africa

Middle East & North Africa

South Asia

East Asia & the Pacific

Europe & Central Asia

Latin America & the Caribbean

Sources: *CIDA, Statistical Report on ODA 2004-05.*

Table 7: Canadian Multilateral Official Development Assistance by Agency and by Country (2004-05)

(Estimated in millions of Canadian dollars)

Regions and Countries	UN and other Multilateral Organizations	International Financial Institutions (IFIs)	Total Multilateral	Multilateral/ Bilateral Ratio	UN Agencies/ IFIs Ratio
	1	2	3	4	5
SUB-SAHARAN AFRICA					
Angola	5.41	0.91	6.32	2.14	5.95
Benin	4.18	2.26	6.44	0.57	1.85
Botswana	3.03	0.15	3.18	1.63	20.20
Burkina Faso	6.77	4.27	11.04	0.63	1.59
Burundi	6.85	1.84	8.69	1.40	3.72
Cameroon	5.11	2.94	8.05	0.20	1.74
Cape Verde	2.96	0.57	3.53	5.52	5.19
Central African Republic	4.98	0.15	5.13	6.41	33.20
Chad	6.28	2.25	8.53	1.27	2.79
Comoros	3.07	0.26	3.33	18.50	11.81
Congo, Dem. Rep.	13.63	6.54	20.17	0.71	2.08
Congo, Rep.	3.50	0.97	4.47	7.84	3.61
Côte d'Ivoire	6.50	1.21	7.71	1.31	4.76
Equatorial Guinea	3.01	0.15	3.16	7.52	20.07
Eritrea	3.62	1.27	4.89	1.17	2.85
Ethiopia	12.72	13.62	26.34	0.32	0.93
Gabon	3.04	0.15	3.19	1.39	20.27
Gambia	3.55	0.85	4.40	2.37	4.18
Ghana	5.68	9.67	15.35	0.30	0.59
Guinea	4.41	1.70	6.11	0.48	2.59
Guinea-Bissau	3.85	0.91	4.76	3.69	4.23
Kenya	6.69	3.17	9.86	0.42	2.11
Lesotho	3.44	0.87	4.31	4.23	3.95
Liberia	4.89	0.15	5.04	2.47	32.60
Madagascar	5.61	8.82	14.43	0.62	0.64
Malawi	6.36	2.82	9.18	0.48	2.26
Mali	7.37	2.82	10.19	0.17	2.61
Mauritania	3.84	1.49	5.33	1.44	2.58
Mauritius	3.01	0.21	3.22	3.70	14.33
Mozambique	9.03	5.93	14.96	0.25	1.52
Namibia	3.38	0.22	3.60	3.13	15.36
Niger	6.54	2.43	8.97	0.75	2.69
Nigeria	12.84	4.28	17.12	0.67	3.00
Rwanda	5.71	4.40	10.11	0.92	1.30
São Tomé and Principe	2.85	0.30	3.15	9.00	9.50
Senegal	5.00	5.87	10.87	0.28	0.85
Seychelles	2.98	0.19	3.17	12.19	15.68
Sierra Leone	5.77	1.32	7.09	1.07	4.37
Somalia	5.30	0.15	5.45	1.15	35.33
South Africa	3.96	0.74	4.70	0.27	5.35
Sudan	10.07	0.49	10.56	0.39	17.49
Swaziland	3.09	0.22	3.31	3.41	14.05
Tanzania	8.78	14.08	22.86	0.49	0.62
Togo	3.84	0.17	4.01	1.19	22.59
Uganda	7.72	9.72	17.44	1.09	0.79
Zambia	5.75	4.95	10.70	0.31	1.16
Zimbabwe	4.03	0.15	4.18	0.36	26.87
Total Sub-Saharan Africa	**260.00**	**128.60**	**388.60**	**0.53**	**2.02**
MIDDLE EAST and NORTH AFRICA					
Algeria	3.41	0.15	3.56	4.75	19.20
Djibouti	3.19	0.47	3.66	7.18	6.79
Egypt	4.15	2.48	6.63	0.36	1.67
Iran	1.71	0.00	1.71	na	na
Iraq	3.48	0.10	3.58	0.08	34.80
Jordan	3.98	0.24	4.22	0.46	16.58
Lebanon	3.79	0.28	4.07	1.32	13.54

Table 7 *(continues)* ▶

Regions and Countries	UN and other Multilateral Organizations	International Financial Institutions (IFIs)	Total Multilateral	Multilateral/ Bilateral Ratio	UN Agencies/ IFIs Ratio
	1	2	3	4	5
Libya	0.00	..	...	...	...
Morocco	3.66	0.83	4.49	0.79	4.41
Oman	0.00	..	...	...	...
Saudi Arabia	0.06	0.00	0.06	...	...
Syria	3.12	0.38	3.50	1.54	8.21
Tunisia	3.01	0.27	3.28	-12.62	11.15
West Bank and Gaza	9.53	0.13	9.66	0.37	73.31
Yemen	4.88	2.78	7.66	5.67	1.76
Total Middle East and North Africa	**47.97**	**8.11**	**56.08**	**0.50**	**5.91**
SOUTH ASIA					
Afghanistan	9.02	2.48	11.50	0.11	3.64
Bangladesh	13.34	16.91	30.25	0.46	0.74
Bhutan	2.48	0.40	2.88	2.18	6.20
India	22.46	27.12	49.58	1.15	0.72
Maldives	2.43	0.27	2.70	0.39	9.00
Nepal	6.64	2.01	8.65	0.81	3.08
Pakistan	10.39	20.32	30.71	1.61	0.48
Sri Lanka	3.11	2.55	5.66	0.11	1.22
Total South Asia	**69.87**	**72.06**	**141.93**	**0.47**	**0.97**
EAST ASIA and the PACIFIC					
Cambodia	5.56	1.64	7.20	0.76	3.39
China	9.01	10.99	20.00	0.54	0.82
Indonesia	6.32	3.91	10.23	0.11	1.62
Korea, Dem. Rep.	2.19	0.28	2.47	0.51	7.82
Laos	3.67	1.21	4.88	1.21	3.03
Malaysia	2.19	0.26	2.45	1.84	8.42
Mongolia	2.35	1.50	3.85	2.45	1.57
Myanmar	5.15	0.00	5.15	10.96	...
Papua New Guinea	3.14	0.11	3.25	5.08	28.55
Philippines	3.38	1.35	4.73	0.23	2.50
Thailand	2.30	0.33	2.63	0.29	6.97
Timor-Leste	2.66	0.10	2.76	0.68	26.60
Vietnam	6.19	11.68	17.87	0.47	0.53
Oceania	41.95	1.21	43.16	7.18	18.92
Total East Asia and the Pacific	**96.06**	**34.57**	**130.63**	**0.58**	**2.78**
EUROPE and CENTRAL ASIA					
Albania	2.78	1.99	4.77	5.48	1.40
Armenia	2.58	2.38	4.96	3.44	1.08
Azerbaijan	2.69	1.49	4.18	2.04	1.81
Belarus	0.00	0.00	0.00	0.00	...
Bosnia and Herzegovina	2.33	5.42	7.75	0.71	0.43
Bulgaria	0.00	0.00	0.00	0.00	...
Croatia	1.75	0.43	2.18	3.96	4.07
Czech Republic	0.00	0.00	0.00	0.00	...
Estonia	0.00	0.00	0.00	0.00	...
Georgia	2.90	2.33	5.23	1.28	1.24
Hungary	0.00	0.00	0.00	0.00	...
Kazakhstan	2.14	0.26	2.40	1.83	8.23
Kyrgyzstan	2.58	0.85	3.43	3.50	3.04
Latvia	0.00	0.00	0.00	0.00	...
Lithuania	0.00	0.00	0.00	0.00	...
Macedonia, FYR	2.53	0.40	2.93	6.98	6.33
Moldova	2.63	0.85	3.48	4.14	3.09
Poland	0.00	0.00	0.00	0.00	...
Romania	0.00	0.00	0.00	0.00	...
Russia	0.00	0.00	0.00	0.00	...

Table 7 *(continues)* ►

Regions and Countries	UN and other Multilateral Organizations	International Financial Institutions (IFIs)	Total Multilateral	Multilateral/ Bilateral Ratio	UN Agencies/ IFIs Ratio
	1	2	3	4	5
Serbia and Montenegro	2.61	4.39	7.00	0.66	0.59
Slovenia	0.00	0.00	0.00	0.00	0.00
Slovakia	0.00	0.00	0.00	0.00	...
Tajikistan	3.14	1.50	4.64	0.81	2.09
Turkey	2.22	0.40	2.62	-0.90	5.55
Turkmenistan	2.11	0.10	2.21	24.56	21.10
Ukraine	0.00	0.00	0.00	0.00	...
Uzbekistan	2.96	0.22	3.18	2.18	13.45
Total Europe and Central Asia	37.95	23.01	60.96	0.39	1.65

LATIN AMERICA and the CARIBBEAN

Regions and Countries	1	2	3	4	5
Argentina	1.23	0.67	1.90	0.53	...
Belize	1.71	0.15	1.86	2.30	11.40
Bolivia	2.42	4.06	6.48	0.42	...
Brazil	2.05	2.66	4.71	0.37	0.77
Chile	1.34	0.83	2.17	0.43	1.61
Colombia	1.96	0.90	2.86	0.26	2.18
Costa Rica	1.47	0.56	2.03	0.54	2.63
Cuba	1.63	0.08	1.71	0.16	...
Dominica	1.98	0.19	2.17	1.09	10.42
Dominican Republic	1.61	0.12	1.73	0.49	13.42
Ecuador	1.86	1.29	3.15	0.38	1.44
El Salvador	1.46	0.51	1.97	0.38	2.86
Grenada	1.50	0.16	1.66	0.15	9.38
Guatemala	2.05	0.29	2.34	0.23	7.07
Guyana	2.09	0.61	2.70	0.28	3.43
Haiti	4.34	0.30	4.64	0.04	14.47
Honduras	2.12	4.28	6.40	0.27	0.50
Jamaica	1.92	0.08	2.00	0.16	24.00
Mexico	1.81	2.05	3.86	0.63	0.88
Nicaragua	2.52	4.76	7.28	0.72	0.53
Panama	1.45	0.49	1.94	1.49	2.96
Paraguay	1.50	0.09	1.59	0.47	16.67
Peru	2.59	0.92	3.51	0.19	2.82
St. Kitts and Nevis	1.47	0.07	1.54	0.85	21.00
St. Lucia	1.97	0.12	2.09	0.90	16.42
St. Vincent and the Grenadines	1.51	0.08	1.59	0.74	18.88
Suriname	1.01	0.08	1.09	0.87	12.63
Trinidad and Tobago	1.61	0.07	1.68	0.80	23.00
Uruguay	1.28	0.20	1.48	0.64	6.40
Venezuela	1.53	0.07	1.60	0.93	21.86
Total Latin America and the Caribbean	54.99	26.74	81.73	0.27	2.06
Regional Programs	279.12	241.71	520.83	3.30	1.15
Total ODA Allocated	989.97	579.16	1,569.13	0.60	1.71
Of which:					
LDCs	233.87	112.29	346.16	0.44	2.08
Low Income Countries	360.41	230.60	591.01	0.53	1.56
Middle Income Countries	199.67	58.13	257.80	0.44	3.43
Countries not Specified	307.38	2.38	309.76	3.18	129.15
Unallocable by Country	0	0	0	0	0
Total ODA	969.97	579.16	1,549.13	0.57	1.67

Table 7

Sources: *CIDA, Statistical Report on ODA 2004-05.*

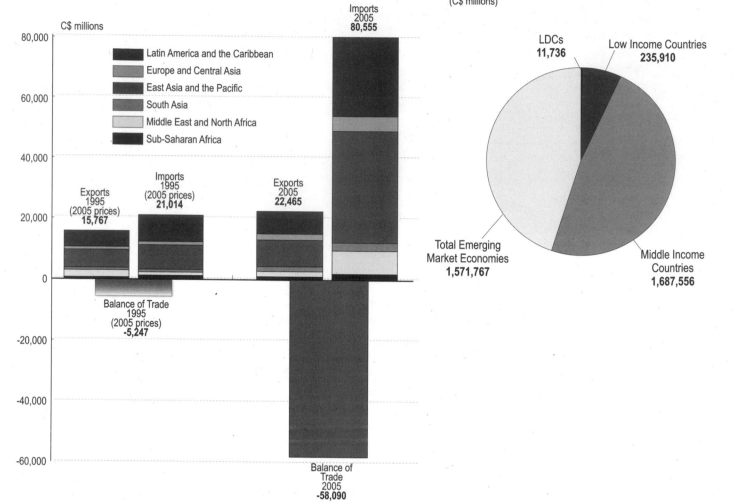

Chart 8.1: Comparative Canadian Balance of Merchandise Trade with Developing Countries (1995 and 2005)

C$ millions

Legend:
- Latin America and the Caribbean
- Europe and Central Asia
- East Asia and the Pacific
- South Asia
- Middle East and North Africa
- Sub-Saharan Africa

Exports 1995 (2005 prices) **15,767**

Imports 1995 (2005 prices) **21,014**

Exports 2005 **22,465**

Imports 2005 **80,555**

Balance of Trade 1995 (2005 prices) **-5,247**

Balance of Trade 2005 **-58,090**

Chart 8.2: Distribution of Trade Partners by Income Group (2005)
(C$ millions)

LDCs **11,736**

Low Income Countries **235,910**

Total Emerging Market Economies **1,571,767**

Middle Income Countries **1,687,556**

Sources: *CIDA, Statistical Report on ODA 2004-05.*

Figure 8.3: Top 10 Export and Import Countries in 2005

	Exports	C$ millions	%		Imports	C$ millions	%
1	China	6,647.19	29.6	1	China	29,515.28	36.6
2	Mexico	3,215.84	14.3	2	Mexico	14,593.89	18.1
3	Brazil	1,061.07	4.7	3	Algeria	4,170.70	5.2
4	India	1,033.83	4.6	4	Brazil	3,142.68	3.9
5	Indonesia	682.74	3.0	5	Malaysia	2,610.82	3.2
6	Russia	512.97	2.3	6	Thailand	1,981.11	2.5
7	Venezuela	512.71	2.3	7	Venezuela	1,829.38	2.3
8	Thailand	428.34	1.9	8	India	1,785.85	2.2
9	Colombia	409.47	1.8	9	Russia	1,728.03	2.2
10	Saudi Arabia	395.24	1.8	10	Saudi Arabia	1,701.35	2.1
	Top 10 Total	**14,899.40**	**66.3**		**Top 10 Total**	**63,059.08**	**78.3**
	Total Canadian Exports	**22,465.76**			**Total Canadian Imports**	**80,555.46**	

Sources: *CIDA, Statistical Report on ODA 2004-05.*

Table 8: Canadian Balance of Merchandise Trade with Developing Countries (1995 and 2005)

(In thousands of Canadian dollars)

Regions and Countries	Total Exports 2005	Total Imports 2005	Balance of Trade 2005	Total Exports 1995 (2005 prices)	Total Imports 1995 (2005 prices)	Balance of Trade 1995 (2005 prices)	Real % Change Per Year Exports 1995-2005	Real % Change Per Year Imports 1995-2005	Total Tariff Revenue Collected 2005	Average Tariff Rate (%) 2005
	1	2	3	4	5	6	7	8	9	10
SUB-SAHARAN AFRICA										
Angola	71,366	332,668	-261,302	4,292	11,506	-7,214	32.5	40.0	0.32	0.00
Benin	3,412	8	3,404	7,367	28	7,339	-7.4	-11.6	0.00	0.04
Botswana	6,165	997	5,168	5,946	142	5,804	0.4	21.5	33.72	3.38
Burkina Faso	14,194	215	13,979	2,900	76	2,824	17.2	11.0	0.65	0.30
Burundi	2,530	381	2,149	1,860	251	1,610	3.1	4.3	2.17	0.57
Cameroon	14,869	10,049	4,820	18,398	9,883	8,514	-2.1	0.2	28.54	0.28
Cape Verde	420	20	400	33	..	..	29.0	...	0.26	1.27
Central African Republic	667	210	457	248	168	80	10.4	2.3	0.38	0.18
Chad	5,626	13	5,613	1,602	102	1,501	13.4	-18.6	0.38	2.94
Comoros	830	96	734	8	574	-566	59.7	-16.4	0.06	0.06
Congo, Dem. Rep.	10,940	270	10,670	40,788	42,365	-1,577	-12.3	-39.7	2.81	1.04
Congo, Rep.	14,112	1,324	12,788	921	883	37	31.4	4.1	13.31	1.01
Côte d'Ivoire	10,628	134,189	-123,561	13,579	27,005	-13,426	-2.4	17.4	110.20	0.08
Equatorial Guinea	2,035	247,269	-245,234	187	3	184	27.0	211.8	1.27	0
Eritrea	1,206	37	1,169	..	..	..	...	...	0.34	0.92
Ethiopia	25,788	8,647	17,141	10,463	7,101	3,362	9.4	2.0	6.97	0.08
Gabon	10,259	1,363	8,896	2,054	473	1,581	17.5	11.2	0.10	0.01
Gambia	254	37	217	142	19	123	6.0	6.9	0.57	1.51
Ghana	91,377	29,057	62,320	33,523	11,838	21,685	10.5	9.4	56.05	0.19
Guinea	7,523	29,113	-21,590	4,426	12,798	-8,371	5.4	8.6	1.58	0
Guinea-Bissau	38	3	35	80	..	..	-7.2	...	0	2
Kenya	37,689	16,011	21,678	18,713	18,234	479	7.3	-1.3	603.17	3.80
Lesotho	297	14,539	-14,242	215	3,577	-3,361	3.3	15.1	182.05	1.25
Liberia	3,504	13,414	-9,910	458	249	210	22.6	49.0	1.41	0
Madagascar	743	14,340	-13,597	974	13,392	-12,418	-2.7	0.7	304.28	2.12
Malawi	2,749	1,395	1,354	7,153	2,398	4,755	-9.1	-5.3	27.17	2.05
Mali	6,324	216	6,108	10,754	7,777	2,977	-5.2	-30.1	2.90	1.35
Mauritania	2,852	592	2,260	2,589	175	2,414	1.0	13.0	9.03	1.53
Mauritius	1,890	5,773	-3,883	3,967	21,145	-17,178	-7.1	-12.2	488.72	8.47
Mozambique	16,494	786	15,708	19,299	238	19,061	-1.6	12.7	1.82	0.74
Namibia	1,334	56,279	-54,945	3,265	42,348	-39,083	-8.6	2.9	3.81	0.01
Niger	5,066	3,065	2,001	1,385	8,463	-7,078	13.9	-9.7	10.01	0.33
Nigeria	90,775	176,724	-85,949	28,663	555,088	-526,425	12.2	-10.8	4.84	0
Rwanda	2,273	360	1,913	4,056	138	3,918	-5.6	10.1	0.26	0.07
São Tomé and Principe	42	115	-73	8	9	-1	18.5	29.7	0.39	0.34
Senegal	22,654	641	22,013	11,742	983	10,759	6.8	-4.2	5.08	0.79
Seychelles	839	3,096	-2,257	170	547	-376	17.3	18.9	7.55	0.24
Sierra Leone	4,419	2,428	1,991	649	4,974	-4,325	21.1	-6.9	40.12	1.65
Somalia	1,262	110	1,152	1,347	24	1,324	-0.7	16.6	2.94	2.38
South Africa	400,632	697,930	-297,298	356,711	395,720	-39,008	1.2	5.8	3,669.19	0.56
Sudan	110,252	80,434	29,818	2,654	166	2,488	45.2	85.6	0.69	0
Swaziland	2,675	3,858	-1,183	34	976	-942	54.7	14.7	151.50	3.93
Tanzania	29,430	159,214	-129,784	14,236	3,621	10,615	7.5	46.0	27.77	0.02
Togo	10,161	546	9,615	1,636	43,475	-41,839	20.0	-35.5	0.81	0.15
Uganda	9,570	3,122	6,448	12,434	8,088	4,346	-2.6	-9.1	47.92	1.54
Zambia	15,373	429	14,944	10,504	3,832	6,673	3.9	-19.7	1.04	0.24
Zimbabwe	5,706	2,234	3,472	17,599	9,627	7,972	-10.7	-13.6	16.95	0.86
Total Sub-Saharan Africa	1,079,244	2,053,617	-974,373	680,032	1,270,475	-590,442	4.7	4.9	5,871.16	0.29
MIDDLE EAST and NORTH AFRICA										
Algeria	220,066	4,170,699	-3,950,633	583,017	329,557	253,460	-9.3	28.9	4.41	0
Djibouti	1,980	34	1,946	2,142	..	..	-0.8	...	0.05	0.15
Egypt	304,541	142,035	162,506	143,846	17,876	125,969	7.8	23.0	4,193.18	2.96
Iran	256,154	44,470	211,684	471,941	115,529	356,411	-5.9	-9.1	411.17	0.93
Iraq	72,519	1,206,427	-1,133,908	244	68	176	76.7	165.9	1.90	0
Jordan	116,694	8,746	107,948	13,637	1,097	12,540	23.9	23.1	1,160.33	13.27

Table 8 *(continues)* ▶

Regions and Countries	Total Exports 2005	Total Imports 2005	Balance of Trade 2005	Total Exports 1995 (2005 prices)	Total Imports 1995 (2005 prices)	Balance of Trade 1995 (2005 prices)	Real % Change Per Year Exports 1995-2005	Real % Change Per Year Imports 1995-2005	Total Tariff Revenue Collected 2005	Average Tariff Rate (%) 2005
	1	2	3	4	5	6	7	8	9	10
Lebanon	43,260	10,851	32,409	52,569	4,062	48,507	-1.9	10.3	174.67	1.73
Libya	73,869	92,289	-18,420	76,788	..	..	-0.4	...	..	..
Morocco	73,869	150,775	-76,906	207,192	66,749	140,443	-9.8	8.5	2,333.40	1.55
Oman	19,583	4,659	14,924	26,535	947	25,588	-3.0	17.3	..	..
Saudi Arabia	395,243	1,701,346	-1,306,103	557,452	476,213	81,240	-3.4	13.6	..	..
Syria	63,951	21,766	42,185	23,033	25,911	-2,878	10.8	-1.7	313.53	1.44
Tunisia	38,221	33,164	5,057	115,694	4,142	111,552	-10.5	23.1	2,447.31	7.41
West Bank and Gaza	...	...	...	...	...	...	...	...	..	..
Yemen	37,592	187	37,405	20,791	53	20,738	6.1	13.4	0.49	0.26
Total Middle East and North Africa	**1,717,542**	**7,587,448**	**-5,869,906**	**2,294,881**	**1,042,205**	**1,252,676**	**-2.9**	**22.0**	**11,040.44**	**0.15**
SOUTH ASIA										
Afghanistan	17,882	461	17,421	7,180	402	6,778	9.6	1.4	11.97	2.60
Bangladesh	98,751	490,102	-391,351	99,109	95,766	3,342	-0.0	17.7	5,535.50	1.13
Bhutan	51	16	35	19	0	19	10.6	...	0.02	0.12
India	1,033,829	1,785,849	-752,020	477,153	513,742	-36,589	8.0	13.3	101,931.24	5.71
Maldives	6,831	393	6,438	405	40	366	32.6	25.7	7.08	1.80
Nepal	5,851	12,635	-6,784	4,968	4,725	243	1.7	10.3	347.32	2.75
Pakistan	309,436	247,667	61,769	135,313	193,902	-58,589	8.6	2.5	29,872.44	12.06
Sri Lanka	120,634	109,135	11,499	23,257	72,506	-49,249	17.9	4.2	12,076.56	11.08
Total South Asia	**1,593,265**	**2,646,258**	**-1,052,993**	**747,404**	**881,083**	**-133,679**	**7.9**	**11.6**	**149,782.14**	**5.66**
EAST ASIA and the PACIFIC										
Cambodia	2,336	131,485	-129,149	4,463	706	3,757	-6.3	68.7	2,824.43	2.15
China	6,647,189	29,515,276	-22,868,087	3,618,311	4,402,378	-784,067	6.3	21.0	1,183,718.06	4.01
Indonesia	682,736	955,864	-273,128	680,158	566,713	113,445	0.0	5.4	40,884.93	4.28
Korea, Dem. Rep.	19,831	49	19,782	1,382	724	658	30.5	-23.6	163,954	3
Laos	765	6,987	-6,222	627	2,568	-1,940	2.0	10.5	109.61	1.57
Malaysia	346,547	2,610,822	-2,264,275	588,495	1,470,605	-882,110	-5.2	5.9	27,086.22	1.04
Mongolia	13,666	157,852	-144,186	..	..	..	...	...	497.25	0.32
Myanmar	367	11,081	-10,714	1,230	13,446	-12,216	-11.4	-1.9	..	..
Papua New Guinea	5,677	2,852	2,825	5,269	1,735	3,535	0.7	5.1	0.83	0.03
Philippines	341,204	921,320	-580,116	357,330	472,012	-114,683	-0.5	6.9	21,013.12	2.29
Thailand	428,343	1,981,111	-1,552,768	612,069	961,983	-349,914	-3.5	7.5	56,569.08	2.86
Timor-Leste	92	799	-707	..	..	..	...	...	0.08	0
Vietnam	188,878	559,025	-370,147	32,374	72,213	-39,840	19.3	22.7	49,020.24	8.77
Oceania	12,097	14,184	-2,087	5,405	29,260	-23,855	8.4	-7.0	0.00	0.00
Total East Asia and the Pacific	**8,689,728**	**36,868,707**	**-28,178,979**	**5,907,113**	**7,994,343**	**-2,087,230**	**3.9**	**16.5**	**1,545,677.54**	**4.19**
EUROPE and CENTRAL ASIA										
Albania	5,168	1,263	3,905	2,221	1,018	1,203	8.8	2.2	..	..
Armenia	4,665	1,765	2,900	566	118	448	23.5	31.1	188.97	11.34
Azerbaijan	13,881	456	13,425	552	55	497	38.1	23.5	1.61	0.35
Belarus	7,845	20,000	-12,155	837	8,011	-7,174	25.1	9.6	547.65	2.74
Bosnia and Herzegovina	2,230	2,727	-497	268	43	225	23.6	51.5	..	..
Bulgaria	45,498	89,287	-43,789	6,466	49,247	-42,781	21.5	6.1	5,663.68	6.44
Croatia	18,277	25,376	-7,099	17,476	14,140	3,335	0.5	6.0	1,255	5.08
Czech Republic	130,678	303,772	-173,094	69,283	71,977	-2,694	6.6	15.5	4,121.48	1.39
Estonia	25,951	51,097	-25,146	7,163	11,394	-4,231	13.7	16.2	742.40	1.46
Georgia	7,202	47,639	-40,437	646	445	201	27.3	59.6	19.65	0.04
Hungary	50,700	219,965	-169,265	44,993	42,853	2,141	1.2	17.8	4,334.91	2.00
Kazakhstan	100,930	36,825	64,105	2,291	11,274	-8,982	46.0	12.6	37.80	0.10
Kyrgyzstan	3,399	21,483	-18,084	9,878	996	8,882	-10.1	35.9	51.76	0.24
Latvia	34,407	14,074	20,333	5,546	5,854	-308	20.0	9.2	789.96	5.77
Lithuania	28,035	508,542	-480,507	3,393	23,460	-20,067	23.5	36.0	2,561.34	0.50
Macedonia, FYR	9,203	4,090	5,113	2,145	2,563	-418	15.7	4.8	452.94	12.99
Moldova	898	20,005	-19,107	1,296	8,891	-7,595	-3.6	8.4	458.92	2.31
Poland	228,914	532,649	-303,735	127,410	114,409	13,000	6.0	16.6	15,655.84	3.00
Romania	149,260	209,281	-60,021	22,800	56,779	-33,979	20.7	13.9	8,916.75	4.28

Table 8 (continues) ▶

Regions and Countries	Total Exports 2005	Total Imports 2005	Balance of Trade 2005	Total Exports 1995 (2005 prices)	Total Imports 1995 (2005 prices)	Balance of Trade 1995 (2005 prices)	Real % Change Per Year Exports 1995-2005	Real % Change Per Year Imports 1995-2005	Total Tariff Revenue Collected 2005	Average Tariff Rate (%) 2005
	1	2	3	4	5	6	7	8	9	10
Russia	512,973	1,728,027	-1,215,054	209,181	472,731	-263,550	9.4	13.8	2,813.94	0.17
Serbia and Montenegro	7,390	13,272	-5,882	..	..	..	...	...	..	..
Slovak Republic	18,414	122,048	-103,634	15,415	28,091	-12,676	1.8	15.8	5,809.30	4.79
Tajikistan	1,594	94	1,500	140	63	77	27.6	4.1	11.68	12.34
Turkey	450,216	637,314	-187,098	308,562	142,444	166,118	3.9	16.2	29,620.38	4.65
Turkmenistan	29,040	3,881	25,159	1,379	6	1,373	35.6	92.0	239.02	6.16
Ukraine	72,581	296,208	-223,627	47,559	16,358	31,201	4.3	33.6	1,563.29	0.53
Uzbekistan	8,549	56,589	-48,040	1,258	5,853	-4,595	21.1	25.5	81.92	0.14
Total Europe and Central Asia	1,967,898	4,967,729	-2,999,831	908,724	1,089,072	-100,340	8.0	16.4	85,940.19	1.73
LATIN AMERICA and the CARIBBEAN										
Argentina	154,551	452,545	-297,994	254,907	161,222	93,685	-4.9	10.9	1,964.63	0.47
Belize	6,347	9,650	-3,303	4,651	11,126	-6,476	3.2	-1.4	46.31	0.48
Bolivia	13,937	24,814	-10,877	11,700	21,248	-9,548	1.8	1.6	116.64	0.47
Brazil	1,061,073	3,142,683	-2,081,610	1,408,193	985,131	423,062	-2.8	12.3	39,407.32	1.27
Chile	379,647	1,663,035	-1,283,388	405,857	264,667	141,190	-0.7	20.2	809.44	0.05
Colombia	409,474	582,618	-173,144	384,711	353,035	31,676	0.6	5.1	9,975.20	1.71
Costa Rica	80,353	353,169	-272,816	49,291	154,789	-105,498	5.0	8.6	2,002.90	0.57
Cuba	319,995	552,861	-232,866	283,438	304,532	-21,094	1.2	6.1	228.50	0.04
Dominica	4,584	774	3,810	2,078	2,287	-209	8.2	-10.3	18.43	2.38
Dominican Republic	134,027	120,002	14,025	83,786	67,509	16,276	4.8	5.9	5,697.76	4.88
Ecuador	151,599	114,437	37,162	82,420	13,096	69,324	6.3	24.2	2,892.20	2.53
El Salvador	53,449	56,057	-2,608	24,882	41,431	-16,549	7.9	3.1	4,679.32	8.35
Grenada	6,955	943	6,012	4,164	620	3,544	5.3	4.3	3.36	0.36
Guatemala	167,598	206,522	-38,924	45,530	88,615	-43,085	13.9	8.8	5,218.40	2.53
Guyana	15,329	147,206	-131,877	8,949	162,499	-153,550	5.5	-1.0	10.89	0.01
Haiti	30,375	25,104	5,271	30,765	2,762	28,002	-0.1	24.7	2,216.12	8.83
Honduras	40,840	129,857	-89,017	21,623	47,259	-25,636	6.6	10.6	11,400.51	8.86
Jamaica	144,300	393,022	-248,722	106,213	189,990	-83,777	3.1	7.5	440.38	0.12
Mexico	3,215,835	14,593,893	-11,378,058	1,221,910	5,078,540	-3,856,630	10.2	11.1	18,374.14	0.13
Nicaragua	18,736	54,437	-35,701	8,770	10,005	-1,234	7.9	18.5	1,013.30	1.88
Panama	52,005	44,667	7,338	50,519	21,158	29,361	0.3	7.8	61.28	0.14
Paraguay	8,513	15,269	-6,756	13,047	3,373	9,675	-4.2	16.3	66.23	0.43
Peru	242,888	1,357,850	-1,114,962	150,601	91,207	59,394	4.9	31.0	4,845.57	0.36
St. Kitts and Nevis	5,376	7,873	-2,497	2,745	2,823	-78	7.0	10.8	154.11	1.96
St. Lucia	7,020	512	6,508	13,760	1,181	12,579	-6.5	-8.0	5.26	1.03
St. Vincent and the Grenadines	6,972	124	6,848	3,093	182	2,911	8.5	-3.8	0.02	0.02
Suriname	10,038	184,361	-174,323	4,918	329	4,588	7.4	88.3	2.62	0.00
Trinidad and Tobago	141,301	237,217	-95,916	104,020	18,025	85,994	3.1	29.4	67.17	0.03
Uruguay	22,257	130,820	-108,563	27,320	23,395	3,924	-2.0	18.8	12,657.45	9.72
Venezuela	512,708	1,829,375	-1,316,667	414,970	614,584	-199,614	2.1	11.5	779.60	0.04
Total Latin America and the Caribbean	7,418,082	26,431,697	-19,013,615	5,228,830	8,736,622	-3,507,792	3.6	11.7	125,155.06	0.47
Total Developing Countries	22,465,759	80,555,456	-58,089,697	15,766,984	21,013,800	-5,246,816	3.6	14.4	1,923,466.53	2.39
Of which:										0.00
LDCs	593,075	1,593,218	-1,000,143	348,188	297,031	51,157	5.5	18.3	11,736.10	0.74
Low Income Countries	3,157,404	5,873,019	-2,715,615	1,831,191	2,304,887	-473,696	5.6	9.8	235,910.37	4.02
Middle Income Countries	19,308,355	74,682,437	-55,374,082	13,935,793	18,708,912	-4,773,120	3.3	14.8	1,687,556.16	2.26
Total Other Countries (excluding US)	41,831,168	90,148,075	-48,316,907	66,260,408	62,634,432	3,625,976	-4.5	3.7	860,067.13	0.95
Total Emerging Market Economies	17,534,678	65,653,933	-48,119,255	11,765,367	17,121,852	-5,356,485	4.1	14.4	1,571,767.46	2.39
United States	343,311,370	208,873,078	134,438,292	190,173,511	130,334,014	59,839,497	6.1	4.8	279,231.85	0.13
Total World	407,608,297	379,576,609	28,031,688	272,200,902	213,982,246	58,218,656	4.1	5.9	3,062,765.52	0.81

Note: Bold-italicized countries are not included in Canadian ODA totals (see Technical Notes).

Sources: *Statistics Canada, Exports by Country January-December 2006, Imports by Country January-December 2006, Exports by Country January-December 1997, Imports by Country January-December 1997.*
Finance Canada, International Trade Policy Division, 2007.

Figure 9.1: Top 10 FDI Countries in 2006

	Countries	C$ millions	%	Region
1	Hungary	9,938	7.58	Europe and Central Asia
2	Brazil	8,244	6.29	Latin America and the Caribbean
3	Chile	5,171	3.94	Latin America and the Caribbean
4	Mexico	4,369	3.33	Latin America and the Caribbean
5	Argentina	3,981	3.04	Latin America and the Caribbean
6	Indonesia	3,127	2.38	South Asia
7	Peru	2,910	2.22	Latin America and the Caribbean
8	Dominican Republic	1,847	1.41	Latin America and the Caribbean
9	China	1,563	1.19	East Asia and the Pacific
10	Thailand	972	0.74	East Asia and the Pacific
	Top 10 Total	**42,122**	**32.12**	
	Total Canadian FDI	**131,152**		

Figure 9.2: Countries for which Canadian FDI Data is Kept Confidential

	Number of countries		
Regions	Data kept confidential	Total	%
	1	2	3
Sub-Saharan Africa	39	47	83.0
Middle East and North Africa	13	15	86.7
South Asia	5	9	55.6
East Asia and the Pacific	6	15	40.0
Europe and Central Asia	15	28	53.6
Latin America and the Caribbean	23	31	74.2
Total Developing Countries	**101**	**145**	**69.7**

Note: *For an explanation of this Figure, please read Technical Notes*

Chart 9.3: Stock of Canadian Foreign Investment Abroad by Income Group and Region (2006)

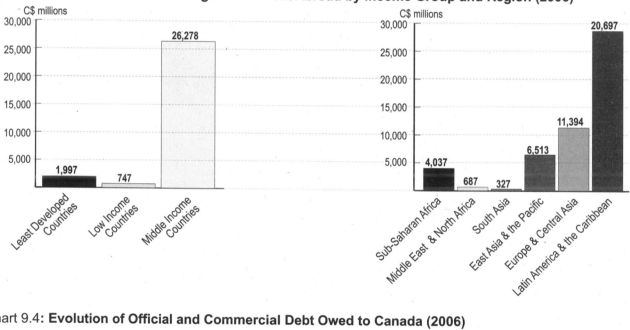

Chart 9.4: Evolution of Official and Commercial Debt Owed to Canada (2006)

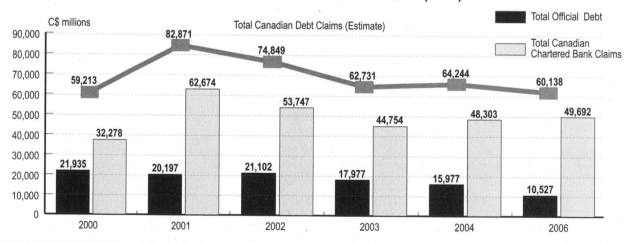

Sources: *Finance Canada, International Finance and Economics Analysis Division.*
Bank of Canada, Banking and Financial Statistics Canada, Balance of Payments Division.
Statistics Canada, Balance of Payments Division.

Table 9: Finance and Investment Flows Between Canada and Developing Countries (2006)

(In millions of Canadian dollars)

Regions and Countries	Public or Official Debt			Private or Commercial Debt	Total Canadian Debt Claims (Estimate) 31-Mar-2007	Stock of Foreign Direct Investment Abroad 2006	Stock of Foreign Direct Investment in Canada 2006
	Non-Concessional 31-Mar-2007	Concessional 31-Mar-2007	Total Official Debt 31-Mar-2007	Total Canadian Chartered Bank Claims 31-Mar-2007			
	1	2	3	4	5	6	7
SUB-SAHARAN AFRICA							
Angola	..	..	..	..	..	X	X
Benin	..	..	..	..	..	X	X
Botswana	..	..	..	..	..	X	X
Burkina Faso	..	..	..	..	..	X	X
Burundi	..	..				..	..
Cameroon	0.1	0.0	0.1	..	0.1	X	X
Cape Verde	..	..	..		..	..	..
Central African Republic	..	..	..	..	..	X	X
Chad	..	..	..	..	..	..	..
Comoros	..	..	..	..	..	..	..
Congo, Dem. Rep.	46.5	0	46.5	..	46.5	X	X
Congo, Rep.	36.5	0	36.5	..	36.5	X	X
Côte d'Ivoire	144.2	0	144.2	..	144.2	X	X
Equatorial Guinea	..	..	..	..	..	..	..
Eritrea	..	..	..	..	..	X	X
Ethiopia	0	0	0	..	0.1	X	X
Gabon	34.8	10	44.4	..	44.4	X	X
Gambia	..	..	..	..	..	X	X
Ghana	0.3	0	0.3	..	0.3	X	X
Guinea	..	..	..	..	..	X	X
Guinea-Bissau	..	..				X	X
Kenya	33.0	6.8	39.8	..	39.8	X	X
Lesotho	..	..	..	..	..	X	X
Liberia	..	..	..	..	..	X	X
Madagascar	..	..	..	..	..	X	X
Malawi	..	..	..	..	..	X	X
Mali	..	..	..	..	..	X	X
Mauritania	..	..	..	..	..	X	X
Mauritius	..	..			..	X	X
Mozambique	19.5	0	19.5	..	19.5	X	X
Namibia	..	..	..	..	..	X	X
Niger	..	..	..	..	..	X	X
Nigeria	31.4	0	31.4	..	31.4	X	X
Rwanda	..	..	..	..	..	X	X
São Tomé and Principe	..	..			..	..	..
Senegal	7.2	0	7.2	..	7.2	X	X
Seychelles	..	..	..	..	..	X	X
Sierra Leone	..	..	..	..	..	X	X
Somalia	..	..	..			..	..
South Africa	49.8	0	49.8	846	895.8	774	1250
Sudan	10.7	0	10.7	..	10.7	X	X
Swaziland	..	..	..	..	..	X	X
Tanzania	..	..	..	..	..	X	X
Togo	..	..	..	..	..	X	X
Uganda	..	..	..	..	..	X	X
Zambia	..	..	..	..	..	X	X
Zimbabwe	..	..	..	..	..	27	X
Sub-Saharan Africa unspecified	..	..	..	291	291.0	3,236	11
Total Sub-Saharan Africa	**414**	**16**	**430**	**1,137**	**1,567.5**	**4,037**	**1,261**
MIDDLE EAST and NORTH AFRICA							
Algeria	244	34	278	229	506.8	278	X
Djibouti	..	..	..		..	..	..
Egypt	203	55	259	..	258.7	158	X
Iran	24	0	24	..	24.3	X	X
Iraq	304	0	304	..	304.4	X	X
Jordan	27	0	27	..	26.8	X	X

Table 9 *(continues)* ▶

Regions and Countries	Public or Official Debt			Private or Commercial Debt		Stock of Foreign Direct Investment Abroad	Stock of Foreign Direct Investment in Canada
	Non-Concessional 31-Mar-2007	Concessional 31-Mar-2007	Total Official Debt 31-Mar-2007	Total Canadian Chartered Bank Claims 31-Mar-2005	Total Canadian Debt Claims (Estimate) 31-Mar-2005	2006	2006
	1	2	3	4	5	6	7
Lebanon	0	0	0	..	0.1	x	x
Libya	..	..	..	..	..	x	x
Morocco	1	102	103	..	102.6	x	x
Oman	96	0	96	..	95.9	x	x
Saudi Arabia	2	0	2	275	276.6	x	x
Syria	..	..	..	..	..	x	x
Tunisia	10	57	67	..	67.0	x	x
West Bank and Gaza	..	..	..	..	..	..	..
Yemen	..	..	..	..	..	251	x
Middle East and North Africa unspecified	..	..	..	1,908	1,908.0	0	0
Total Middle East and North Africa	**911**	**248**	**1,159**	**2,412**	**3,571.2**	**687**	**0**
SOUTH ASIA							
Afghanistan	..	..	..	..	..	..	..
Bangladesh	..	..	..	..	..	x	x
Bhutan	..	..	..	..	..	..	..
India	713	54	767	1,720	2,486.9	327	201
Maldives	1	0	1	..	0.9	..	..
Nepal	..	..	..	..	..	x	x
Pakistan	121	448	569	..	568.8	x	x
Sri Lanka	0	92	92	..	92.1	x	x
South Asia unspecified	..	..	0	..	0.0	..	..
Total South Asia	**835**	**594**	**1,429**	**1,720**	**3,148.7**	**327**	**201**
EAST ASIA and the PACIFIC							
Cambodia	..	..	..	..	..	x	x
China	1,182	533	1,715	1,205	2,919.5	1,563	1,297
Indonesia	467	223	691	..	690.7	3,127	x
Korea, Dem. Rep.	..	..	..	..	..	x	x
Laos	..	..	..	..	..	..	..
Malaysia	19	2	20	1,428	1,448.1	568	118
Mongolia	0	0	0	..	..	x	x
Myanmar	0	8	8	..	8.3	x	x
Papua New Guinea	..	..	..	..	..	x	x
Philippines	179	2	181	238	418.5	141	1
Thailand	52	26	77	313	390.1	972	2
Timor-Leste	..	..	..	..	..	..	..
Vietnam	71	0	71	..	70.6	142	x
Oceania	..	..	..	..	..	..	..
East Asia and the Pacific unspecified	..	..	..	746	746.0	..	..
Total East Asia and the Pacific	**1,969**	**793**	**2,762**	**3,930**	**6,691.8**	**6,513**	**1,418**
EUROPE and CENTRAL ASIA							
Albania	..	..	..	..	..	x	x
Armenia	..	..	..	..	..	x	x
Azerbaijan	..	..	..	..	..	..	..
Belarus	..	..	..	..	..	..	..
Bosnia and Herzegovina	5	0	5	..	4.8	..	..
Bulgaria	..	..	..	..	..	x	x
Croatia	13	0	13	..	12.7	x	x
Czech Republic	..	..	..	..	..	189	x
Estonia	..	..	..	..	..	x	x
Georgia	..	..	..	..	..	x	x
Hungary	..	..	..	..	..	9,938	x
Kazakhstan	81	0	81	..	..	x	x
Kyrgyzstan	..	..	0	..	0.0	x	x
Latvia	..	..	..	..	..	x	x
Lithuania	..	..	..	..	..	x	x
Macedonia, FYR	..	..	..	..	..	0	0
Moldova	..	..	..	..	..	0	0

Table 9 *(continues)* ▶

Regions and Countries	Public or Official Debt			Private or Commercial Debt			
	Non-Concessional 31-Mar-2007	Concessional 31-Mar-2007	Total Official Debt 31-Mar-2007	Total Canadian Chartered Bank Claims 31-Mar-2005	Total Canadian Debt Claims (Estimate) 31-Mar-2005	Stock of Foreign Direct Investment Abroad 2006	Stock of Foreign Direct Investment in Canada 2006
	1	2	3	4	5	6	7
Poland	..	..	..	148	148.0	451	x
Romania	..	..	..	..	..	16	x
Russia	..	..	..	50	50.0	x	x
Serbia and Montenegro	135	0	135	..	134.9	..	..
Slovak Republic	..	..	..	..	..	x	x
Tajikistan	..	..	..	..	..	x	x
Turkey	60	112	171	..	171.1	800	x
Turkmenistan	..	..	..	..	..	x	x
Ukraine	1	0	1	..	0.7	x	x
Uzbekistan	..	..	..	..	..	..	..
Europe and Central Asia unspecified	..	..	..	993	993.0	..	..
Total Europe and Central Asia	**293**	**112**	**405**	**1,191**	**1,515.2**	**11,394**	**0**
LATIN AMERICA and the CARIBBEAN							
Argentina	241	0	241	139	379.8	3,981	5
Belize	..	..	..	..	..	x	x
Bolivia	10	1	11	..	10.9	87	x
Brazil	501	0	501	1,744	2,244.8	8,244	9,405
Chile	524	1	525	4,078	4,602.9	5,171	x
Colombia	7	0	7	..	6.9	453	1
Costa Rica	0	0	0	..	0.1	448	x
Cuba	24	10	34	..	33.9	x	x
Dominica	..	..	0	..	..	x	x
Dominican Republic	259	4	263	..	262.8	1,847	x
Ecuador	44	5	48	..	48.3	46	x
El Salvador	18	0	18	..	17.8	x	x
Grenada	..	..	..	..	..	x	x
Guatemala	2	2	4	..	4.2	x	x
Guyana	..	..	..	..	..	41	x
Haiti	28	0	28	..	28.2	x	x
Honduras	1	0	1	..	0.7	101	x
Jamaica	68	7	75	..	75.0	x	x
Mexico	1,783	0	1,783	22,289	24,071.7	4,369	277
Nicaragua	..	..	..	..	..	x	x
Panama	15	0	15	721	735.7	149	55
Paraguay	0	0	0	..	0.2	x	x
Peru	239	0	239	331	569.5	2,910	x
St. Kitts and Nevis	..	..	..	..	..	0	0
St. Lucia	..	..	..	..	..	x	x
St. Vincent and the Grenadines	..	..	..	..	..	0	0
Suriname	..	..	..	..	..	x	x
Trinidad and Tobago	91	0	91	1,480	1,571.0	276	x
Uruguay	..	..	..	..	..	x	x
Venezuela	459	0	459	367	826.4	574	x
Latin America and the Caribbean unspecified	..	..	0	8,153	8,153.0	..	..
Total Latin America and the Caribbean	**4,312**	**29**	**4,342**	**39,302**	**43,643.8**	**28,697**	**9,743**
Total Developing Countries	**8,735**	**1,792**	**10,527**	**49,692**	**60,138.2**	**131,152**	**27,075**
Of which:							
LDCs	113	8	121	130	251.1	1,997	2,248
Low Income Countries	1,729	740	2,470	3,210	5,679.0	747	201
Middle Income Countries	7,005	1,052	8,058	9,110	17,167.6	26,277	43,445
Unspecified Countries	0	0	0	12,091	12,091.0	3,236	11

Note: *An X indicates that data is confidential.*

Sources: *Finance Canada, International Finance and Economics Analysis Division.*
Bank of Canada, Banking and Financial Statistics Canada, Balance of Payments Division.
Statistics Canada, Balance of Payments Division.

Chart 10.1 Evolution Over Time of Permanent Residents by Category (1980 to 2006)

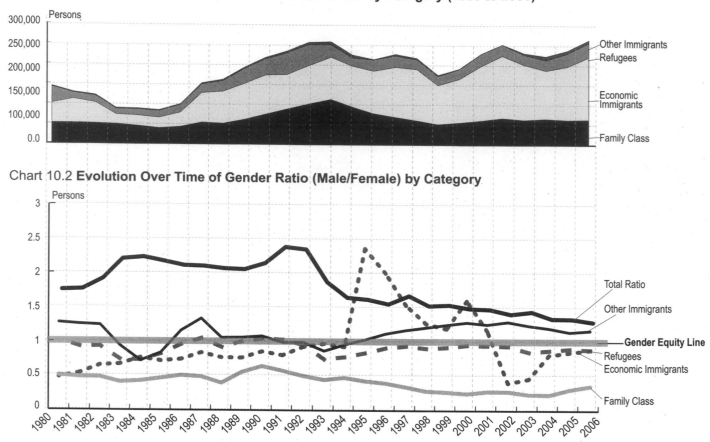

Other Immigrants
Refugees
Economic Immigrants
Family Class

Chart 10.2 Evolution Over Time of Gender Ratio (Male/Female) by Category

Total Ratio
Other Immigrants
Gender Equity Line
Refugees
Economic Immigrants
Family Class

Chart 10.3 Permanent Residents in Canada (2006)
Chart 10.3.a: By Region and Gender

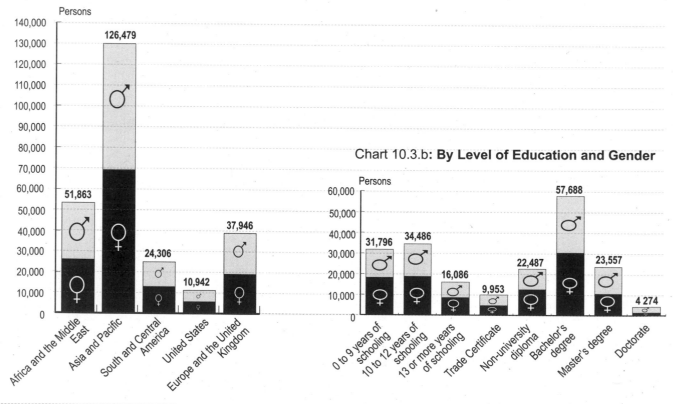

Chart 10.3.b: By Level of Education and Gender

Source: *Citizenship and Immigration Canada, Facts and Figures 2006: Immigration Overview, Permanent and Temporary Residents.*

Chart 10.4: Gender Ratios Among Permanent Residents in 2006

Chart 10.4.a: By Source Region

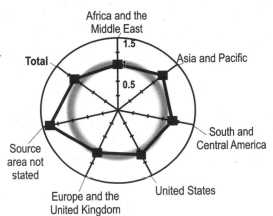

Chart 10.4.b: By Level of Education

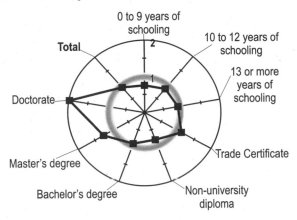

Chart 10.5: Gender Ratios of Foreign Workers by Occupational Skill Level Over Time (1997 to 2006)

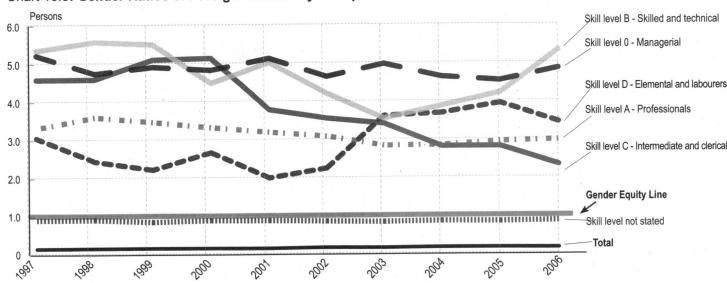

Chart 10.6: Inflow of Foreign Workers, Students and Humanitarian Population Over Time

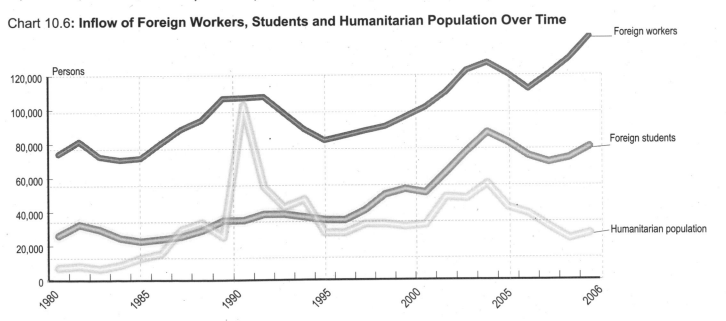

Source: *Citizenship and Immigration Canada, Facts and Figures 2006: Immigration Overview, Permanent and Temporary Residents.*

Map 10.1: **Permanent Residents Flow Into Canada (2006)**

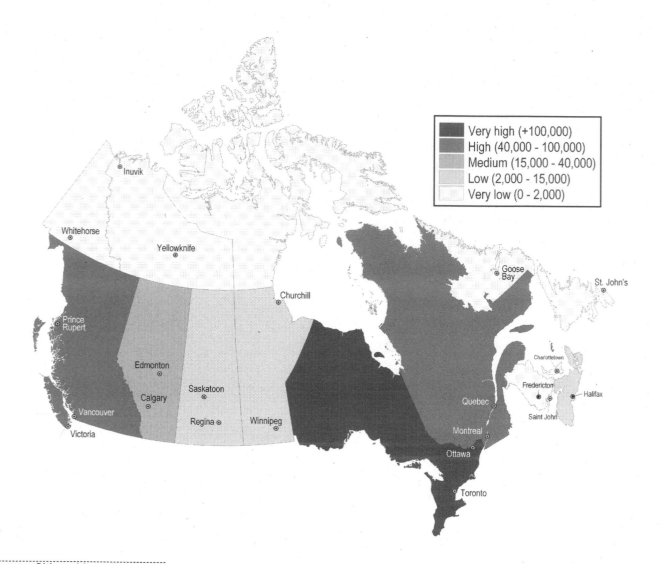

Very high (+100,000)
High (40,000 - 100,000)
Medium (15,000 - 40,000)
Low (2,000 - 15,000)
Very low (0 - 2,000)

Source: *Citizenship and Immigration Canada, Facts and Figures 2006: Immigration Overview, Permanent and Temporary Residents.*

Table 10: **Permanent and Temporary Residents in Canada (1997, 2001 and 2006)**

Table 10.1: **Flow of Temporary Workers by Occupational Skill Level and Gender in Canada (1997, 2001 and 2006)**

Occupational skill level	1997 ♀		1997 ♂		Ratio ♂/♀	2001 ♀		2001 ♂		Ratio ♂/♀	2006 ♀		2006 ♂		Ratio ♂/♀
	#	%	#	%		#	%	#	%		#	%	#	%	
Skill level 0 - Managerial	461	2.2	2,406	4.4	5.22	509	1.7	2,616	3.7	5.14	645	1.7	3,142	4.2	4.87
Skill level A - Professionals	6,093	29.7	20,205	36.8	3.32	7,518	25.6	24,099	33.8	3.21	5,656	15.0	16,994	22.7	3.00
Skill level B - Skilled and technical	1,705	8.3	9,120	16.6	5.35	2,354	8.0	11,849	16.6	5.03	2,265	6.0	12,102	16.2	5.34
Skill level C - Intermediate and clerical	3,123	15.2	14,324	26.1	4.59	5,307	18.1	20,187	28.3	3.80	10,119	26.8	23,800	31.8	2.35
Skill level D - Elemental and labourers	263	1.3	806	1.5	3.06	302	1.0	608	0.9	2.01	795	2.1	2,758	3.7	3.47
Skill level not stated	8,907	43.3	8,097	14.7	0.91	13,340	45.5	11,917	16.7	0.89	18,263	48.4	16,118	21.5	0.88
Total	20,552	100.0	54,958	100.0	2.67	29,330	100.0	71,276	100.0	2.43	37,743	100.0	74,914	100.0	1.98

Source: *Citizenship and Immigration Canada, Facts and Figures 2006: Immigration Overview, Permanent and Temporary Residents.*

Table 10 *(continues)* ▶

Table 10.2: Permanent Residents by Source Area and Gender in Canada (1997, 2001 and 2006)

	1997				Ratio ♂/♀	2001				Ratio ♂/♀	2006				Ratio ♂/♀
	♀		♂			♀		♂			♀		♂		
Region	#	%	#	%		#	%	#	%		#	%	#	%	
Africa and the Middle East	17,711	16.2	20,084	18.9	1.13	22,817	18.0	25,421	20.6	1.11	25,281	19.5	26,582	21.8	1.05
Asia and Pacific	60,309	55.0	56,761	53.4	0.94	68,240	53.7	64,704	52.3	0.95	67,322	52.0	59,157	48.4	0.88
South and Central America	9,379	8.6	8,043	7.6	0.86	10,929	8.6	9,282	7.5	0.85	12,655	9.8	11,651	9.5	0.92
United States	2,791	2.5	2,238	2.1	0.80	3,260	2.6	2,651	2.1	0.81	5,542	4.3	5,400	4.4	0.97
Europe and the United Kingdom	19,500	17.8	19,174	18.0	0.98	21,753	17.1	21,542	17.4	0.99	18,637	14.4	19,309	15.8	1.04
Source area not stated	2	0.0	6	0.0	3.00	15	0.0	19	0.0	1.27	64	0.0	47	0.0	0.73
Total	109,692	100.0	106,306	100.0	0.97	127,014	100.0	123,619	100.0	0.97	129,501	100.0	122,146	100.0	0.94

Table 10.3: Permanent Residents by Top Source Countries (1997, 2001 and 2006)

Country	1997			2001			2006		
	#	%	Rank	#	%	Rank	#	%	Rank
China, People's Republic of	18,526	8.6	3	40,365	16.1	1	33,080	13.2	1
India	19,615	9.1	2	27,904	11.1	2	30,753	12.2	2
Philippines	10,872	5.0	6	12,928	5.2	4	17,717	7.0	3
Pakistan	11,239	5.2	5	15,354	6.1	3	12,332	4.9	4
United States	5,030	2.3	9	5,911	2.4	6	10,943	4.4	5
Colombia	7,486	3.5	7	5,746	2.3	7	7,073	2.8	6
United Kingdom	4,657	2.2	10	5,360	2.1	10	6,542	2.6	7
Korea, Republic of	4,001	1.9	11	9,608	3.8	5	6,178	2.5	8
Iran	571	0.3	60	2,967	1.2	21	5,813	2.3	9
France	2,858	1.3	17	4,428	1.8	12	4,915	2.0	10
Romania	5,071	2.4	8	5,520	2.2	9	4,490	1.8	12
Sri Lanka	3,916	1.8	12	5,589	2.2	8	4,393	1.8	13
Russia	3,735	1.7	14	4,073	1.6	13	2,851	1.1	20
Taiwan	13,324	6.2	4	3,114	1.2	19	2,823	1.1	22
Hong Kong	22,250	10.3	1	1,965	0.8	29	1,489	0.6	33
Yugoslavia (former)	1,384	0.6	35	2,803	1.1	22	126	0.1	120
Top 10 source countries	118,070	54.7		134,285	23.6		135,346	53.8	
Other countries	97,968	45.4		116,356	46.4		116,303	46.2	
Total	216,038	100.0		250,641	100.0		251,649	100.0	

Table 10.4: Permanent Residents by Category and Gender in Canada (1997, 2001 and 2006)

	1997				Ratio ♂/♀	2001				Ratio ♂/♀	2006				Ratio ♂/♀
	♀		♂			♀		♂			♀		♂		
Category	#	%	#	%		#	%	#	%		#	%	#	%	
Family Class	35,851	32.7	24,089	22.7	0.67	40,738	32.1	26,049	21.1	0.64	41,988	32.4	28,516	23.3	0.68
Economic Immigrants	61,523	56.1	66,828	62.9	1.09	73,182	57.6	82,538	66.8	1.13	66,361	51.2	71,896	58.9	1.08
Refugees	10,818	9.9	13,489	12.7	1.25	12,995	10.2	14,924	12.1	1.15	15,801	12.2	16,691	13.7	1.06
Other Immigrants	1,500	1.4	1,900	1.8	1.27	99	01	107	0.1	1.08	5,344	4.1	5,038	4.1	0.94
Category not stated	0	0.0	0	0.0	...	0	0.0	1	0.0	...	7	0.0	5	0.0	0.71
Total	109,692	100	106,306	100.0	0.97	127,014	100.0	123,619	100.0	0.97	129,501	100.0	122,146	100.0	0.94

Source: *Citizenship and Immigration Canada, Facts and Figures 2006: Immigration Overview, Permanent and Temporary Residents.*

Table 10 (continues) ▶

Table 10.5: Permanent Residents 15 Years of Age or Older by Gender and Level of Education (1997, 2001 and 2006)

Level of Education	1997 ♀ #	%	♂ #	%	Ratio ♂/♀	2001 ♀ #	%	♂ #	%	Ratio ♂/♀	2006 ♀ #	%	♂ #	%	Ratio ♂/♀
0 to 9 years of schooling	6,590	0.10	10,961	0.07	0.66	16,871	0.09	12,938	0.07	0.77	18,168	0.09	13,628	0.07	0.75
10 to 12 years of schooling	22,156	0.13	17,079	0.10	0.77	18,627	0.10	20,152	0.10	1.08	18,721	0.09	15,765	0.08	0.84
13 or more years of schooling	7,347	0.04	6,400	0.04	0.87	9,709	0.05	7,235	0.04	0.75	8,527	0.04	7,559	0.04	0.89
Trade Certificate	8,384	0.05	7,277	0.04	0.87	4,679	0.02	7,692	0.04	1.64	4,717	0.02	5,236	0.03	1.11
Non-University Diploma	7,352	0.04	6,340	0.04	0.86	10,125	0.05	6,455	0.03	0.64	12,524	0.06	9,963	0.05	0.80
Bachelor's Degree	18,590	0.11	22,247	0.13	1.20	30,571	0.16	20,694	0.11	0.68	30,301	0.15	27,387	0.14	0.90
Master's Degree	4,038	0.02	7,555	0.05	1.87	7,215	0.04	6,609	0.03	0.92	10,501	0.05	13,056	0.07	1.24
Doctorate	698	0.00	2,029	0.01	2.91	1,038	0.01	2,050	0.01	1.97	1,433	0.01	2,841	0.01	1.98
Total	85,155	0.52	79,888	0.48	0.94	98,835	0.51	83,825	0.43	0.85	104,892	0.52	95,435	0.48	0.91

*Applies to those 15 years of age or older.

Table 10.6: Permanent Residents by Labour Market Intention and Occupational Skill Level (1997, 2001 and 2006)

Occupational Skill Level	1997 #	%	2001 #	%	2006 #	%
Skill level 0 - Managerial	3,305	1.5	4,873	1.9	8,123	3.2
Skill level A - Professionals	31,224	14.5	46,708	18.6	31,214	12.4
Skill level B - Skilled and technical	23,214	10.7	18,248	7.3	14,493	5.8
Skill level C - Intermediate and clerical	7,096	3.3	6,931	2.8	6,538	2.6
Skill level D - Elemental and labourers	1,037	0.5	1,152	0.5	607	0.2
Occupational Skill level identified	65,876	30.5	77,912	31.1	60,975	24.2
New workers - 15 years of age or older	42,587	19.7	51,848	20.7	67,850	27.0
Industrial codes - 15 years of age or older	2,864	1.3	1,631	0.7	712	0.3
Intending to work	111,327	51.5	131,391	52.4	129,537	51.5
Children under 15 years of age	50,965	23.6	57,288	22.9	51,322	20.4
Students 15 years of age or older	19,825	9.2	21,877	8.7	27,633	11.0
Retirees 15 years of age or older	6,682	3.1	7,206	2.9	6,421	2.6
Other non-workers 15 years of age or older	27,216	12.6	32,863	13.1	36,497	14.5
Labour market intention not stated	23	0.0	16	0.0	239	0.1
Total	216,038	100.0	250,641	100.0	251,649	100.0

Table 10.7: Refugees by Source Area (1997, 2001 and 2006)

Region	1997 #	%	2001 #	%	2006 #	%
Africa and the Middle East	7,975	32.8	9,663	34.6	10,226	31.5
Asia and Pacific	7,201	29.6	9,858	35.3	10,567	32.5
South and Central America	1,752	7.2	2,657	9.5	7,597	23.4
United States	54	0.2	55	0.2	1,246	3.8
Europe and the United Kingdom	7,321	30.1	5,683	20.4	2,763	8.5
Source area not stated	5	0.0	3	0.0	93	0.3
Total Refugees	24,308	100.0	27,919	100.0	32,492	100.0

Source: *Citizenship and Immigration Canada, Facts and Figures 2006: Immigration Overview, Permanent and Temporary Residents.*

Technical Notes

General Comments

Virtually all data in these tables is available or derived from existing, publicly accessible information issued by the Government of Canada, the Organization for Economic Co-operation and Development (OECD), the World Bank, and United Nations agencies. The North-South Institute selects the data for this annex chiefly for its development interest. However, data availability, including annual updates, also is an important factor. Some additions (and deletions) have been made to this year's report.

Selection of Developing Countries

The statistical annex lists developing countries under country groupings which reflect the eight Millennium Development Goals (MDGs) reference regions as set by the World Bank. Regional country groupings are the following:

- Sub-Saharan Africa,
- Middle East and North Africa,
- South Asia,
- East Asia and the Pacific,
- Europe and Central Asia, and
- Latin America and the Caribbean.

Tables 2 through 4 and 7 through 9 list this common set of developing countries. The Europe and Central Asia grouping includes 12 countries that are ineligible for Official Development Assistance (ODA) according to the criteria of the OECD Development Assistance Committee (DAC). The treatment of these countries is discussed below.

None of the countries on the list is a dependent or colonial territory. However, the following entities listed in these tables and identified in italics—Hong Kong, the West Bank and Gaza, Oceania, Taiwan, and former Yugoslavia —are not "independent countries." Hong Kong became the Hong Kong Special Administrative Region (SAR) of China on July 1, 1997. The West Bank and Gaza, at the time of writing, had not yet been granted independent status.

Oceania comprises the Cook Islands, Fiji, Kiribati, the Marshall Islands, Micronesia, Nauru, Palau, Samoa, the Solomon Islands, Tonga, Tuvalu, and Vanuatu.

ODA Ineligible Countries

There are 13 countries categorized as "developing" that were ineligible for official development assistance in 2004-05. These are: Belarus, Bulgaria, the Czech Republic, Estonia, Hungary, Latvia, Lithuania, Poland, Romania, the Russian Federation, the Slovak Republic, Slovenia, and Ukraine.

Although these countries may receive "official assistance" from Canada and other donors, that aid is not included in calculations of official development assistance (ODA). Statistics for these countries are excluded from regional, world, and income-based totals in Tables 3, 4 and 7.

Year of Coverage

Data generally is given for the latest calendar year for which complete information exists—normally 2005. However, in the case of Official Development Assistance in Tables 3 through 7, the figures are for fiscal year 2004-05 (April 1, 2004 to March 31, 2005). In other cases where the data is not for calendar year 2005, the relevant date is indicated. Some statistics were readily available for 2006 however, in some cases information from 2004 was used — see the Human Development Index (HDI).

Symbols

Following Statistics Canada's Standard Table symbols (http://www.statcan.ca/english/concepts/definitions/guide-symbol.htm), symbols in this annex are used as follows:

. = not available for any reference period

.. = not available for a specific reference period

... = not applicable

0 = true zero or a value rounded to zero

Unless otherwise indicated, figures are in Canadian dollars.

Income-Grouped Totals

Sub-totals for country income-groupings can be found at the bottom of columns in Tables 2 through 4 and 7 through 10. These groupings follow the World Bank's classification of countries by income level, as listed in the UNDP *Human Development Report* and in CIDA's *Statistical Report on Development Assistance* for fiscal year 2004-05.

The list of least developed countries (LDCs), low income countries, and middle income countries is provided below.

Least developed countries: Afghanistan, Angola, Bangladesh, Benin, Bhutan, Burkina Faso, Burundi, Cambodia, Cape Verde, Central African Republic, Chad, Comoros, Democratic Republic of the Congo, Djibouti, Equatorial Guinea, Eritrea, Ethiopia, Gambia, Guinea, Guinea-Bissau, Haiti, Kiribati, Lao People's Democratic Republic, Lesotho, Liberia, Madagascar, Malawi, Maldives, Mali, Mauritania, Mozambique, Myanmar, Nepal, Niger, Rwanda, Samoa, São Tomé and Principe, Senegal, Sierra Leone, Solomon Islands, Somalia, Sudan, Timor-Leste, Togo, Tuvalu, Uganda, United Republic of Tanzania, Vanuatu, Yemen, and Zambia.

Low-income countries: Afghanistan, Bangladesh, Benin, Bhutan, Burkina Faso, Burundi, Cambodia, Central African Republic, Chad, Comoros, Democratic Republic of the Congo, Côte d'Ivoire, Ethiopia, Gambia, Ghana, Guinea, Guinea-Bissau, Haiti, India, Kenya, Democratic Republic of Korea, Kyrgyzstan, Lao People's Democratic Republic, Liberia, Lithuania, Madagascar, Malawi, Mali, Mauritania, Mongolia, Mozambique, Myanmar, Nepal, Niger, Nigeria, Pakistan, Papua New Guinea, Rwanda,

São Tomé and Principe, Senegal, Sierra Leone, Solomon Islands, Somalia, Sudan, Tajikistan, Tanzania, Timor-Lesté, Togo, Uganda, Uzbekistan, Vietnam, Yemen, Rep., Zambia, and Zimbabwe.

Middle-income countries: Albania, Algeria, Argentina, Armenia, Belarus, Belize, Bolivia, Bosnia and Herzegovina, Botswana, Brazil, Bulgaria, Cape Verde, Chile, China, Colombia, Costa Rica, Croatia, Cuba, Czech Republic, Djibouti, Dominica, Dominican Republic, Ecuador, Egypt, El Salvador, Estonia, Fiji, Gabon, Grenada, Guatemala, Guyana, Honduras, Hungary, Iran, Iraq, Jamaica, Jordan, Kazakhstan, Kiribati, Latvia, Lebanon, Libya, Lithuania, Macedonia FYR, Malaysia, Maldives, the Marshall Islands, Mauritius, Mexico, Micronesia, Morocco, Namibia, Northern Mariana Islands, Oman, Palau, Panama, Paraguay, Peru, Philippines, Poland, Romania, Russia, Saint Kitts and Nevis, Saint Lucia, Saint Vincent and the Grenadines, Samoa, Saudi Arabia, Serbia and Montenegro, Seychelles, Slovak Republic, South Africa, Sri Lanka, Suriname, Swaziland, Syria, Thailand, Tonga, Trinidad and Tobago, Tunisia, Turkey, Turkmenistan, Ukraine, Uruguay, Vanuatu, Venezuela, and the West Bank and Gaza.

Note that totals by income-group may differ from totals for all developing countries because income-group totals are based on country-specific information only, while overall totals for developing countries also include allocations to regions that cannot be attributed to specific countries.

Emerging Market Economies

In Table 8 this country grouping is included alongside the income-based grouping. This grouping is not, strictly speaking, income based because it includes low, middle, and high-income countries (but no LDCs). These are countries that are considered to have fairly dynamic economies, which have already undergone significant levels of industrial and financial development, and achieved substantial integration into international capital markets. The countries (included in the "Emerging-market indicators" section of The Economist, as of December 13, 2006) are: Argentina, Brazil, Chile, China, Czech Republic, Egypt, Hong Kong, Hungary, India, Indonesia, Iran, Israel, Malaysia, Mexico, Nigeria, Pakistan, Philippines, Poland, Russia, Saudi Arabia, Singapore, South Africa, South Korea, Taiwan, Thailand, Turkey, Ukraine and Venezuela.

Tables

Table 1 Canada and other High Human Development Economies: Selected Indicators (2004 – 2005).

Table 1.1 includes the 22 OECD DAC Member Countries and two other high-income OECD Member Countries (Iceland and the Republic of Korea). Table 1.2 includes 14 other high-income countries. The HDI and gender-related development index (GDI) are from the UNDP's *Human Development Report 2006*. The GNI per capita (PPP$) figures are from the World Bank's *World Development Indicators (WDI) 2006*. Data on foreign aid and net private

financial flows are taken from the OECD's DAC *Development Cooperation Report 2006*. Numbers for the shares of exports to and imports from developing countries are from the IMF's *Direction of Trade Statistics Yearbook 2006*.

Again, per capita incomes were reported in PPP$ rather than US$. The PPP$ is a more accurate standardization of the 'value in consumption' of income across all reporting countries. This denomination, therefore, forms a better basis for comparative incomes across countries. In addition, exchange rate changes can significantly alter the recorded US$ incomes of countries from year to year, even when it is averaged (as in the World Bank's Atlas method) and can therefore give misleading information about actual changes in domestic income.

Table 2 The Developing Countries: Selected Indicators (2004, 2005 and 2006)

Figures on the GDI, HDI, Adult Literacy, and Under-5 Mortality rates are taken from the UNDP's *Human Development Report 2006*. Figures on GNI per capita, total GDP, annual GDP per capita growth rate, population, present value of debt/GNI (a new column), external debt/GNI, total debt service/GNI and aid/GNI are taken from the World Bank's *World Development Indicators and Global Development Finance (GDF) 2006*, available online at: www.worldbank.org.

Country groupings totals for columns 1, 2, 3, 5, 7, and 8 are weighted by population. Country groupings totals for columns 9, 10, and 11 are weighted by GNI (current $US). Population figures for 2004 and 2005 are taken from the World Bank's *WDI 2006*.

As in Table 1, per capita estimates are also reported in PPP$. The justification given above applies here as well.

Table 3 Canadian Official Development Assistance: Basic Data (2004-05)

Table 4 Canadian Bilateral ODA by Channel and by Country (2004-05)

Table 5 Canadian Biltilateral ODA by Sector (2004-05)

Table 6 Canadian Technical Assistance to Developing Countries (1999-2005)

Table 7 Canadian Multilateral ODA by Channel and by Country (2004-05)

The basic data on Canadian official development assistance in Tables 3 through 7 are taken or derived from the "*Statistical Report on Development Assistance*" for fiscal year 2004-05, published by CIDA's International Development Information Centre. Information in the tables is taken from "Table L: Country-to-Country ODA Disbursements by Sector and Percentage", "Table M: Total Disbursements by Country", "Table N: Experts on Assignment Abroad by Area of Expertise", "Table O: Experts on Assignment

Abroad by Region of Assignment", "Table P: Students and Trainees supported by CIDA by Region of Origin and Location of Study" and "Table Q: Students and Trainees supported by CIDA by Field of Study". To ensure conformity with CIDA totals, aid allocations for developing countries, which do not match NSI criteria (such as South Korea and Bahamas), are included as Regional, Africa, Caribbean, Latin America, and Asia, and as Other: Americas, Asia, and Europe. Information on Canada's rank among other bilateral donors in recipient countries is derived from the OECD's *Geographic Distribution of Financial Flows to Aid Recipients 2000-2006*.

In Table 3, for better comparison purposes the 1994-95 total bilateral ODA flows have been translated into 2005 prices using the Consumer Price Index (CPI). Included under the classification "Unallocable by Country" at the bottom of Tables 3, 4 and 7 are imputed administrative costs, interest costs, other government department costs and services, provincial government support to development, CIDA's Public Outreach (Development Information) Program as well as other costs.

Finally, in Table 7, the imputed shares of Canadian Multilateral Assistance by Channel and Country were taken from "Table M: Total Disbursements by Country" and ratios were obtained by comparing disbursement of main multilateral channels: United Nations organizations and other Multilateral Channels as well as International Financial Institutions (IFIs).

Table 8 Canadian Balance of Trade with Developing Countries (2005)

The data on exports and imports are obtained from Statistics Canada *Catalogues # 65-003* and *# 65-006* for 2005 and 1995. Export and import prices for 1995 were translated into real terms using the respective implicit price indices (Fisher index formula). The Department of Finance provided the information on total tariff revenue collected on imports from developing countries and average tariff rate, disaggregated by country.

Table 9 Finance and Investment Flows between Canada and Developing Countries (2006)

Data on the stock of public Canadian claims were made available by Finance Canada's International Finance and Economic Analysis Division and by Export Development Canada (EDC). Data on the stock of private Canadian claims were taken from the *Bank of Canada's Banking and Financial Statistics*, April 2007.

Public or official debt is constituted by non-concessional and concessional loans.

Non-concessional loans are: EDC's Corporate Account (sovereign and commercial) loans which include principal outstanding, recognized accrued revenue, and unrecognized accrued revenue; EDC's non-concessional loans under the Canada Account; Department of Finance loans;

and the Canadian Wheat Board loans (sovereign and commercial).

Concessional loans are: CIDA loans; and EDC's concessional loans under the Canada Account.

Private or commercial debt includes total claims booked worldwide vis-à-vis non-residents by Canadian chartered banks.

Statistics Canada's Balance of Payments Division provided the figures on Canadian direct investment abroad in developing countries and foreign direct investment by developing countries in Canada. The symbol "x" in the two columns relating to foreign direct investment signals that data are not available in order to protect confidentiality. Hence, country-grouping and income-grouping totals underestimate the total stock of foreign investment.

Table 10 Permanent and Temporary Residents in Canada (1997, 2001 and 2006)

Citizenship and Immigration Canada's website (http://www.cic.gc.ca/english/resources/statistics/facts2006/index.asp) was the source of data on population inflows from other countries to Canada. *Facts and Figures 2006 - Immigration Overview: Permanent and Temporary Residents* provided information on immigration flows generally disaggregated by permanent residents and temporary residents. Data were further disaggregated by gender, in the following categories: occupational skill level, source areas and top source areas, categories, level of education, and refugees.

Whenever data permitted, a "gender ratio" was generated. We have introduced Gender Equity Lines and Circles to show the gender relations across different series. Below, you will find a more detailed explanation on how to interpret these charts.

This edition of the *Canadian Development Report Statistical Annex 2008* introduces data on Temporary Foreign Workers, relating to The North-South Institute's ongoing research on temporary labour migration (See Table 10).

Definitions used by Citizenship and Immigration Canada (CIC), are applied to table 10. See Box A, page 136.

Box A: Citizenship and Immigration Canada Definitions

Category. Four immigration categories are shown for permanent residents: family class, economic immigrants, refugees and other immigrants. The economic immigrant category is further divided into: principal applicants, and spouses and dependants.

Economic immigrants: Permanent residents selected for their skills and ability to contribute to Canada's economy; including, skilled workers, business immigrants, provincial or territorial nominees and live-in caregivers.

Family class: Permanent residents sponsored by a Canadian citizen or a permanent resident living in Canada who is 18 years of age or over. This includes spouses and partners; parents and grandparents; and others (i.e., dependent children, children under the age of 18 whom the sponsor intends to adopt in Canada, brothers, sisters, nephews, nieces and grandchildren who are orphans under 18 years of age, or any other relative if the sponsor has no relative as described above). Fiancé(e)s are no longer designated as a component of the family class under the Immigration and Refugee Protection Act.

Foreign workers: This category includes individuals who enter Canada to work on a temporary basis. Every foreign worker must have been issued a work permit but may also have been issued other types of permits or authorizations. The foreign worker category excludes foreign students who may have been issued a work permit associated with their studies or status as a student and individuals who have been issued a work permit for humanitarian reasons, such as refugee claimants.

Immigration Act (1976): Federal legislation respecting immigration to Canada. The Immigration Act of 1976 became law in 1978 and remained in effect until June 27, 2002.

Immigration and Refugee Protection Act (IRPA): Federal legislation respecting immigration to Canada and the granting of refugee protection to people who are displaced, persecuted or in danger. IRPA received royal assent on November 1, 2001, and came into effect on June 28, 2002.

Independent immigrants: The independent immigrant category is a pre-IRPA immigration category that includes skilled workers selected for their labour market skills and business immigrants selected on the basis of their business experience and other related skills.

Level of education: Eight levels of education have been determined for permanent residents who are 15 years of age or older, based on the number of years of schooling or the certificate, diploma or degree obtained.

- **0 to 9 years of schooling**
- **10 to 12 years of schooling**
- **13 or more years of schooling**, with no additional certificate, diploma or degree
- **Trade certificate**: completion of vocational training at non-university educational institutions

- **Non-university diploma**: completion of a diploma program not at the university or trade level
- **Bachelor's degree**: completion of a bachelor's program at the university level
- **Master's degree**: completion of a master's program at the university level
- **Doctoral degree**: completion of a doctoral program at the university level

Occupational skill level: Five skill levels, based on the National Occupational Classification, have been determined for permanent residents 15 years of age or older as well as for foreign workers.

- **Skill level O (managerial)**: management occupations
- **Skill level A (professionals)**: professional occupations in business and finance; natural and applied sciences; health; social science, education, government service, and religion; and art and culture. Educational or training requirements: university degree.
- **Skill level B (skilled and technical)**: skilled or technical occupations in administration and business; natural and applied sciences; health; law, social service, education, and religion; art, culture, recreation and sport; sales and service; as well as trades and skilled transport and equipment operators; skilled occupations in primary industries; and processing, manufacturing and utilities supervisors and skilled operators. Educational or training requirements: two to three years of post-secondary education, or two to five years of apprenticeship training, or three to four years of secondary school and more than two years of on-the-job training, occupation-specific training courses or specific work experience.
- **Skill level C (intermediate and clerical)**: clerical occupations; assisting occupations in health services; intermediate occupations in sales and services; transport, equipment operations, installation and maintenance; primary industries; as well as processing and manufacturing machine operators and assemblers. Educational or training requirements: one to four years of secondary school education, or up to two years of on-the-job training, training courses or specific work experience
- **Skill level D (elemental and labourers)**: elemental sales and service occupations and labourers in construction; primary industries; and processing, manufacturing and utilities. Educational or training requirements: no formal educational requirements; short work demonstration or on-the-job training

Permanent residents: People who have been granted permanent resident status in Canada. Permanent residents must live in Canada for at least 730 days (two years) within a five-year period or risk losing their status. Permanent residents have all the rights guaranteed under the Canadian Charter of Rights and Freedoms such as equality rights, legal rights, mobility rights, freedom of religion, freedom of expression and

freedom of association. They do not, however, have the right to vote in elections.

Refugees: Permanent residents in the refugee category include government-assisted refugees, privately sponsored refugees, refugees landed in Canada and refugee dependants (i.e., dependants of refugees landed in Canada, including spouses and partners living abroad or in Canada). With the introduction of IRPA, "refugees" are referred to as "Protected persons".

Skilled workers: Economic immigrants selected for their ability to participate in the labour market and to establish themselves economically in Canada. Skilled workers are assessed on the basis of selection criteria that stress education, language ability and skilled work experience rather than a specific occupation. Before IRPA, the skilled worker category included assisted relatives and independent immigrants.

Source area: Five major world regions are shown: Africa and the Middle East, Asia and Pacific, South and Central America, the United States, and Europe and the United Kingdom.

Source countries: Refers to the principal country of last permanent residence (CLPR) for all permanent residents and temporary residents, unless otherwise indicated. For refugee claimants, source country refers to the principal country of alleged persecution (COAP). The ranking of the top ten source countries is based on the annual flow or stock in the most recent year.

Temporary resident flow: This represents the number of temporary residents identified as entering the CIC system (and presumably the country) for the first time. CIC commonly measures the annual flow of foreign workers, foreign students and the humanitarian component of the temporary resident population. Flows are calculated as of the earliest effective date of any valid permit issued to a temporary resident. Seasonal workers are counted each time they re-enter the system.

Temporary residents: Foreign nationals who are lawfully in Canada on a temporary basis under the authority of a temporary permit. Temporary residents include foreign workers, foreign students, the humanitarian population and other temporary residents. The humanitarian population includes refugee claimants and temporary residents allowed to remain in Canada on humanitarian grounds and who are not categorized as either foreign workers or foreign students. The other category of temporary residents includes people in Canada on a temporary basis who are not under the authority of a work permit or a study permit and who are not refugee claimants. The other category of temporary residents is not profiled in this publication.

Province or territory: Refers to the province or territory of intended destination in Canada.

Figures, Charts and Maps

The Canadian Development Report 2008 Statistical Annex includes charts, figures and Geographical Information System (GIS) maps.

In this edition, enhanced graphics have been added to all basic bar, pie and composite charts to convey an additional level of information. All charts carry both axes (x and y) which are properly labelled and each series has its own value depicted accordingly.

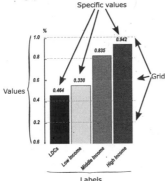

Certain pie charts included in this annex are constructed by merging three levels of distribution:

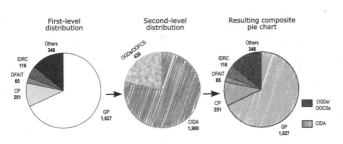

Several bar charts included in this annex break values down into gender components in order to convey gender ratios. Gender symbols are placed on bar portions that correspond to each gender value:

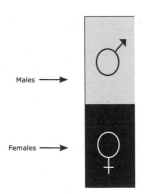

In addition, this volume introduces radar charts ("spider web charts") in order to illustrate gender distribution for different series. Radar charts are used to display changes in values relative to a value set to 1, which denotes a parity value. The closer the value is to 1 (Gender Equity Circle) the closer it denotes gender parity.

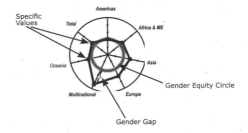

Gender ratios are also depicted over time, and built around a Gender Equity Line. Statistics for men and women are equal when they converge at the Gender Equity Line. A value above the Gender Equity Line or outside the Gender Equity Circle indicates more men than women. A value below the Gender Equity Line or inside the Gender Equity Circle indicates more women than men, in any given category.

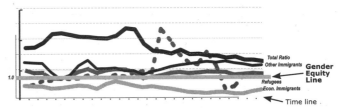

Chart 10.2 Evolution Over Time of Gender Ratio (Male/Female) by Category

Stacked bar charts are used to compare individual values to cumulative data for each category. The bars in a stacked bar chart are divided into categories and together represent a total.

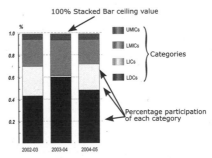

Chart 5.1: Comparative Net Canadian Disbursements Across Category of Recipients (2002 to 2005)

There are some stacked areas plotted against a time-line and accompanied by trend lines for the same period. Values for each time-specific series are combined and then projected over time:

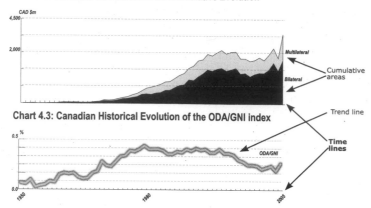

Chart 4.2 Canadian Historical ODA: A Cumulative Evolution

Chart 4.3: Canadian Historical Evolution of the ODA/GNI index

Secondary tables

Also included are secondary tables containing additional information relative to main tables or other charts.

Top Ten Recipients of Gross ODA/OA

		(USD million)
1	Iraq	229
2	Afghanistan	73
3	Ethiopia	62
4	Haiti	60
5	Indonesia	56
6	Ghana	50
7	Bangladesh	50
8	Mozambique	42
9	Mali	40
10	Cameroon	39

"Figure 9.2: Countries for which Canadian FDI data is kept confidential" shows the number of countries for which data on Canadian Foreign Direct Investment is kept confidential. Column 1 provides the absolute number of countries; column 2 is the total number of countries in each region and column 3 is the percentage of countries for which confidentiality about FDI is maintained.

Figure 9.2: **Countries for which Canadian FDI Data is Kept Confidential**

Regions	Number of countries		
	Data kept confidential	Total	%
	1	2	3
Sub-Saharan Africa	39	47	83.0
Middle East and North Africa	13	15	86.7
South Asia	5	9	55.6
East Asia and the Pacific	6	15	40.0
Europe and Central Asia	15	28	53.6
Latin America and the Caribbean	23	31	74.2
Total Developing Countries	**101**	**145**	**69.7**

Maps

The GIS maps correspond to data contained in Table 1 and Table 10 and show socio-economic indicators overlaid on geographic contexts.

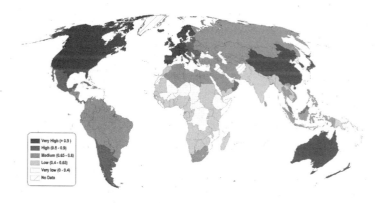

Map 1.1: UNDP Human Development Index by Region (2005)

Organization Acronyms

CIDA: Canadian International Development Agency

DAC: Development Assistance Committee (Organisation for Economic Co-operation and Development)

DFAIT: Foreign Affairs and International Affairs Canada

ICHRDD: International Centre for Human Rights and Democratic Development (now Rights and Democracy)

IDRC: International Development Research Centre

IHA: International Humanitarian Assistance

UN: United Natlons

UNDP: United Nations Development Programme

Marquis Book Printing Inc.

Québec, Canada

2007